# Romanian
## PHRASE BOOK
## & DICTIONARY

### Easy to use features
- Handy thematic color-coding
- Quick Reference Section—opposite page
- Tipping Guide—inside back cover
- Quick reply panels throughout

# How best to use this phrase book

● We suggest that you start with the **Guide to pronunciation** (pp. 6-8), then go on to **Some basic expressions** (pp. 9-15). This gives you not only a minimum vocabulary, but also helps you get used to pronouncing the language. The phonetic transcription throughout the book enables you to pronounce every word correctly.

● Consult the **Contents** pages (3-5) for the section you need. In each chapter you'll find travel facts, hints and useful information. Simple phrases are followed by a list of words applicable to the situation.

● Separate, detailed contents lists are included at the beginning of the extensive **Eating out** and **Shopping guide** sections (Menus, p. 38, Shops and services, p. 97).

● If you want to find out how to say something in Romanian, your fastest look-up is via the **Dictionary** section (pp. 164-189). This not only gives you the word, but is also cross-referenced to its use in a phrase on a specific page.

● If you wish to learn more about constructing sentences, check the **Basic grammar** (pp. 159-163).

● Note the **colour margins** are indexed in Romanian and English to help both listener and speaker. And, in addition, there is also an index in Romanian for the use of your listener.

● Throughout the book, this symbol 👉 suggests phrases your listener can use to answer you. If you still can't understand, hand this phrase book to the Romanian-speaker to encourage pointing to an appropriate answer. The English translation for you is just alongside the Romanian.

**Contacting the Editors**
Every effort has been made to provide accurate information in this publication, but changes are inevitable. The publisher cannot be responsible for any resulting loss, inconvenience or injury. We would appreciate it if readers would call our attention to any errors or outdated information by contacting Berlitz Publishing, 95 Progress Street, Union, NJ 07083, USA. Fax: 1-908-206-1103

Reprinted 2002                                                      Printed in Singapore

4

# Contents

**Acknowledgements**
We are particularly grateful to Ani Price and Isabella Preoteasa for
their help in the preparation of this book.

# Guide to pronunciation

This chapter is intended to make you familiar with the phonetic transcription we have devised, and to help you get used to the sound system of Romanian. Note that Romanian uses some dia-critical letters—letters with accent marks—which we don't use in English.

The imitated pronunciation should be read as if it were English (based on Standard British pronunciation), except for any spe-cial rules set out below. It is based on Standard British pro-nunciation, though we have tried to take account of General American pronunciation also.

Letters written in **bold** should be pronounced louder, though in Romanian stress is not as marked as in English.

### The Romanian language

Romanian is relatively easy to read and write since it is a pho-netic language in which all letters are pronounced. With the exception of the two typical sounds â and î, all the other sounds are easy to identify with English approximations. Originating in the Latin language brought by Roman colonists in 101–275 AD, Romanian has much in common with French, Italian, Spanish and Portuguese.

Through the centuries the Romanian territories have been crossed by migrating tribes of Germanic, Slav and Magyar ori-gin, each contributing words of their own vocabulary to the Romanian language. Some words of Greek and Turkish origin are a reminder of the political dominance exercised by these two powers from the Middle Ages until Romanian indepen-dence in 1877.

## Consonants

| Letter | Approximate pronunciation | Symbol | Example | |
|--------|---------------------------|--------|---------|---|
| b, d, f, l, m, n, p, t, v, w, x, z | are pronounced as in English | | | |
| c | 1) like c in cake | c | cartofi | kartof$^y$ |
| | 2) followed by e or i like ch in cheese | ch | ceas cineva | cheas cheeneva |
| ch | like k in kettle | k | chibrit | kibreet |
| g | 1) like g in girl | g | rog | rog |
| | 2) when followed by e or i, like g in gender | j | ginere | jeenereh |
| gh | like g in girl | gh | ghete | geteh |
| h | like h in hand | h | hartă | harter |
| j | like s in pleasure | zh | jucărie | zhuceree-eh |
| r | rolled consonant similar to the Scottish r | r | roată | rwater |
| s | like s in sun | s | student | stoodent |
| ş | like sh in short | sh | şiret | sheeret |
| ţ | like ts in bits | ts | ţară | tsarer |

## Vowels

| a | like the vowel sound in cut | a | alfabet | alfabet |
|---|-----------------------------|---|---------|---------|
| ă | like er at the end of teacher; but the r should not be pronounced | er | masă | maser |
| â | pronounced exactly like î below; it only occurs in a few words | i | ro- mâneşte | romineshteh |

| e | 1) like the **e** in t**e**n; | e | **elev** | elev |
| | this is also pronounced at the end of the word, but to avoid confusion is represented **eh** | eh | **carte** | carteh |
| | 2) at the beginning of certain words, like **ye** in **yes** | ye | **este** | **ye**steh |
| i | 1) like **ee** in b**ee** | ee | **intrare** | eentrareh |
| | 2) If unstressed at the end of a word, **i** may be scarcely audible, softening the preceding consonant | y | **bani** | ban^y |
| î | there's no exact equivalent in English; it resembles the **o** in less**o**n, kingd**o**m | ï | **înțeleg** | ïntseleg |
| o | like vowel sound in sp**o**rt, without pronouncing the **r** | o | **copil** | kop**ee**l |
| u | like **oo** in b**oo**k | oo | **munte** | **moo**nteh |

## Diphthongs

Diphthongs are combinations of a vowel and a semi-vowel, pronounced as one syllable. Practically all vowels in Romanian can act as semi-vowels in diphthongs. The following dipthongs are the most frequent.

| ai | like **igh** in h**igh** | igh | **mai** | migh |
| au | like **ow** in c**ow** | a^oo | **stau** | sta^oo |
| ău | like **o** in g**o** | oh | **rău** | roh |
| ea | 1) no exact equivalent in English; sounds almost like **a** in bat | a | **dimineața** | deemeenatsa |
| | 2) at the end of the word like **aye** in l**aye**r | eh-a | **prea** | preh-a |

---

\* Hyphens are sometimes inserted between sounds to avoid confusion.

| ei | like **ay** in b**ay** | ay | **lei** | **l**ay |
| eu | no equivalent in English; start pronouncing the **e** of bed then draw your lips together to make a brief **oo** sound | e^oo | **leu** | **le**^oo |
| ia | like **ya** in **ya**rd | ya | **iarbă** | **yar**ber |
| ie | like **ye** in **ye**llow | ye | **ieftin** | **ye**fteen |
| io | like **yo** in **yo**nder | yo | **dic-ţionar** | deectsyo**nar** |
| iu | like **ew** in f**ew** | yoo | **iubire** | yoo**beer**eh |
| oa | like **wha** in **wha**t | wa | **poate** | **pwa**teh |
| oi | like **oy** in b**oy** | oy | **doi** | doy |
| ua | like **wa** in **wa**tch | wah | **luati** | l**wah**ts^y |
| uă | similar to **ue** in infl**ue**nce | wer | **două** | do-**wer** |

## Pronunciation of the Romanian alphabet

| A ah | G geh | N neh | Ţ tseh |
| Ă er | H hah | O oh | U oo |
| Â ‡ | I ee | P peh | V veh |
| B beh | Î ‡ | R reh | W dooblu-veh |
| C cheh | J zheh | S seh | X eeks |
| D deh | K kah | Ş sheh | Y eegrek |
| E eh | L leh | T teh | Z zeh |
| F feh | M meh | | |

# Some basic expressions

| | | |
|---|---|---|
| Yes. | **Da.** | da |
| No. | **Nu.** | noo |
| Please. | **Vă rog.** | ver rog |
| Thank you. | **Mulţumesc.** | mooltsoomesc |
| Thank you very much. | **Mulţumesc foarte mult.** | mooltsoomesc fwarteh moolt |
| That's all right/ You're welcome. | **Nu aveţi pentru ce.** | noo avets<sup>y</sup> pentroo cheh |

## Greetings *Formule de salut*

| | | |
|---|---|---|
| Good morning. | **Bună dimineaţa.** | booner deemeenatsa |
| Good afternoon. | **Bună ziua.** | booner zeewah |
| Good evening. | **Bună seara.** | booner sara |
| Good night. | **Noapte bună.** | nwapteh booner |
| Goodbye. | **La revedere.** | la revedereh |
| See you later. | **Pe curînd.** | peh coorind |
| Hello/Hi! | **Bună!** | booner |
| This is Mr./Mrs./ Miss... | **Vă prezint pe domnul/doamna/domnişoara...** | ver prezeent peh domnool/ dwamna/domnishwara |
| How do you do? (Pleased to meet you.) | **Încîntat de cunoştinţă.** | incintat deh coonoshteentser |
| How are you? | **Ce mai faceţi?** | cheh migh fachets<sup>y</sup> |
| Very well, thanks. And you? | **Mulţumesc bine, şi dumneavoastră?** | mooltsoomesc beeneh shee doomnavwastrer |
| How's life? | **Cum vă merg treburile?** | coom ver merg trebooreeleh |
| Fine. | **Bine.** | beeneh |
| I beg your pardon? | **Poftim?** | pofteem |

| | | |
|---|---|---|
| Excuse me. (May I get past?) | **Pardon, vă rog.** | pardon ver rog |
| Sorry! | **Scuzaţi-mă, vă rog.** | scoozatsee-mer ver rog |

## Questions *Întrebări*

| | | |
|---|---|---|
| Where? | **Unde?** | oondeh |
| How? | **Cum?** | coom |
| When? | **Cînd?** | cind |
| What? | **Ce?** | cheh |
| Why? | **De ce?** | de cheh |
| Who? | **Cine?** | cheeneh |
| Which? | **Care?** | careh |
| Where is...? | **Unde este...?** | oondeh yesteh |
| Where are...? | **Unde sînt...?** | oondeh sint |
| Where can I find/ get...? | **Unde pot găsi/de unde pot lua...?** | oondeh pot gersee/deh oondeh pot lwa |
| How far? | **Este departe?** | yesteh departeh |
| How long? | **Cît timp durează?** | cit teemp doorazer |
| How much/ How many? | **Cîţi/cîte?** | cits<sup>y</sup>/citeh |
| How much does this cost? | **Cît costă?** | cit coster |
| When does... open/ close? | **Cînd se deschide/ închide...?** | cind seh deskeedeh/ inkeedeh |
| What do you call this/that in Romanian? | **Cum se zice asta în româneşte?** | coom seh zeecheh asta in romineshteh |
| What does this/that mean? | **Ce înseamnă asta?** | cheh insamner asta |

## Do you speak...? *Vorbiţi...?*

| | | |
|---|---|---|
| Do you speak English? | **Vorbiţi englezeşte?** | vorbeets<sup>y</sup> englezeshteh |
| Does anyone here speak English? | **Vorbeşte cineva aici englezeşte?** | vorbeshteh cheeneva aeech<sup>y</sup> englezeshteh |
| I don't speak Romanian. | **Nu vorbesc româneşte.** | noo vorbesc rominehshteh |
| Could you speak more slowly? | **Puteţi să vorbiţi mai rar, vă rog?** | pootets<sup>y</sup> ser vorbeets<sup>y</sup> migh rar ver rog |

| Could you repeat that? | **Puteţi să repetaţi asta?** | pootets<sup>y</sup> ser repetats<sup>y</sup> asta |
|---|---|---|
| Could you spell it? | **Cum se scrie?** | coom seh scree-eh |
| How do you pronounce this? | **Cum se pronunţă asta?** | coom seh pro**noont**ser asta |
| Could you write it down, please? | **Vreţi să-mi scrieţi asta?** | vrets<sup>y</sup> serm<sup>y</sup> **scree**-ets<sup>y</sup> asta |
| Can you translate this for me? | **Puteţi să-mi traduceţi, vă rog, asta?** | pootets<sup>y</sup> serm<sup>y</sup> tra**doo**chets<sup>y</sup> ver rog asta |
| Can you translate this for us? | **Vreţi să ne traduceţi asta, vă rog?** | vrets<sup>y</sup> ser neh tra**doo**chets<sup>y</sup> asta ver rog |
| Could you point to the... in the book, please? | **Puteţi să ne arătaţi... în carte, vă rog?** | pootets<sup>y</sup> ser neh arer**tats**<sup>y</sup>... în carteh ver rog |
| word | **cuvînt** | coo**vint** |
| phrase | **frază** | **fraz**er |
| sentence | **propoziţie** | propo**zeets**yeh |
| Just a moment. | **Un moment.** | oon mo**ment** |
| I'll see if I can find it in this book. | **Să văd dacă-l pot găsi în această carte.** | ser verd **dac**erl pot ger**see** în a**chas**ter **cart**eh |
| I understand. | **Înţeleg.** | int**seleg** |
| I don't understand. | **Nu înţeleg.** | noo int**seleg** |
| Do you understand? | **Înţelegeţi?** | int**selejets**<sup>y</sup> |

## Can/May...? *Pot/Îmi permiteţi...?*

| Can I have...? | **Pot avea...?** | pot a**veh**-a |
|---|---|---|
| Can we have...? | **Putem avea...?** | **poo**tem a**veh**-a |
| Can you show me...? | **Puteţi să-mi arătaţi...?** | pootets<sup>y</sup> serm<sup>y</sup> arer**tats**<sup>y</sup> |
| I can't. | **Nu pot** | noo pot |
| Can you tell me...? | **Puteţi să-mi spuneţi...?** | pootets<sup>y</sup> serm<sup>y</sup> **spoonets**<sup>y</sup> |
| Can you help me? | **Puteţi să mă ajutaţi?** | pootets<sup>y</sup> ser mer a**zhootats**<sup>y</sup> |
| Can I help you? | **Vă pot ajuta cu ceva?** | ver pot a**zhoota** coo **cheva** |
| Can you direct me to...? | **Puteţi să-mi spuneţi cum să ajung la...?** | pootets<sup>y</sup> serm<sup>y</sup> **spoonets**<sup>y</sup> coom ser a**zhoong** la |

**Do you want...?** *Vreți să...?*

| I'd like... | **Aş vrea...** | ash vreh-a |
| We'd like... | **Am dori...** | am doree |
| What do you want? | **Ce doriți?** | cheh doreets<sup>y</sup> |
| Could you give me...? | **Puteți să-mi dați...?** | pootets<sup>y</sup> serm<sup>y</sup> dats<sup>y</sup> |
| Could you bring me...? | **Vreți să-mi aduceți...?** | vrets<sup>y</sup> serm<sup>y</sup> adoochets<sup>y</sup> |
| Could you show me...? | **Puteți să-mi arătați...?** | pootets<sup>y</sup> serm<sup>y</sup> arertats<sup>y</sup> |
| I'm looking/searching for... | **Caut...** | caoot |
| I'm hungry. | **Mi-e foame.** | myeh fwameh |
| I'm thirsty. | **Mi-e sete.** | myeh seteh |
| I'm tired. | **Sînt obosit(ă).** | sint oboseet(er) |
| I'm lost. | **M-am rătăcit.** | mam rertercheet |
| It's important. | **Este important.** | yesteh eemportant |
| It's urgent. | **Este urgent.** | yesteh oorjent |

**It is/There is...** *Este/Există...*

| It is... | **Este...** | yesteh |
| Is it...? | **Este...?** | yesteh |
| It isn't... | **Nu este...** | noo yesteh |
| Here it is. | **Aici e.** | aeech<sup>y</sup> yeh |
| Here they are. | **Aici sînt.** | aeech<sup>y</sup> sint |
| There it is. | **Acolo este.** | acolo yesteh |
| There they are. | **Acolo sînt.** | acolo sint |
| There is/There are... | **Există...** | egzeester |
| Is there/Are there...? | **Există...?** | egzeester |
| There isn't/aren't... | **Nu există...** | noo egzeester |
| There isn't/aren't any. | **Nu există nici una.** | noo egzeester neech<sup>y</sup> oona. |

## It's... *Este...*

| | | |
|---|---|---|
| beautiful/ugly | **frumos/urît** | fro**o**mos /**oo**rit |
| better/worse | **mai bine/mai rău** | migh **bee**neh/migh roh |
| big/small | **mare/mic** | **ma**reh/meec |
| cheap/expensive | **ieftin/scump** | yef**t**een/scoomp |
| early/late | **devreme/tîrziu** | dev**r**emeh/t**i**rz**yoo** |
| easy/difficult | **uşor/greu** | oo**shor**/gre°° |
| free (vacant)/ occupied | **liber/ocupat** | **lee**ber/oco**o**pat |
| full/empty | **plin/gol** | pleen/gol |
| good/bad | **bun/rău** | boon/roh |
| heavy/light | **greu/uşor** | gre°°/oo**shor** |
| here/there | **aici/acolo** | a**ee**ch'/a**co**lo |
| hot/cold | **fierbinte/rece** | f**y**er**b**inteh/**r**echeh |
| near/far | **aproape/departe** | apr**wa**peh/de**par**teh |
| next/last | **următorul/ultimul** | oorme**r**to**r**ool/**oo**lteemool |
| old/new | **vechi/nou** | vek'/no°° |
| old/young | **bătrîn/tînar** | ber**t**rin/**t**iner |
| open/shut | **deschis/închis** | des**kees**/in**kees** |
| quick/slow | **repede/încet** | **r**epedeh/in**chet** |
| right/wrong | **bine/rău** | **bee**neh/roh |

## Quantities *Cantităţi*

| | | |
|---|---|---|
| a little/a lot | **puţin/mult** | poot**seen**/moolt |
| few/a few | **puţini/cîţiva** | poot**seen**'/c**i**ts'va |
| much | **mult** | moolt |
| many | **mulţi** | moolts' |
| more/less (than) | **mai mult/mai puţin (decît)** | migh moolt/migh poot**seen** (de**cit**) |
| enough/too | **destul/prea** | des**tool**/pra |
| some/any | **nişte/oricare** | **neesh**teh/o**r**eecareh |

# A few more useful words *Alte cuvinte utile*

| | | |
|---|---|---|
| above | **deasupra** | dasoopra |
| after | **după** | dooper |
| and | **şi** | shee |
| at | **la** | la |
| before (time) | **înainte** | inaeenteh |
| behind | **înapoi** | inapoy |
| below | **dedesubt** | dedesoobt |
| between | **între** | intreh |
| but | **dar** | dar |
| down | **jos** | zhos |
| downstairs | **la parter** | la par**ter** |
| during | **în timpul** | in **teem**pool |
| for | **pentru** | **pen**troo |
| from | **de la** | deh la |
| in | **în** | in |
| inside | **înăuntru** | iner-**oon**troo |
| near | **lîngă** | **lin**ger |
| never | **niciodată** | neechyo**da**ter |
| next to | **lîngă/aproape** | **lin**ger/a**prwa**peh |
| none | **niciunul (niciuna)** | neech$^y$-**oo**nool (neech$^y$-**oon**na) |
| not | **nu** | noo |
| nothing | **nimic** | nee**meec** |
| now | **acum** | a**coom** |
| on | **pe** | peh |
| only | **numai** | **noo**migh |
| or | **sau** | sa$^{oo}$ |
| outside | **afară** | a**far**er |
| perhaps | **poate** | **pwa**teh |
| since | **de atunci încoace** | deh a**toonch**$^y$ in**cwa**cheh |
| soon | **curînd** | coo**rind** |
| then | **atunci** | a**toonch**$^y$ |
| through | **prin** | preen |
| to | **pînă la** | **pi**ner la |
| too (also) | **de asemenea** | deh-a**se**meneh-a |
| towards | **spre** | spreh |
| under | **sub/dedesubt** | soob/dede**soobt** |
| until | **pînă** | **pi**ner |
| up | **sus** | soos |
| upstairs | **la etaj** | la e**tazh** |
| very | **foarte** | **fwar**teh |
| with | **cu** | coo |
| without | **fără** | **fer**rer |
| yet | **încă** | **in**cer |

# Arrival

Whether you come by train, plane or car you will have to go through customs formalities. If you did not obtain a visa in advance through your travel agency or Romanian Consulate, you can get one at road crossing points or the airport.

*Note*: Rail travellers *cannot* have a visa issued on the spot.

> **GHISEUL DE PASAPOARTE**
> PASSPORT CONTROL

The Romanian international airport Otopeni (*otopen*) is situated 18 km from the centre of Bucharest. Although a regular bus service links the airport to the centre, petrol shortages and mechanical problems can cause disruptions. Taxis are probably the most reliable method of transport to and from the airport.

| | | |
|---|---|---|
| Here's my passport. | **Poftiți pașaportul.** | pofteets<sup>y</sup> pashaportool |
| I'll be staying... | **O să stau...** | o ser sta<sup>oo</sup> |
| a few days | **cîteva zile** | cîteva zeeleh |
| a week | **o săptămînă** | o serpterminer |
| two weeks | **două săptămîni** | do-wer serptermin<sup>y</sup> |
| a month | **o lună** | o looner |
| I don't know yet. | **Nu știu încă.** | noo shtee<sup>oo</sup> încer |
| I'm here on holiday. | **Sînt (aici) în vacanță.** | sînt (aeech<sup>y</sup>) in vacantser |
| I'm here on business. | **Sînt/Am venit în interes de serviciu.** | sînt/am veneet in eenteres deh serveechyoo |
| I'm just passing through. | **Sînt în trecere doar.** | sînt in trechereh dwar |

If things become difficult:

| | | |
|---|---|---|
| I'm sorry, I don't understand. | **Regret, nu înțeleg.** | regret noo intseleg |
| Does anyone here speak English? | **Vorbește cineva engleza aici?** | vorbeshteh cheeneva engleza aeech<sup>y</sup> |

> **LA VAMA**
> CUSTOMS

After collecting your baggage at the airport (*aeroport*) you have a choice: use the green exit if you have nothing to declare, or leave via the red exit if you have items to declare (in excess of those allowed).

| **bunuri de declarat** | **nimic de declarat** |
|:---:|:---:|
| goods to declare | nothing to declare |

The import and export of Romanian currency is prohibited, but there is no restriction on the amount of foreign currency visitors can bring into the country.

The chart below shows what you can bring in duty-free.

|  |  |  |
|:---:|:---:|:---:|
| Cigarettes | Spirits (Liquor) | Wine |
| 200 | 2 litres | 4 litres |

| | | |
|---|---|---|
| I have nothing to declare. | **Nu am nimic de declarat.** | noo am nee**meec** deh decla**rat** |
| I have... | **Am...** | am |
| a carton of cigarettes | **un cartuş de ţigări** | oon car**toosh** deh tseeg**err**ᵛ |
| a bottle of whisky | **o sticlă de wisky** | o **stee**cler deh **wees**kee |
| It's for my personal use. | **E pentru mine.** | yeh **pen**troo **mee**neh |
| It's a gift. | **Este un cadou.** | **yes**teh oon ca**do**°° |

| **Paşaportul, vă rog.** | Your passport, please. |
|---|---|
| **Aveţi ceva de declarat?** | Do you have anything to declare? |
| **Vă rog să deschideţi acest sac.** | Please open this bag. |
| **Trebuie să plătiţi vamă pentru aceast obiect.** | You'll have to pay duty on this. |
| **Mai aveţi bagaje?** | Do you have any more luggage? |

## Baggage—Porter *Hamal*

Baggage-porters are available only at the airport. Luggage trolleys are hard to come by at train stations, although you can ask a taxi driver to help you.

| | | |
|---|---|---|
| Porter! | **Hamal!/Alo!** | hamal/alo |
| Please take (this)... | **Vă rog luaţi (acest)...** | ver rog lwats<sup>y</sup> (**achest**) |
| | | |
| luggage | **bagaj** | bagazh |
| suitcase | **valiză** | valeezer |
| (travelling) bag | **sac de voiaj** | sac de voyazh |
| That one is mine. | **Aceea este a mea.** | acheya yesteh a meh-a |
| Take this luggage... | **Duceţi acest bagaj...** | doochets<sup>y</sup> achest bagazh |
| | | |
| to the bus | **la autobuz** | la aootobooz |
| to the luggage lockers | **la cabinele de bagaje** | la cabeeneleh de bagazheh |
| to the taxi | **la taxi** | la taxee |
| How much is that? | **Cît costă?** | cît coster |
| There's one piece missing. | **Lipseşte un bagaj.** | leepseshteh oon bagazh |
| Where are the luggage trolleys (carts)? | **Unde sînt cărucioarele de bagaje?** | oondeh sînt cerroochywareleh deh bagazheh |

## Changing money *Schimb valutar*

Foreign currency can be changed at airports, banks, most hotels and currency exchange offices in major cities. Avoid changing a large amount of money at the beginning of your visit as you may not easily be able to change it back. Never change money with street dealers; you're only likely to be cheated.

| | | |
|---|---|---|
| Where's the nearest currency exchange office? | **Unde este un birou de schimb prin apropiere?** | oondeh yeste oon beero<sup>oo</sup> deh skeemb preen apropyereh |
| Can you change these traveller's cheques (checks)? | **Pot încasa nişte cecuri de voiaj?** | pot încasa neeshteh checoor<sup>y</sup> deh voyazh |

BANK—CURRENCY, see page 129

| I want to change some dollars/pounds. | **Vreau să schimb niște dolari/lire sterline.** | vrea⁰⁰ ser skeemb **neesh**teh dolar**ᵛ**/**leer**eh sterleeneh |
| Can you change this into lei? | **Puteți schimba aceşti bani în lei?** | poo**tets**ᵛ skeemba achesht**ᵛ** ban**ᵛ** in lay |
| What's the exchange rate? | **Care este cursul?** | careh **yes**teh **coor**sool |

## Where is...? *Unde este...?*

| Where is the...? | **Unde este...?** | **oon**deh **yes**teh |
| booking office | **agenţia de voiaj** | ajent**see**-a deh vo**yazh** |
| duty (tax)-free shop | **magazinul 'duty free'** | maga**zee**nool 'duty free' |
| newsstand | **chioşcul de ziare** | **kyosh**cool deh **zyar**eh |
| restaurant | **restaurantul** | restau**ran**tool |
| How do I get to...? | **Cum se ajunge la...?** | coom seh a**zhoon**jeh la |
| Is there a bus into town? | **Ce autobuz merge în oraş?** | cheh auto**booz mer**jeh in o**rash** |
| Where can I get a taxi? | **De unde pot lua un taxi?** | deh **oon**deh pot lwa oon taxee |
| Where can I hire (rent) a car? | **Unde pot închiria o maşină?** | **oon**deh pot inkeer**eea** o ma**shee**ner |

## Hotel reservation *Rezervare la hotel*

| Do you have a hotel guide (directory)? | **Aveţi un ghid cu hoteluri?** | a**vets**ᵛ oon geed coo hoteloor**ᵛ** |
| Could you reserve a room for me? | **Puteţi să-mi rezervaţi o cameră?** | poo**tets**ᵛ serm**ᵛ** rezer**vats**ᵛ o **camer**er |
| in the centre | **în centru** | in **chen**troo |
| near the railway station | **lîngă gară** | **lin**ger **gar**er |
| a single room | **o cameră cu un pat** | o **camer**er coo oon pat |
| a double room | **o cameră cu două paturi** | o **camer**er coo **do**-wer **pat**oor**ᵛ** |
| not too expensive | **nu prea scumpă** | noo preh-a **scoom**per |
| Where is the hotel/ guesthouse? | **Unde este hotelul/ hotelul pensiune?** | **oon**deh **yes**teh **hotel**ool/ **hotel**ool pensy**oo**neh |
| Do you have a street map? | **Aveţi o hartă a oraşului?** | a**vets**ᵛ o **har**ter a orashoo**loo**y |

HOTEL/ACCOMMODATION, see page 22

## Car hire (rental) *Inchirieri auto*

There are car rental facilities at the airport and in major cities. The main rental offices are the National Tourist Office (ONT) and the Romanian Automobile Club (ACR). You must be at least 21 years old and have held a full driving licence for more than one year. Your hotel can help you with further information, or contact The National Tourist Office. The Intercontinental Hotel provides a chauffeur-driven limousine rental service for its guests.

| | | |
|---|---|---|
| I'd like to hire (rent) a car. | **Aş vrea să închiriez o maşină.** | ash vreh-**a** ser ɨnkeeree-**ez** o masheener |
| small | **un autoturism** | oon aoototoo**reesm** |
| medium-sized | **de capacitate medie** | deh capachee**tateh** **med**yeh |
| large | **mare** | **mareh** |
| automatic | **automată** | aooto**mater** |
| I'd like it for a day/ a week. | **Pentru o zi/o săp-tămînă.** | **pen**troo o zee/o serpter**mi**ner |
| Are there any week-end arrangements? | **Ce tarife aveţi pen-tru sfîrşit de săptă-mînă?** | cheh ta**reefeh** a**vets**ʸ **pen**troo sfɨr**sheet** deh serpter**miner** |
| Do you have any special rates? | **Ce reduceri faceţi?** | cheh re**doocher**ʸ **fachets**ʸ |
| What's the charge per day/week? | **Cît costă locaţia pe zi/săptămînă?** | cɨt **coster** lo**catsya** peh zee/serpter**miner** |
| Is mileage included? | **Kilometrajul este inclus?** | keelometra**zhool** **yeste** een**cloos** |
| What's the charge per kilometre? | **Cît costă pe kilo-metru?** | cɨt **coster** peh keelo**metroo** |
| I'd like to leave the car in... | **Aş vrea să las maşina în...** | ash vreh-**a** ser las ma**sheena** ɨn |
| I'd like full insurance. | **Doresc o asigurare integrală.** | do**resc** o aseegoo**rareh** eente**graler** |
| How much is the deposit? | **Ce avans trebuie să las?** | cheh **avans** tre**booyeh** ser las |
| I have a credit card. | **Pentru plată am carte de credit.** | **pen**troo **plater** am **carteh** deh **credeet** |
| Here's my driving licence. | **Poftim carnetul de conducere.** | pof**teem** carne**tool** deh con**doochereh** |

CAR, see page 75

## Taxi *Taxi*

Metered vehicles, both state owned (GETAX) and private (TAXIP), are available in Bucharest and all larger towns. Taxi drivers can issue a receipt for the fare on request. It is customary to give a tip in addition to the amount shown on the meter. Taxis are generally rather old Romanian cars and are easily identified by a light on top of the vehicle.

| Where can I get a taxi? | **De unde pot lua un taxi, vă rog?** | deh **oon**deh pot lwa oon taxee ver rog |
| Where is the taxi rank (stand)? | **Unde este staţia de taxi?** | **oon**deh **yes**teh **stat**sya deh taxee |
| Could you get me a taxi? | **Puteţi să-mi comandaţi un taxi, vă rog?** | poo**tets**ʸ serm**ʸ** coman**dats**ʸ oon taxee ver rog |
| What's the fare to...? | **Cît costă pînă la...?** | cît **cos**ter **pi**ner la...? |
| How far is it to...? | **Este departe pînă la...?** | **yes**teh de**par**teh **pi**ner la...? |
| Take me to... | **Vreau să merg la...** | vrau ser merg la |
| this address | **adresa aceasta** | adresa a**chas**ta |
| the airport | **aeroport** | a-ero**port** |
| the town centre | **în centru** | in **chen**troo |
| the... Hotel | **la hotelul...** | la hote**lool**... |
| the railway station | **la gară** | la **gar**er |
| Turn at the next corner. | **Cotiţi la colţul următor.** | co**teets**ʸ la **colt**sool oormer**tor** |
| left/right | **la stînga/la dreapta** | la **stin**ga/la **drap**ta |
| Go straight ahead. | **Mergeţi drept înainte.** | mer**jets**ʸ drept inaa**een**teh |
| Please stop here. | **Vă rog, opriţi aici.** | ver rog o**preets**ʸ a**eech**ʸ |
| I'm in a hurry. | **Mă grăbesc.** | mer grer**besc** |
| Could you drive more slowly? | **Aţi putea să conduceţi mai încet?** | ats**ʸ** pooteh-a ser condoo**chets**ʸ migh in**chet** |
| Could you help me carry my luggage? | **Vreţi să mă ajutaţi la bagaje?** | vrets**ʸ** ser mer azhoo**tats**ʸ la ba**gazh**eh |
| Could you wait for me? | **Puteţi să mă aşteptaţi?** | poo**tets**ʸ ser mer ashtep**tats**ʸ |
| I'll be back in 10 minutes. | **Mă întorc peste zece minute.** | mer **in**torc **pes**teh **ze**cheh mee**noo**teh |

# Hotel—Other accommodation

Although you are advised to book ahead if you intend to stay during the peak holiday season, hotel rooms are not difficult to come by; a room will generally be found for foreign travellers. However, Romania is not yet well equipped for independent tourists – hotels tend to cater mainly for business travellers or for package tours to the Black Sea resorts, spa towns or cities linked with the life of Count Dracula.

**hotel**
(hotel)

Hotels in Romania are classified from five-star to one-star, or de luxe. Few offer full or half board, or even bed and breakfast, though this is changing. Most rooms in three-star hotels have en-suite bathrooms and toilets. In two-star and one-star hotels the bathroom and toilet are shared, and visitors are advised to bring their own essentials, like soap and toilet paper. Usually the price includes a room only and any meals will be charged separately or paid for in the dining room.

In general, and particularly outside Bucharest, foreigners are expected to pay in Western currency, preferably in US dollars; most hotels do not yet accept credit cards.

It is unwise to leave valuables in hotel rooms of any category.

**motel**
(motel)

There are an increasing number of motels in Romania, catering specifically for the motorist.

**camera mobilată**
(camera mobeelater)

Rented accommodation in private flats and houses is becoming increasingly available to visitors. Details may be available at the local tourist office; otherwise taxi drivers can be a useful source of information.

**caminul de studenti**
(cameenool deh stoodent’ÿ)

Youth hotels, run by the student travel service, CTT, are situated in major towns; these give preference to large groups and are open only in July and August, but are inexpensive if booked directly at the hostel.

| | | |
|---|---|---|
| **cabane**<br>(cabaneh) | A network of chalets for hikers in the mountains; cheap and friendly, though not necessarily comfortable, these cabins are listed in the official *Cabane Turistice* map. | |

| | | |
|---|---|---|
| Can you recommend a hotel? | **Puteţi să-mi recomandaţi un hotel?** | pootets<sup>y</sup> serm<sup>y</sup> recomandats<sup>y</sup> oon hotel |
| Are there any self-catering flats (apartments) vacant? | **Ce apartamente aveţi libere?** | cheh apartamenteh avets<sup>y</sup> leebereh |
| I'd like a private room. | **Vreau o cameră particulară.** | vra<sup>oo</sup> o camer parteecoolarer |

## Checking in—Reception *La recepţie*

| | | |
|---|---|---|
| My name is... | **Mă numesc...** | mer noomesc |
| I have a reservation. | **Am o rezervare.** | am o rezervareh |
| We've reserved two rooms/ an apartment. | **Am rezervat două camere/un apartament.** | am rezervat do-wer camereh/oon apartament |
| Here's the confirmation. | **Aceasta este confirmarea.** | achasta yesteh confeermareh-a |
| Do you have any vacancies? | **Aveţi camere libere?** | avets<sup>y</sup> camereh leebereh |
| I'd like a... | **Aş vrea...** | ash vreh-a |
| single room | **o cameră cu un pat** | o camer coo oon pat |
| double room | **o cameră cu două paturi** | o camer coo do-wer patoor<sup>y</sup> |
| We'd like a room... | **Am dori o cameră...** | am doree o camer |
| with twin beds | **cu două paturi** | coo do-wer patoor<sup>y</sup> |
| with a double bed | **cu pat dublu** | coo pat doobloo |
| with a bath | **cu baie** | coo bayeh |
| with a shower | **cu duş** | coo doosh |
| with a balcony | **cu balcon** | coo balcon |
| with a view | **cu vedere la stradă** | coo vedereh la strader |
| at the front | **la faţadă** | la fatsader |
| at the back | **la interior** | la eenteryor |
| It must be quiet. | **Trebuie să fie liniştită.** | trebooyeh ser fee-eh leeneeshteeter |
| Is there...? | **Este/Există ...?** | yesteh/egzeester |
| air conditioning | **aer condiţionat** | a-er condeetsyonat |
| a conference room | **o sală de conferinţe** | o saler deh confereentseh |

CHECKING OUT, see page 31

Hotel

| a laundry service | serviciu de spălătorie | serveechyoo deh sperlertoree-eh |
| a private toilet | toaletă individuală | to-aleter eendeeveedwaler |
| a radio/television in the room | un radio/un televizor în cameră | oon radyo/oon televeezor in camerer |
| a swimming pool | o piscină | o peescheener |
| hot water | apă caldă | aper calder |
| room service | servicii la cameră | serveechee la camerer |
| running water | apă curentă | aper coorenter |
| Could you put an extra bed/a cot in the room? | Puteţi pune încă un pat/un pătuţ în cameră, vă rog? | pootetsʸ pooneh incer oon pat/oon pertoots in camerer ver rog |

## How much? *Cît costă?*

| What's the price...? | Cît costă? | cit coster |
| per day | pe zi | peh zee |
| per week | pe săptămînă | peh serpterminer |
| for bed and breakfast | pentru cazare şi micul dejun | pentroo cazareh shee meecool dezhoon |
| excluding meals | fără mese | ferrer meseh |
| for full board (A.P.) | pensiune completă | pensyooneh completer |
| for half board (M.A.P.) | demi pesiune | demee pensyooneh |
| Does that include...? | Aceasta include şi...? | achasta eencloodeh shee |
| breakfast | micul dejun | meecool dezhoon |
| service | serviciul | serveechyool |
| Is there any reduction for children? | Faceţi reduceri de tarif pentru copii? | fachetsʸ redoocherʸ deh tareef pentroo copeeh |
| Do you charge for the baby? | Se plăteşte pentru copii mici? | seh plerteshteh pentroo copeeh meechʸ |
| That's too expensive. | E preha scump. | yeh preh-a scoomp |
| Do you have anything cheaper? | Aveţi ceva mai ieftin? | avetsʸ cheva migh yefteen |
| Is electricity included in the rental? | Electricitatea este inclusă în chirie? | electreecheetata yesteh eenclooser in keeree-eh |

## How long? *Cît timp (vreţi să staţi)?*

| We'll be staying... | O să stăm... | o ser sterm |
| overnight only | numai o noapte | noomigh o nwapteh |
| a few days | cîteva zile | citeva zeeleh |

NUMBERS, see page 147

| a week (at least) | o săptămînă (cel puţin) | o serpterminer (chel pootseen) |
| I don't know yet. | Nu ştiu încă. | noo shtee°° încer |

### Decision *Decizie*

| May I see the room? | Pot să văd camera, vă rog? | pot ser verd camera ver rog |
| That's fine. I'll take it. | E bine, o iau. | yeh beeneh o ya°° |
| No. I don't like it. | Nu-mi place. | noom$^y$ placheh |
| It's too... | Este prea... | yesteh preh-a |
| cold/hot | rece/caldă | recheh/calder |
| dark/small | intunecoasă/mică | întoonecwaser/meecer |
| noisy | zgomotoasă | zgomotwaser |
| I asked for a room with a bath. | Am cerut o cameră cu baie. | am cheroot o camerer coo bayeh |
| Do you have anything...? | Aveţi ceva...? | avets$^y$ cheva |
| better | mai bun | migh boon |
| bigger | mai mare | migh mareh |
| cheaper | mai ieftin | migh yefteen |
| quieter | mai liniştit | migh leeneeshteet |
| Do you have a room with a better view? | Aveţi o cameră cu vedere mai bună? | avets$^y$ o camerer coo vedereh migh booner |

### Registration *Înregistrare*

Upon arrival at a hotel you'll be asked to fill in a registration form (*formular*).

| Numele/Prenumele | Name/First name |
| Oraşul/Strada/Numărul | Home town/Street/Number |
| Naţionalitatea/Ocupaţia | Nationality/Occupation |
| Data/Locul naşterii | Date/Place of birth |
| Sosit din... /Cu destinaţia... | Coming from... /Going to... |
| Numărul de paşaport | Passport number |
| Locul/Data emiterii | Place/Date |
| Semnătura | Signature |

| What does this mean? | Ce înseamnă aceasta? | cheh însamner achasta |
| What's my room number? | Ce număr are camera mea? | cheh noomerr areh camera meh-a |

| | |
|---|---|
| **May I see your passport, please?** | Pașaportul, vă rog? |
| **Would you mind filling in this registration form?** | Vă rog să completați acest formular. |
| **Please sign here.** | Vă rog să semnați în locul acesta. |
| **How long will you be staying?** | Cît doriți să stați? |

| | | |
|---|---|---|
| Will you have our luggage sent up? | **Vreți să ne trimiteți bagajul în cameră?** | vrets$^y$ ser neh treemeetetsy bagazhool ïn camerer |
| Where can I park my car? | **Unde pot parca mașina?** | oondeh pot parca masheena |
| Does the hotel have a garage? | **Există un garaj al hotelului?** | egzeester oon garazh al hoteloolooy |
| I'd like to leave this in the hotel safe. | **Aș vrea să las aceasta în seiful hotelului.** | ash vreh-a ser las achasta ïn seyfool hotelooloy |

### Hotel staff   *Personalul hotelului*

| hall porter | **valet** | valet |
|---|---|---|
| maid | **cameristă** | camereester |
| manager | **director** | deerector |
| porter | **portar** | portar |
| receptionist | **recepționist(ă)** | recheptsyoneest(er) |
| switchboard operator | **telefonistă** | telefoneester |
| waiter | **chelner** | kelner |
| waitress | **chelneriță** | kelnereetser |

If you want to address members of staff, use a general introductory phrase: *Fiți amabil, vă rog . . .* —feets$^y$ amabeel ver rog.

### General requirements   *Servicii—Informații*

| | | |
|---|---|---|
| The key to room..., please. | **Dați-mi vă rog cheia de la camera numărul...** | datseem$^y$ ver rog keya deh la camera noomerrool |
| Could you wake me at... please? | **Puteți să mă sculați la ora..., vă rog?** | pootets$^y$ ser mer scoolats$^y$ la ora... ver rog |
| When is breakfast/ lunch/dinner served? | **Cînd se servește micul dejun/prînzul/cina?** | cïnd seh serveshteh meecool dezhoon/prïnzool/cheena |

NUMBERS, see page 147/TELLING THE TIME, see page 153

| May we have breakfast in our room, please? | **Putem avea micul dejun în cameră, vă rog?** | pootem aveh-a meecool dezhoon in camerer ver rog |
| Is there a bath on this floor? | **Există o baie pe palierul acesta?** | egzeester o bayeh peh palyerool achesta |
| What's the voltage? | **Ce voltaj are circuitul electric?** | cheh voltazh areh cheercooeeetool electreec |
| Where's the shaver socket (outlet)? | **Există o priză pentru aparatul de ras?** | egzeester o preezer pentroo aparatool deh ras |
| Can you find me a...? | **Puteți să-mi găsiți...?** | pootets<sup>y</sup> serm<sup>y</sup> gerseets<sup>y</sup> |
| babysitter | **îngrijitoare de copii/baby sitter** | ingreezheetwareh deh copeey/'babysitter' |
| secretary | **secretară** | secretarer |
| typewriter | **mașină de scris** | masheener deh screes |
| May I have a/an/some...? | **Aveți...?** | avets<sup>y</sup> |
| ashtray | **o scrumieră** | o scroomyerer |
| bath towel | **un prosop de baie** | oon prosop deh bayeh |
| (extra) blanket | **o pătură (în plus)** | o pertoorer (in ploos) |
| envelopes | **plicuri** | pleecoor<sup>y</sup> |
| (more) hangers | **(cîteva) umerașe** | (cîteva) oomerasheh |
| hot-water bottle | **o buiotă cu apă fierbinte** | o booyoter coo aper fyerbeenteh |
| ice cubes | **cuburi de gheață** | cooboor<sup>y</sup> deh gyatser |
| needle and thread | **ac și ață** | ac shee atser |
| (extra) pillow | **(încă o) pernă** | (incer o) perner |
| reading lamp | **lampă de citit** | lamper deh cheeteet |
| soap | **săpun** | serpoon |
| writing paper | **hîrtie de scris** | hirtee-eh deh screes |
| Where's the...? | **Unde este...?** | oondeh yesteh |
| bathroom | **baia** | baya |
| dining-room | **sala de mese/sufrageria** | sala deh meseh/soofrajereea |
| electricity meter | **contoarul** | contwarool |
| emergency exit | **ieșirea de incendiu** | yesheereh-a deh eenchendyoo |
| hairdresser's | **coaforul/frizeria** | cwaforool/freezereea |
| lift (elevator) | **liftul** | leeftool |
| Where are the toilets? | **Unde este toaleta?** | oondeh yesteh to-aleta |

BREAKFAST, see page 40

## Telephone—Post (mail) *Telefon—Poştă*

| | | |
|---|---|---|
| Can you get me Constanţa 123-45-67? | **Puteţi să-mi faceţi legătura cu Constanţa 123 45 67?** | pootets<sup>y</sup> serm<sup>y</sup> fachets<sup>y</sup> legertoora coo Constantsa 123 45 67 |
| Do you have any stamps? | **Aveţi timbre?** | avets<sup>y</sup> **teem**breh |
| Would you post this for me, please? | **Fiţi amabil, puteţi să-mi puneţi acest plic la poştă?** | feets<sup>y</sup> amabeel pootets<sup>y</sup> serm<sup>y</sup> **poo**nets<sup>y</sup> achest pleec la **posh**ter |
| Are there any letters for me? | **Am vreo scrisoare?** | am vro scree**swa**reh |
| Are there any messages for me? | **Am vreun mesaj?** | am vroon me**sazh** |
| How much is my telephone bill? | **Cît vă datorez pentru convorbirile telefonice?** | cît ver datorez pentroo convorbee**reel**eh telefo**neech**eh |

## Difficulties *Dificultăţi—Probleme*

| | | |
|---|---|---|
| The... doesn't work. | **Nu funcţionează...** | noo foonctsyo**naz**er |
| air conditioning | **aerul condiţionat** | a-erool condeetsyo**nat** |
| bidet | **bideul** | beede-**ool** |
| fan | **ventilatorul** | venteela**tor**ool |
| heating | **încălzirea** | incerl**zee**reh-a |
| light | **lumina** | loo**mee**na |
| radio | **radioul** | **rad**yo-ool |
| television | **televizorul** | tele**veez**orool |
| The tap (faucet) is dripping. | **Robinetul curge.** | robee**net**ool **coor**jeh |
| There's no hot water. | **Nu este apă caldă.** | noo **yes**teh aper **cal**der |
| The washbasin is blocked. | **Chiuveta este înfundată.** | kyoo**vet**a **yes**teh **in**foon**dat**er |
| The window is jammed. | **Fereastra este blocată.** | fe**ras**tra **yes**teh blo**cat**er |
| The curtains are stuck. | **Perdelele sînt blocate.** | per**del**eleh sint blo**cat**eh |
| The bulb is burned out. | **Becul s-a ars.** | **bec**ool sa ars |
| My bed hasn't been made up. | **Patul nu a fost făcut.** | **pat**ool noo a fost fer-**coot** |

POST OFFICE AND TELEPHONE, see page 132

| The... is broken. | **Nu funcţionează...** | noo foonctsyonazer |
|---|---|---|
| blind | **jaluzelele** | zhaloozeleleh |
| lamp | **lampa** | lampa |
| plug | **ştecherul** | shtekerool |
| shutter | **oblonul** | oblonool |
| switch | **butonul/întrerupâ-torul** | bootonool/intreroopertorool |
| Can you get it repaired? | **Îl puteţi da la reparat?** | il pootets$^y$ da la reparat |

## Laundry—Dry cleaner's *Spălătorie—Curăţătorie*

There are laundry services in most big towns. Look for the sign
*Nufărul*—**noo**ferrool.

| I'd like these clothes... | **Aş vrea să las aceste rufe...** | ash vreh-a ser las achesteh roofeh |
|---|---|---|
| cleaned | **pentru curăţat** | pentroo coorertsat |
| ironed | **pentru călcat** | pentroo cerlcat |
| pressed | **pentru călcat** | pentroo cerlcat |
| washed | **pentru spălat** | pentroo sperlat |
| When will they be ready? | **Cînd vor fi gata?** | cind vor fee gata |
| I need them... | **Am nevoie de ele...** | am nevoyeh deh yeleh |
| today | **azi** | az$^y$ |
| tonight | **deseară** | desarer |
| tomorrow | **mîine** | miyneh |
| before Friday | **înainte de vineri** | inaeenteh deh veener$^y$ |
| Can you... this? | **Puteţi...?** | pootets$^y$ |
| mend | **repara aceasta** | repara achasta |
| patch | **pune un petec** | pooneh oon petec |
| stitch | **coase aceasta** | cwaseh achasta |
| Can you sew on this button? | **Puteţi coase acest nasture?** | pootets$^y$ cwaseh achest nastooreh |
| Can you get this stain out? | **Puteţi scoate pata aceasta?** | pootets$^y$ scwateh pata achasta |
| Is my laundry ready? | **Sînt gata rufele mele?** | sint gata roofeleh meleh |
| This isn't mine. | **Aceasta nu este a mea.** | achasta noo yesteh a meh-a |

| There's something missing. | **Lipsește ceva.** | leepseshteh cheva |
| There's a hole in this. | **Aceasta are o gaură.** | achasta areh o **ga**-oorer |

## Hairdresser—Barber *Coafor—Frizer*

| Is there a hairdresser/ beauty salon in the hotel? | **Există un salon de coafură/un salon de cosmetică în hotel?** | egzeester oon salon deh cwafoorer/oon salon deh cosmeteecer in hotel |
| Can I make an appointment for Tuesday? | **Pot să-mi fixez o oră pentru marți, vă rog?** | pot serm<sup>y</sup> feexez o o-rer pentroo marts<sup>y</sup> ver rog |
| I'd like a cut and blow dry. | **Aș vrea o tunsoare și un pieptănat.** | ash vreh-a o toonswareh shee oon pyepternat |
| I'd like a haircut, please. | **Aș vrea o tunsoare, vă rog.** | ash vreh-a o toonswareh ver rog |
| blow-dry | **un pieptănat** | oon pyepternat |
| colour rinse | **un șampon colorant** | oon shampon colorant |
| dye | **un vopsit** | oon vopseet |
| face pack | **o mască** | o mascer |
| hair gel | **un gel de păr** | oon jel deh perr |
| highlights | **un decolorat** | oon decolorat |
| manicure | **o manechiură** | o manekyoorer |
| (perm)anent wave | **un permanent** | oon permanent |
| setting lotion | **un fixativ** | oon feexateev |
| shampoo and set | **șampon și bigudi-uri** | shampon shee beegoodee-oor<sup>y</sup> |
| with a fringe (bangs) | **cu breton** | coo breton |
| I'd like a shampoo for... hair. | **Un spălat cu șampon pentru...** | oon sperlat coo shampon pentroo |
| normal/dry/ greasy (oily) | **păr normal/uscat/ gras** | perr normal/ooscat/gras |
| Do you have a colour chart? | **Aveți o paletă de culori?** | avets<sup>y</sup> o paleter deh coolor<sup>y</sup> |
| Don't cut it too short. | **Nu tundeți prea scurt.** | noo toondets<sup>y</sup> preh-a scoort |
| A little more off the... | **Puțin mai scurt...** | pootseen migh scoort |
| back | **la spate** | la spateh |
| neck | **pe gît** | peh git |
| sides | **în părți** | in perrts<sup>y</sup> |
| top | **în vîrful capului** | in virfool capoolooy |

DAYS OF THE WEEK, see page 151

| I don't want any hairspray. | **Nu vreau fixativ.** | noo vra°° feexa**teev** |
| I'd like a shave. | **Vreau un ras.** | vra°° oon ras |
| Would you trim my..., please? | **Vreți să-mi aranjați... vă rog?** | vrets<sup>y</sup> serm<sup>y</sup> aranzhats<sup>y</sup>... ver rog |
| beard | **barba** | barba |
| moustache | **mustața** | moostatsa |
| sideboards (sideburns) | **perciunii** | perchyooneey |

## Checking out *La plecare*

| May I have my bill, please? | **Nota de plată, vă rog?** | nota deh plater ver rog |
| I'm leaving early in the morning. | **Plec mîine dimineață.** | plec miyneh deemeenatser |
| Please have my bill ready. | **Vă rog să pregătiți nota de plată.** | ver rog ser pregerteets<sup>y</sup> nota deh plater |
| We'll be checking out around noon. | **O să părăsim hotelul în jurul orei douăsprezece.** | o ser perrerseem hotelool in zhoorool oray do-wersprezecheh |
| I must leave at once. | **Trebuie să plec imediat.** | trebooyeh ser plec eemedyat |
| Is everything included? | **Este totul inclus?** | yesteh totool eencloos |
| Can I pay by credit card? | **Pot plăti cu cartea de credit?** | pot plertee coo carteh-a deh credeet |
| I think there's a mistake in the bill. | **Cred că este o greșeală în nota de plată.** | cred cer yesteh o greshaler in nota deh plater |
| Can you get us a taxi? | **Ne puteți comanda un taxi?** | neh pootets<sup>y</sup> comanda oon taxee |
| Could you have our luggage brought down? | **Puteți să ne aduceți bagajul în hol, vă rog?** | pootets<sup>y</sup> ser neh adoochets<sup>y</sup> bagazhool in hol ver rog |
| Here's the forwarding address. | **Aceasta este adresa pentru expedierea curierului.** | achasta yesteh adresa pentroo expedyereh-a cooryeroolooy |
| You have my home address. | **Aveți adresa mea de acasă.** | avets<sup>y</sup> adresa meh-a deh acaser |
| It's been a very enjoyable stay. | **Am avut un sejur minunat.** | am avoot oon sezhoor meenoonat |

DAYS OF THE WEEK, see page 151

## Camping *Camping*

Camping facilities of a standard acceptable to foreign visitors are almost non-existent in Romania. However, you can obtain a list of designated camp sites from Romanian National Tourist Offices. If you are travelling by caravan you can stop almost anywhere, though be sure to take plenty of provisions with you as shopping in the countryside can be difficult.

| | | |
|---|---|---|
| Is there a camp site near here? | Există un teren de camping în apropiere? | egzeester oon teren deh campeeng in apropyereh |
| Can we camp here? | Putem face un camping aici? | pootem facheh oon campeeng aeech<sup>y</sup> |
| Do you have room for a tent/caravan? | Aveți spațiu pentru un cort/o rulotă? | avets<sup>y</sup> spatsyoo pentroo oon cort/o rooloter |
| What's the charge...? | Cît costă? | cit coster |
| per day | pe zi | peh zee |
| per person | de persoană | deh perswaner |
| for a car | pentru o mașină | pentroo o masheener |
| for a tent | pentru un cort | pentroo oon cort |
| for a caravan (trailer) | pentru o rulotă | pentroo oh rooloter |
| Is tourist tax included? | Taxa turistică este inclusă? | taxa tooreesteecer yesteh eenclooser |
| Is there/Are there (a)...? | Este/Există...? | yesteh/egzeester |
| drinking water | apă potabilă | aper potabeeler |
| electricity | electricitate | electreecheetateh |
| playground | teren de joacă | teren de zhwacer |
| restaurant | restaurant | resta<sup>oo</sup>rant |
| shopping facilities | magazin | magazeen |
| swimming pool | piscină | pees-cheener |
| Where are the showers/toilets? | Unde sînt dușurile/toaletele? | oondeh sint dooshooreeleh/to-aleteleh |
| Where can I get butane gas? | De unde putem cumpăra gaz butan? | deh oondeh pootem coomperra gaz bootan |
| Is there a youth hostel near here? | Ce cazare aveți pentru tineret? | cheh cazareh avets<sup>y</sup> pentroo teeneret |

CAMPING EQUIPMENT, see page 106

# Eating out

Romania offers a variety of places where you can eat and drink, ranging from simple snack bars to luxury restaurants (*restaurant*—resta°°**rant**). Although most restaurants are still state-run by the Ministry of Tourism, a number of new private eating establishments have begun to open up, especially in Bucharest.

Most restaurants still display the category markings I, II and III; the higher the category, the higher the price you can expect to pay. Many of the larger hotels have a category I restaurant. You will also see self-service restaurants where a good range of traditional Romanian dishes is offered at reasonable prices.

Romania does not have many eating places serving foreign cuisine, although you will find a few good Chinese and Turkish restaurants in Bucharest. Here are some other places to look for.

**Autoservire**
(a°°toser**vee**reh)

Inexpensive, self-service canteen.

**Berărie**
(berer**yeh**)

A public house where you can drink Romanian beer as well as foreign brands. Women do not usually frequent these serious drinking dens.

**Braserie**
(braser**yeh**)

A combined bar, café and restaurant usually offering a good variety of dishes at reasonable prices. Service is provided at the table.

**Bufet**
(boo**fet**)

This is a small restaurant found in railway stations where you'll be served traditional Romanian food. The *Bufet expres* is a stand-up cafeteria for quick meals of rather limited choice.

**Cafe-bar**
(cafeh-**bar**)

Serves hot beverages, soft and alcoholic drinks, and is a convenient place for a quick snack. Cafe-bars are similar to the *snack bar*, which also offers a range of light meals and drinks.

**Cofetărie**
(cofe**terryeh**)

This is a cake shop that also serves coffee, ice cream and soft drinks. Tea is generally served only in large hotels.

| **Han** (han) | A large restaurant, usually with rustic decor, serving moderately priced food and drinks. Some have Romanian folk music entertainment in the evening. |
| **Podgorie** (podgoryeh) | A wine bar serving drinks only; you won't be able to eat here. |

## Meal times  *Mesele zilei*

Traditionally Romanians have three meals per day:
Breakfast (*micul dejun*) is normally served between 7 and 10am and is generally based on bread and cheese, or jam and butter on bread, served with tea or coffee.

Lunch (*masa de prînz* or *dejunul*) is served from 12am until 2pm, and is the main meal of the day for most people in Romania. They will generally start with borsh or soup and follow with a stew or roast. Home-made cakes such as pancakes, fritters or petits fours will end the meal. Romanians like to drink wine mixed with sparkling mineral water with their meal, and a cup of Turkish coffee to finish.

Dinner (*cina*) is taken between 7pm and 10pm. It generally comprises baked meat, pies, souffles, meat rolls, cheese rolls, *mămăligă* (polenta, or cornmeal porridge) with cheese and fried eggs, and home-made yoghurt. In the evening wine, beer or herbal teas are drunk.

Before beginning the meal people wish each other *pofta buna*, the equivalent of *bon appetit*; at the end of the meal they say *sa va fie de bine*—"To your health!"

## Romanian cuisine  *Mîncăruri românești*

Romanians love eating, supported by a long and notable gastronomic tradition. The country offers an intriguing culinary mixture of Latin and Slavic, a love of France with the crossing of influences from Hungary and Turkey. Traditional dishes are based on borsh, stewed vegetables (*ghiveci*), vegetable souffles, pasta, potatoes, polenta and vegetable salads. Romanian dishes are cooked using sunflower or corn oil; butter or lard is used for baking.

An à la carte menu will have a choice of starters: slices of salami or ham, feta cheese and olives, taramasalata, aubergine salad, chicken liver or meat and cheese pastries; subsequent courses will include borsh or soup, roast or grilled meat, cakes or tortes, ice cream and fruit salad. Some restaurants will also serve traditional Romanian dishes such as stewed vegetables with meat (*ghiveci cu carne*) or minced meat with vegetables. Turkish coffee is usually served at the end of the meal.

Although there are no great regional differences in Romanian cuisine, it is generally accepted that Moldavian food is more piquant and offers greater variety.

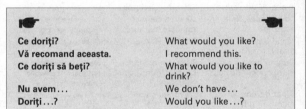

| | |
|---|---|
| **Ce doriţi?** | What would you like? |
| **Vă recomand aceasta.** | I recommend this. |
| **Ce doriţi să beţi?** | What would you like to drink? |
| **Nu avem...** | We don't have... |
| **Doriţi...?** | Would you like...? |

## Hungry? *Vă este foame?*

| | | |
|---|---|---|
| I'm hungry/I'm thirsty. | **Mi-e foame/Mi-e sete.** | myeh **fwa**meh/myeh **se**teh |
| Can you recommend a good restaurant? | **Imi puteţi recomanda un restaurant bun?** | im<sup>y</sup> pootets<sup>y</sup> recoman**da** oon resta<sup>oo</sup>**rant** boon |
| Are there any inexpensive restaurants around here? | **Există vreun restaurant nu prea scump prin apropiere?** | egzeester vreh-**oon** resta<sup>oo</sup>**rant** noo preh-a scoomp preen apro**pye**reh |

If you want to be sure of getting a table in a well-known restaurant, it may be better to book in advance.

| | | |
|---|---|---|
| I'd like to reserve a table for 4. | **Doresc să rezerv o masă pentru patru persoane.** | doresc ser rezerv o maser pentroo patroo perswaneh |
| We'll come at 8. | **O să venim la ora opt.** | o ser veneem la ora opt |
| Could we have a table...? | **Putem avea o masă...?** | pootem aveh-a o maser |
| in the corner | **în colț** | in colts |
| by the window | **lîngă fereastră** | linger ferastrer |
| outside | **afară** | afarer |
| on the terrace | **pe terasă** | peh teraser |
| in a non-smoking area | **în zona de nefumători** | in zona deh nefoomertor[y] |

## Asking and ordering *A cere si a face o comandă*

| | | |
|---|---|---|
| Waiter/Waitress! | **Chelner/Chelneriță!** | kelner/kelnereetser |
| I'd like something to eat/drink. | **Aş vrea ceva de mîncare/băutură.** | ash vreh-a cheva deh mincareh/ber-ootoorer |
| May I have the menu, please? | **Meniul, vă rog.** | meneeool ver rog |
| Do you have a set menu*/local dishes? | **Aveți un meniu cu preț fix/mîncăruri românești?** | avets[y] oon menee[oo] coo prets feex/mincerroor[y] rominesht[y] |
| What do you recommend? | **Ce ne recomandați?** | cheh neh recomandats[y] |
| Do you have anything ready quickly? | **Aveți ceva gata de servit repede?** | avets[y] cheva gata deh serveet repedeh |
| I'm in a hurry. | **Mă grăbesc.** | mer grerbesc |
| I'd like... | **Aş vrea...** | ash vreh-a |
| Could we have a/ an..., please? | **Putem avea ..., vă rog?** | pootem aveh-a... ver rog |
| ashtray | **o scrumieră** | o scroomyerer |
| cup | **o ceaşcă** | o chashcer |
| fork | **o furculiță** | o foorcooleetser |
| glass | **un pahar** | oon pahar |
| knife | **un cuțit** | oon cutseet |
| napkin (serviette) | **un şervețel** | oon shervetsel |

---

* A set menu is a number of pre-chosen courses, usually cheaper than à la carte.

| plate | **o farfurie** | o farfooryeh |
| spoon | **o lingură** | o leengoorer |
| May I have some…? | **Pot avea niște…?** | pot aveh-a **neesh**teh |
| bread | **pîine** | pïyneh |
| butter | **unt** | oont |
| lemon | **lămîie** | lermïyeh |
| oil | **ulei** | oolay |
| pepper | **piper** | peeper |
| salt | **sare** | sareh |
| seasoning | **condimente** | condeementeh |
| sugar | **zahăr** | zaherr |
| vinegar | **oțet** | otset |

## Special diet  *Regim special*

Some useful expressions for those with special requirements:

| I'm on a diet. | **Țin regim.** | tseen rejeem |
| I'm vegetarian. | **Sînt vegetarian.** | sïnt vejetaryan |
| I don't drink alcohol. | **Nu beau alcool.** | noo bea°° alcol |
| I don't eat meat. | **Nu mănînc carne.** | noo merninc carneh |
| I mustn't eat food containing… | **Nu am voie să mănînc mîncare care conține…** | noo am voyeh ser merninc mincareh careh contseeneh |
| flour/fat | **făină/grăsime** | fer-eener/grer-seemeh |
| salt/sugar | **sare/zahăr** | sareh/zaherr |
| Do you have… for diabetics? | **Aveți… pentru diabetici?** | avetsʸ… pentroo dyabeteechʸ |
| cakes | **prăjituri** | prerzheetoorʸ |
| fruit juice | **suc de fructe** | sooc deh froocteh |
| a special menu | **meniu special** | menyoo spechyal |
| Do you have any vegetarian dishes? | **Aveți mîncăruri pentru vegetarieni?** | avetsʸ mincerroorʸ pentroo vejetaryenʸ |
| Can I have an artificial sweetener? | **Aveți zaharină?** | avetsʸ zahareener |

And…

| I'd like some more. | **Mai vreau puțin.** | migh vreh-a°° pootseen |
| Can I have more…, please? | **Mai pot avea puțin…, vă rog?** | migh pot aveh-a pootseen… ver rog |
| Just a small portion. | **Numai puțin.** | noomigh pootseen |
| Nothing more, thanks. | **Nimic altceva, mulțumesc.** | neemeec altcheva multsoomesc |
| Where are the toilets? | **Unde este toaleta?** | oondeh yesteh to-aleta |

## What's on the menu? *Ce aveţi în meniu?*

Under the headings below, you'll find alphabetical lists of dishes that might be offered on a Romanian menu with their English equivalent. You can simply show the book to the waiter. If you want some fruit, for instance, let *him* point to what's available on the appropriate list. Use pages 36 and 37 for ordering in general.

In addition to various à la carte dishes, restaurants usually offer one or more set menus which provide a good meal at a fair price.

**Reading the menu** *In meniu*

Note that some dishes may be priced by weight (per 100 grammes, for example), and you should therefore expect a final price more expensive than that listed on the menu.

For meals without a garnish, you should specify your deisired side dish or the waiter may choose this for you.

If the restaurant has run out of a dish, it may be crossed out on the menu or simply appear without a price. Establishments with a limited choice of dishes may not have a printed menu but a selection of changing daily specials.

| | |
|---|---|
| **meniu fix** | set menu |
| **meniu special** | special menu |
| **listă de vinuri** | wine list |
| **mîcăruri pentru vegetarieni** | vegetarian dishes |
| **specialități le zilei** | specials of the day |
| **preț** | price |

| | | |
|---|---|---|
| **antreuri** | antreoor^y | appetizers |
| **băuturi** | ber-ootoor^y | beverages |
| **bere** | bereh | beer |
| **carne de pasăre** | carneh deh paserreh | poultry |
| **chiftele** | keefteleh | burgers |
| **deserturi** | desertoor^y | desserts |
| **fructe** | froocteh | fruit |
| **fructe de mare** | froocteh deh mareh | seafood |
| **gustări** | goosterr^y | snacks |
| **înghețată** | ingetsater | ice cream |
| **legume** | legoomeh | vegetables |
| **mîncăruri cu ouă** | mincerroor^y coo o-wer | egg dishes |
| **paste făinoase** | pasteh fer-eenwaseh | pasta |
| **pește** | peshteh | fish |
| **salate** | salateh | salads |
| **supe** | soopeh | soups |
| **vînat** | vinat | game |
| **vin** | veen | wine |

## Breakfast *Micul dejun*

The Romanian breakfast can be a very substantial meal consisting of bread or rolls with jam, cheese, salami, fried eggs, tomatoes and coffee or tea. Hotels serve either a continental breakfast of rolls, butter, jam, coffee or tea or a traditional breakfast with eggs, cold meats, cheese or yoghurt. Breakfast cereals are not common in Romania.

| | | |
|---|---|---|
| I'd like breakfast, please. | Aş vrea micul dejun, vă rog. | ash vreh-a meecool dezhoon ver rog |
| I'll have (a/an/some)... | Aş dori... | ash doree |
| bacon and eggs | nişte şuncă şi ouă | neeshteh shooncer shee o-wer |
| boiled egg | un ou fiert | oon oh fyert |
| soft/hard | moale/tare | mwaleh/tareh |
| cereal | nişte fulgi de cereale | neeshteh foolj<sup>y</sup> deh chereh-aleh |
| eggs | nişte ouă | neeshteh o-wer |
| fried eggs | nişte ouă prăjite | neeshteh o-wer prerzheeteh |
| scrambled eggs | nişte ouă jumări | neeshteh o-wer zhoomer<sup>y</sup> |
| poached eggs | nişte ouă ochiuri fierte în apă | neeshteh o-wer okyoor<sup>y</sup> fyerteh in aper |
| fruit juice | nişte suc de fructe | neeshteh sooc deh froocteh |
| grapefruit | grepfrut | grepfroot |
| orange | portocale | portocaleh |
| ham and eggs | nişte şuncă şi ouă | neeshteh shooncer shee o-wer |
| jam | nişte gem | neeshteh jem |
| marmalade | nişte marmeladă | neeshteh marmelader |
| toast | nişte pîine prăjită | neeshteh piyneh prerzheeter |
| yoghurt | un iaurt | oon yaoort |
| May I have some...? | Vreţi să-mi daţi nişte...? | vrets<sup>y</sup> serm<sup>y</sup> dats<sup>y</sup> neeshteh |
| bread | pîine | piyneh |
| butter | unt | oont |
| (hot) chocolate | ciocolată | chyocolater |
| coffee | cafea | cafeh-a |
| decaffeinated | decofeinată | dekofeh-eenater |
| black/with milk | neagră/cu lapte | neh-agrer/coo lapteh |

| honey | **miere** | **my**ereh |
|---|---|---|
| milk | **lapte** | **lap**teh |
| cold/hot | **cald/rece** | cald/**re**cheh |
| pepper | **piper** | **pee**per |
| rolls | **chifle** | **keef**leh |
| salt | **sare** | **sa**reh |
| tea | **ceai** | chay |
| with milk | **cu lapte** | coo **lap**teh |
| with lemon | **cu lămîie** | coo ler**mi**yeh |
| (hot) water | **apă (fierbinte)** | **a**per (fyer**been**teh) |

## Starters (Appetizers) *Antreuri*

A typical Romanian starter is a platter of feta cheese, sliced salami and black olives. In summer you may also be served traditional aubergine salad (*salată de vinete*).

| I'd like an appetizer. | **Aş vrea un antreu.** | ash vreh-**a** oon an**tre**°° |
|---|---|---|
| What would you recommend? | **Ce îmi recoman-daţi?** | cheh im<sup>y</sup> recoman**dats**<sup>y</sup> |

## Cold starters *Aperitive reci*

| cîrnaţi | **cîrnats**<sup>y</sup> | sausages |
|---|---|---|
| cîrnaţi cu usturoi | **cîrnats**<sup>y</sup> coo oostoo**roy** | garlic sausage |
| ciuperci cu maioneză | chyoo**perch**<sup>y</sup> coo ma-yo**ne**zer | mushrooms in mayonnaise |
| covrigei | covree**jay** | savoury pretzels |
| măsline | mers**lee**neh | olives |
| mezeluri | meze**loor**<sup>y</sup> | assortment of cold meats |
| muşchi fillet | **moosh**k<sup>y</sup> fee**leh** | processed pork sirloin |
| pastramă | pas**tram**er | smoked mutton |
| paté de ficat | **pa**teh deh fee**cat** | liver paté |
| roşii | **ro**shee | tomatoes |
| salam | sa**lam** | salami |
| salată de icre | sa**la**ter deh **ee**creh | fish roe salad (taramasalata) |
| salată de vinete | sa**la**ter deh **vee**neteh | aubergine salad |
| sardele | **sar**deleh | sardines |
| şuncă | **shoon**cer | ham |

**ouă umplute**
(o-wer oomplooteh)

Hard-boiled eggs, halved, then filled with paté and topped with mayonnaise.

**piftie de pui**
(peefteeyeh deh pooy)

A traditional Romanian dish of stewed chicken pieces in aspic.

**salată 'boeuf'**
(salater boef)

A salad of diced potatoes, carrots, celery, pickled cucumbers, peas and ham in a mayonnaise dressing.

**salată de crudităţi**
(salater deh croodeeterts$^y$)

Coarsely grated raw celery, carrots and apples in mayonnaise.

**salată orientală**
(salater oryentaler)

Sliced potatoes and olives marinated in a vinegar and onion sauce.

## Hot starters *Aperitive calde*

| | | |
|---|---|---|
| **cabanos prăjit** | cabanos prerjeet | fried pieces of sausage |
| **chifteluţe** | keeftelootseh | fried minced meat balls |
| **creier pané** | creyer paneh | brains in breadcrumbs |
| **crenvurşti** | crenvoorsht$^y$ | boiled sausage |
| **ficăţei de pasăre** | feecertsay deh paserreh | fried or braised chicken liver |
| **frigărui** | freegerrooy | grilled pork kebabs |

**caşcaval pané**
(cashcaval paneh)

Cheese coated in egg and breadcrumbs and deep fried.

**crochete de caşcaval**
(croketeh deh cashcaval)

Grated cheese mixed with egg and flour into croquettes and fried.

**drob de miel**
(drob deh myel)

A dish of chopped lamb's liver and kidneys, mixed with herbs and egg and baked in the oven.

**mititei/mici**
(meeteetay/meech$^y$)

A traditional Romanian dish comprising small, sausage-shaped minced meat rissoles made from a seasoned mixture of various meats, usually served with a garlic sauce.

**pateuri cu carne**
(pateoor$^y$ coo carneh)

Puff pastry cases filled with minced meat.

**ruladă de caşcaval**
(roolader deh cashcaval)

A sponge roll filled with grated cheese and cream.

**ruladă de ciuperci**
(roolader deh chyooperch$^y$)

Mushroom-filled sponge roll.

### Soups and stews  *Supe şi tocane*

The most popular soup in Romania is *borş*. This is a richly flavoured meat and vegetable soup soured with 'borsh' or lemon
juice and dressed with sour cream. The borsh, or souring ingre-
dient, is obtained after wheat bran, cornflour, a sprig of cherry
tree, thyme and basil have been fermented in five or six litres of
water. The resulting brew tastes like sour wine and is rec-
ommended in its own right as an effective hangover cure.
Soup which has been soured with lemon juice or yoghurt is
called *ciorbă*, and you will frequently see this on restaurant
menus instead of *borş*. Soups in the countryside are generally
eaten with *mămăligă*, a yellow cornmeal porridge or polenta.
Vegetarians should specify *fără carne* (**fer**rer **car**neh) when
ordering vegetable soups or stews.

| | | |
|---|---|---|
| **borş de legume** | borsh deh le**goo**meh | vegetable borsh |
| **ciorbă de legume** | **chy**orber deh le**goo**meh | vegetable ciorbă |
| **ghiveci de legume** | gee**vech**ʸ deh le**goo**meh | vegetable stew, with or without meat |
| **supă-cremă de ciuperci** | **soo**per **cre**mer deh chyoo**perch**ʸ | cream of mushroom soup |
| **supă-cremă de legume** | **soo**per **cre**mer deh le**goo**meh | thick vegetable purée soup |
| **supă-cremă de ţelină** | **soo**per **cre**mer deh **tse**leener | cream of celery soup |
| **supă de cartofi** | **soo**per deh car**tof**ʸ | potato soup with vegetables |
| **supă de pasăre** | **soo**per deh pa**ser**reh | clear chicken soup |
| **supă de roşii** | **soo**per deh **ro**shee | tomato soup |
| **tocană** | to**ca**ner | stew |
| **tocană de legume** | to**ca**ner deh le**goo**meh | vegetable stew |
| **tocăniţă de cartofi cu carne** | to**cer**neetser deh car**tof**ʸ coo **car**neh | vegetable stew with meat, usually pork |

| | |
|---|---|
| **borş cu carne de porc** (borsh coo **car**neh deh porc) | Pork boiled with vegetables and seasoned with tarragon, then soured. |
| **borş de văcuţă** (borsh deh ver**coot**ser) | Beef on the bone boiled with vegetables, seasoned with herbs and soured. |
| **borş de viţel** (borsh deh **veet**sel) | Veal boiled with vegetables and seasoned with herbs, then soured. |
| **borş de perişoare** (borsh deh peree**shwa**reh) | Soured, seasoned vegetable soup served with rice-and-meat balls. |

## Main course *Felul întîi*

### Fish and seafood *Peşte şi fructe de mare*

Fish dishes are popular in Romania. They are often piquant, and frequently include vegetables such as carrots, tomatoes and peppers. Seafood is not common. The best fish dishes come from the Danube Delta, most notably *ciorbă pescărească* (a type of fish soup with vegetables) and *saramură de peşte* (grilled fish seasoned with hot paprika and salt). Romania also specializes in fish roe (*icre*), usually carp or pike.

| | | |
|---|---|---|
| I'd like some fish. | **Aş vrea o mîncare de peşte.** | ash vreh-**a** o mîncareh deh peshteh |
| What kind of seafood do you have? | **Ce fructe de mare aveţi?** | cheh **frooc**teh deh mareh avets[y] |
| **biban** | bee**ban** | river perch |
| **caviar** | cavee**ar** | caviar |
| **cegă** | **che**ger | sterlet |
| **cod** | cod | cod |
| **chefal** | ke**fal** | grey mullet |
| **crab** | crab | crab |
| **crap** | crahp | carp |
| **creveţi** | crevets[y] | shrimps |
| **homar** | **ho**mar | lobster |
| **icre** | **ee**creh | fish roe |
| **icre negre** | **ee**creh **neg**reh | caviar |
| **macrou** | ma**croh** | mackerel |
| **plătică** | pler**tee**cer | river bream |
| **raci** | rach[y] | freshwater crayfish |
| **sardele** | sar**del**eh | sardines |
| **scrumbie** | scroom**bee**-eh | shad |
| **ştiucă** | **shtyoo**cer | pike |
| **sturion** | stoo**ryon** | sturgeon |
| **ţipar** | tsee**par** | eel |

| | | |
|---|---|---|
| baked | **copt** | copt |
| fried | **prăjit** | prer**zheet** |
| grilled | **la grătar** | la grer**tar** |
| marinated | **marinată** | maree**nat**er |
| poached | **fiert în apă** | fyert in **ap**er |
| sautéed | **prăjiţi repede în grăsime** | prer**zheets**[y] **re**pedeh in grer**see**meh |
| smoked | **afumat** | afoo**mat** |
| steamed | **în aburi** | in a**boor**[y] |

**chifteluţi de icre**
(keeftelootseh deh eecreh)

Caviar or fish roe dipped in egg and bread-crumbs and fried in oil.

**ghiveci de peşte**
(geevech' deh peshteh)

A typical fish stew with olives, carrots, celery, cucumber and tomato purée.

**marinată de peşte**
(mareenater deh peshteh)

Fish marinated in brine.

**păstrăv afumat**
(perstrerv afoomat)

A traditional dish of trout wrapped in fir tree branches and smoked.

**păstrăv cu orez**
(perstrerv coo orez)

Trout cooked with onion, paprika and curry powder and served with rice.

**peşte à la grecque**
(peshteh a la grec)

Fried fish served with lemon juice and parsley.

**peşte cu usturoi**
(peshteh coo oostooroy)

Fish served in a tangy garlic sauce.

**peşte la cuptor**
(peshteh la cooptor)

A whole fish, generally carp or pike, baked in the oven with tomatoes, carrots and green peppers.

**peşte pané**
(peshteh paneh)

Fish coated in beaten egg and flour, then fried in oil and served with lemon juice.

**sturion la grătar**
(stooryon la grertar)

Grilled sturgeon.

## Meat *Carne*

Romanians eat a lot of meat, particularly pork and beef. At Easter, lamb is eaten. Mutton and goat's meat is normally preferred in autumn when it is specially prepared and accompanied by *must*—new wine.

| I'd like some... | **Aş vrea nişte...** | ash vreh-**a neesh**teh |
|---|---|---|
| beef | **carne de vacă** | **car**neh deh **va**cer |
| lamb | **carne de miel** | **car**neh deh **my**el |
| pork | **carne de porc** | **car**neh deh porc |
| veal | **viţel** | **car**neh deh **veet**sel |

| | | |
|---|---|---|
| caltaboş cu sînge | caltabosh coo sinjeh | black pudding |
| cap de porc | cap deh porc | pig's head |
| chiftele | keefteleh | meatballs |
| cîrnaţi | cirnats<sup>y</sup> | sausage |
| coadă de vacă | cwader deh vacer | oxtail |
| cotlet | cotlet | chop/cutlet |
| escalop | escalop | escalope |
| filet chateaubriand | feeleh chateaubriand | tenderloin |
| friptură | freeptoorer | larded roast |
| friptură la tavă | freeptoorer la taver | pot roast |
| iepure | yepooreh | rabbit |
| limbă | leember | tongue |
| măruntaie de porc | merroontayeh deh porc | chitterlings |
| muşchi de vacă | mooshk<sup>y</sup> deh vacer | sirloin |
| muşchi filet | mooshk<sup>y</sup> feeleh | fillet |
| oaie | wayeh | mutton |
| picioare de porc | peechywareh deh porc | pig's trotters |
| pulpă de miel | poolper de myel | leg of lamb |
| purcel de lapte | poorchel deh lapteh | suckling pig |
| rinichi | reeneek<sup>y</sup> | kidneys |
| slănină | slerneener | bacon |
| spinare | speenareh | saddle |
| şuncă (afumată) | shooncer (afoomater) | (smoked) ham |
| şuncă | shooncer | gammon |

| | | |
|---|---|---|
| baked | **copt** | copt |
| barbecued | **la grătar** | la grertar |
| baked in grease-proof paper | **copt în hîrtie pergament** | copt in hirtee-eh pergament |
| boiled | **fiert** | fyert |
| braised | **fiert înăbuşit** | fyert inerboosheet |
| fried | **prăjit** | prerzheet |
| grilled | **la grătar** | la grertar |
| roast | **prăjit la cuptor** | prerzheet la cooptor |
| sautéed | **prăjit repede în grăsime** | prerzheet repedeh in grerseemeh |
| stewed | **fiert înăbuşit** | fyert inerboosheet |
| very rare | **în sînge** | in sinjeh |
| underdone (rare) | **cu puţin sînge** | coo pootseen sinjeh |
| medium | **potrivit** | potreeveet |
| well-done | **bine prăjit** | beeneh prerzheet |

## Some meat specialities  *Cîteva specialităţi cu carne*

| | | |
|---|---|---|
| biftec à la Sinaia | beeftec a la seenaya | slices of beef steak in a thick sauce |
| carne de vită rasol | carneh deh veeter rasol | stewed beef |
| chiftele | keefteleh | minced meat balls |
| fasole verde cu carne | fasoleh verdeh coocarneh | haricot beans and meat in tomato sauce |
| fleică la grătar | flaycer la grertar | grilled steak, usually with garlic sauce |
| frigărui de porc | freeerrooy deh porc | pork kebabs |
| friptură cu sos | freeptoorer coo sos | roast meat with vegetable sauce |
| friptură la tavă de vacă | freeptoorer la taver deh vacer | oven-roasted beef |
| mazăre cu carne | mazerreh coo carneh | green peas and meat in tomato sauce |
| mîncare de limbă cu maioneză | mincareh deh leember coo mighonezer | stewed tongue in mayonnaise |
| şniţel Cordon-Bleu | shneetsel cordon-blur | breaded beef or pork escalope with ham and cheese |
| şniţel de carne de viţel | shneetsel deh carneh deh veetsel | breaded veal escalope |
| tocană de porc | tocaner deh porc | vegetable stew with pork |
| varză à la Cluj | varzer a la cloozh | shredded cabbage with minced meat and sour cream. |

| | |
|---|---|
| ardei umpluţi (arday oomploots<sup>y</sup>) | Green peppers stuffed with minced meat and rice, topped with sour cream. |
| dovlecei umpluţi (dovlechay oomploots<sup>y</sup>) | Courgettes stuffed with rice and minced meat, served with sour cream. |
| mixed grill ('mixed grill') | An assortment of braised chicken liver, fried sausages and *mititei*, seasoned rissoles made from pork, mutton and beef, served with a piquant garlic sauce. |
| sarmale în foi de varză (sarmaleh în foy deh varzer) | Pickled cabbage leaves stuffed with a mixture of rice, onion, minced beef and herbs, then boiled in a light tomato sauce. This typical Romanian dish is usually served with sour cream and *mămăligă*. |

| | | |
|---|---|---|
| **sarmale în foi de viţă**<br>(sar**ma**leh în foy deh<br>**vee**tser) | Vine leaves stuffed with rice, onion, minced beef and herbs, cooked in tomato sauce and served with sour cream. | |
| **stufat**<br>(stoo**fat**) | Marinated beef, larded and served with a rich marinade of vegetables, garlic, tomato purée and wine. | |
| **tocană de miel**<br>(to**ca**ner deh **my**el) | Lamb and vegetable stew made with okra and white wine, served with slices of *mămăligă* or potatoes. | |
| **tocană de viţel**<br>(to**ca**ner deh vee**tsel**) | A rich veal stew with onions and cream or tomato sauce, served with rice or semolina dumplings. | |

## Game and Poultry *Vînat şi pasăre*

The most popular game in Romania are rabbit and pheasant, while chicken and turkey are also widely appreciated.

| | | |
|---|---|---|
| **bibilică** | beebee**lee**cer | guinea fowl |
| **căprioară** | cerpree**wa**rer | venison |
| **clapon** | cla**pon** | capon |
| **curcan** | coor**can** | turkey |
| **fazan** | fa**zan** | pheasant |
| **gîscă** | **gis**cer | goose |
| **iepure de cîmp** | ye**poo**reh deh cimp | hare |
| **iepure înăbuşit** | ye**poo**reh<br>inerboo**sheet** | jugged hare |
| **lişiţă** | lee**shee**tser | teal |
| **porc mistreţ** | porc mees**trets** | wild boar |
| **porumbel sălbatec** | poroom**bel** serl**ba**tec | pigeon |
| **potîrniche** | potir**nee**keh | grouse |
| **potîrniche** | potir**nee**keh | partridge |
| **prepeliţă** | prepe**lee**tser | quail |
| **pui** | **poo**y | chicken |
| **piept/pulpă/aripă** | **py**ept/**pool**per/<br>a**ree**per | breast/leg/wing |
| **pui la rotisor** | **poo**y la rotee**sor** | barbecued chicken |
| **raţă** | **rat**ser | duck |
| **raţă tînără** | **rat**ser **ti**nerrer | duckling |

These are some of the poultry and game dishes you may come across:

| | | |
|---|---|---|
| **fazan cu smîntînă şi ciuperci** | fazan coo smîntiner shee chyoo**perch**ᵛ | pheasant with cream and mushrooms |
| **ficăţei de pasăre** | feecert**say** deh **pa**serreh | braised or fried chicken liver |
| **friptură de curcan** | freep**too**rer deh coor**can** | roast turkey |
| **friptură de pui** | freep**too**rer deh pooy | roast chicken |
| **găină umplută** | ger**ee**ner oom**ploo**ter | whole chicken stuffed with liver, egg, breadcrumbs and herbs |
| **ghiveci de curcan** | gee**vech**ᵛ deh coor**can** | turkey with aubergines simmered in wine |
| **iepure în vin roşu** | ye**poo**reh in veen **ro**shoo | rabbit cooked in red wine |
| **mîncare de iepure cu măsline** | mî**ca**reh deh ye**poo**reh coo mers**lee**neh | rabbit with olives, served cold |
| **pateu de iepure** | pate°° deh ye**poo**reh | rabbit pie |
| **pilaf de pui** | **pee**laf deh pooy | chicken with rice and herbs |
| **pui cu ciuperci** | pooy coo chyoo**perch**ᵛ | chicken in a mushroom sauce |
| **pui cu mujdei** | pooy coo moozh**day** | roasted chicken with a garlic sauce |
| **pui la ceaun** | pooy la cheh-a**oon** | chicken fried in oil |
| **pui la grătar** | pooy la grer**tar** | whole chicken roasted on a spit over an open fire |
| **raţă pe varză** | **rat**ser peh **var**zer | roast duck served with cabbage |
| **raţă sălbatică cu varză acră** | **rat**ser serl**bat**eecer coo **var**zer **a**crer | wild duck with sauerkraut |

| | |
|---|---|
| **ciulama de pui**<br>(chyoo**la**ma deh pooy) | A traditional Romanian dish consisting of pieces of chicken cooked in a white cream sauce and flavoured with herbs. It is usually eaten with *mămăligă*. |
| **pui cu tarhon**<br>(pooy coo tar**hon**) | A popular Transylvanian dish of chicken with tarragon, sautéed with white wine, root vegetables, green peppers and sour cream |

## Potatoes and polenta  *Cartofi şi mămăligă*

Potatoes are the Romanians' favourite vegetable. In Transylvania they are even used in bread. Cornmeal porridge (polenta) is typically eaten as an accompaniment to most meals in country areas. Dumplings made either with cornmeal and cheese or with semolina are also served with certain soups.

| | | |
|---|---|---|
| borş de cartofi | borsh deh cartof<sup>y</sup> | potato borsh |
| cartofi prăjiţi | cartof<sup>y</sup> prerzheets<sup>y</sup> | chips |
| găluşti | gerloosht<sup>y</sup> | semolina dumplings, served in chicken soup |
| găluşti cu prune | gerloosht<sup>y</sup> coo prooneh | balls of mashed potatoes with plums |
| mămăligă | mermerleeger | polenta (cornmeal mush) |
| musaca de cartofi | moosaca deh cartof<sup>y</sup> | shepherd's pie |
| salata orientală | salata oryentaler | potato salad with onions, fish and black olives |

| | |
|---|---|
| balmuş (balmoosh) | Butter and grated curd cheese wrapped in *mămăligă*, rolled into balls and served very hot with sour cream. They may be filled with ham, mushroom, cheese or boiled egg. |
| tocinei (tocheenay) | A Moldavian speciality of grated potato rissoles, bound with egg and fried in oil. This dish is normally served with sour cream. |

## Rice and pasta  *Orez şi tăiţei*

Rice is a popular staple, and is commonly used in the preparation of traditional dishes such as stuffed vine leaves and chicken pilaf. Different types of pasta are used to add substance to soups, or are served with a variety of tasty sauces. A thin porridge is also made from noodles cooked with milk and sugar.

| | | |
|---|---|---|
| macaroane cu brînză | macarwaneh coo brinzer | macaroni cheese |
| macaroane cu nuci | macarwaneh coo nooch<sup>y</sup> | macaroni with nut sauce |
| supă de găină cu fidea/cu tăiţei | sooper deh gereener coo feedeh-a/coo tereetsay | chicken soup with noodles |

## Sauces  *Sosuri*

The sauces that accompany Romanian dishes are based mainly on tomatoes and cream although wine sauces are also used. Garlic sauce is typically served with grilled meat.

| | | |
|---|---|---|
| **aspic** | aspeec | dressing containing gelatine |
| **ciulama** | chyoolama | white sauce |
| **mujdei de usturoi** | moozh**day** deh oostoo**roy** | garlic sauce |
| **sos de ceapă** | sos deh **chap**er | sauce made with onions, tomatoes, garlic and thyme |
| **sos de muştar** | sos deh **moosh**tar | mustard sauce |
| **sos de piper** | sos deh pee**per** | sauce made with butter, pepper and beef stock |
| **sos de roşii** | sos deh ro**shee** | tomato sauce with cream and herbs |
| **sos de smîntînă** | sos deh smînti**ner** | sour cream sauce |
| **ciulama de piu** (chyoolama deh pyoo) | Chicken cooked in a white sauce made with cream. | |

## Vegetables and salads  *Legume şi salate*

Romanian cuisine has a wide variety of vegetarian dishes, although there are no exclusively vegetarian restaurants. It is possible to ask for *mîncare de post*, which is food without meat, normally associated with religious fasting periods. Otherwise ask for *mîncare fără carne* if you want vegetarian options.

| | | |
|---|---|---|
| **andive** | andeeveh | endive (chicory) |
| **anghinare** | angeenareh | artichokes |
| **ardei (gras)** | arday (gras) | (sweet) peppers |
| **verde/roşu** | **verd**eh/roshoo | green/red |
| **ardei iute** | ard**eey** yooteh | chilli |
| **bame** | bameh | okra |
| **brocoli** | brocolee | broccoli |
| **cartofi dulci** | cartof<sup>y</sup> dooch<sup>y</sup> | sweet potatoes |
| **cartofi** | cartof<sup>y</sup> | potatoes |
| **castane** | castaneh | chestnuts |
| **castravete** | castraveteh | cucumber |
| **ceapă** | chaper | onions |

| ciuperci | chyoo**perch**ʸ | mushrooms |
|---|---|---|
| conopidă | cono**peeder** | cauliflower |
| dovleac | dovleh-**ac** | vegetable marrow |
| dovlecel | dovle**chel** | courgette (zucchini) |
| fasole | **fasoleh** | beans |
|   fasole neagră |   fasoleh neh-**agrer** |   butter beans |
|   fasole verde |   fasoleh **verdeh** |   green beans |
|   fasole mare |   fasoleh **mareh** |   kidney beans |
|   fasole de Lima |   fasoleh deh **leema** |   lima beans |
| fasole fiduluţă | fasoleh feede**lootser** | French beans |
| legume asortate | le**goomeh** asor**tateh** | mixed vegetables |
| linte | **leenteh** | lentils |
| mărar | me**rrar** | dill |
| mazăre | **mazerreh** | peas |
| morcovi | **morcov**ʸ | carrots |
| napi | **nap**ʸ | turnips |
| pară avocado | **parer** avocado | avocado |
| porumb | po**roomb** | sweetcorn |
| praz | praz | leeks |
| ridiche | ree**deekeh** | radishes |
| roşii | **roshee** | tomatoes |
| salată verde | sa**later verdeh** | lettuce |
| secărică | secerr**eecer** | fennel |
| sfeclă | **sfecler** | beets |
| sfeclă roşie | **sfecler** roshee-eh | beetroot |
| spanac | spa**nac** | spinach |
| sparanghel (vîrfuri) | spa**rangel** (vir**foor**ʸ) | asparagus (tips) |
| ţelină | tse**leener** | celery |
| varză | **varzer** | cabbage |
| varză de Bruxelles | **varzer** deh broo**xel** | Brussels sprouts |
| vinătă | vee**nerter** | aubergine (eggplant) |

Vegetables may be served...

| boiled | **fierte** | **fyerteh** |
|---|---|---|
| creamed | **pireu** | **peere**ᵒᵒ |
| diced | **tăiate în cubuleţe** | ter**yateh** in cooboo**letseh** |
| mashed | **pireu** | **peere**ᵒᵒ |
| oven-browned | **rumenite la cuptor** | roome**neeteh** la coop**tor** |
| steamed | **în aburi** | in a**boor**ʸ |
| stewed | **înăbuşite** | iner**boosheeteh** |
| stuffed | **umplute** | oom**plooteh** |

## Specialities *Specialităţi*

| | | |
|---|---|---|
| **borş de legume fără carne** | borsh deh legoomeh ferrer carneh | soured vegetable soup without meat |
| **conopidă murată** | conopeeder moorater | pickled cauliflower |
| **gogonele murate** | gogoneleh moorateh | pickled green tomatoes |
| **iahnie de fasole** | yahnee-eh deh fasoleh | bean purée with garlic sauce |
| **mîncare de fasole** | mincareh deh fasoleh | baked beans |
| **murături** | moorertoor$^y$ | pickles |
| **musaca de vinete** | moosaca deh veeneteh | aubergine moussaka with meat |
| **pilaf de post** | peelaf deh post | rice with mushrooms or vegetables |
| **salată de andive** | salater deh andeeveh | chicory in mayonnaise |
| **salată de castraveţi** | salater deh castrvets$^y$ | sliced cucumbers in vinaigrette |
| **salată de speclă roşie** | salater deh specler roshee-eh | grated beetroot salad dressed with oil and lemon |
| **salată de varză murată** | salater deh varzer moorater | pickled cabbage salad |
| **salată de vinete** | salater deh veeneteh | aubergine salad |
| **salată verde** | salater verdeh | green salad |
| **tocană de legume fără carne** | tocaner deh legoomeh ferrer carneh | meatless vegetable stew |

| | |
|---|---|
| **dovlecei cu mărar şi smîntînă** (dovlechay coo merrar shee smintiner) | Courgettes cooked with dill and sour cream. |
| **salată de ardei copţi** (salater deh arday copts$^y$) | Green peppers grilled over an open fire, skinned, then dressed in vinaigrette. |
| **sarmale de post** (sarmaleh deh post) | Rice, mushrooms and carrots wrapped in vine leaves. |
| **vinete umplute** (veeneteh oomplooteh) | Aubergines stuffed with a seasoned mixture of rice and meat, then baked in tomato sauce or stock made with white wine. |

## Herbs and spices *Mirodenii şi condimente*

Although Romanian food does not contain many spices, the use of herbs is widespread. Virtually no borsh is complete without lovage (*leuştean*), while summer salads are full of dill, parsley, lovage and basil. Some dishes such as parsley stew or tarragon stew are made only using herbs.

| | | |
|---|---|---|
| anason | ana**son** | aniseed |
| ardei iute | ar**day yoo**teh | pimiento |
| arpagic | arpa**jeec** | chives |
| boia | **boya** | paprika |
| busuioc | boosoo**yoc** | basil |
| capere | **caper**eh | capers |
| castraveciori | castrave**chyor**ʸ | gherkins |
| ceapă de apă | **cha**per deh **aper** | shallot |
| chimen | **kee**men | caraway |
| cimbru | **cheem**broo | thyme |
| cuişoare | cooee**shwar**eh | clove |
| foi de dafin | foy deh **da**feen | bay leaf |
| ghimber | **geem**ber | ginger |
| hrean | hreh-**an** | horseradish |
| măcriş | mer**creesh** | watercress |
| măghiran | mergee**ran** | marjoram |
| mărar | **merrar** | dill |
| mentă | **menter** | mint |
| mirodenii asortate | meero**denee** asor**tateh** | mixed herbs |
| muştar | moosh**tar** | mustard |
| nucşoară | nooc**shwar**er | nutmeg |
| pătrunjel | pertroon**zhel** | parsley |
| piper | **peeper** | pepper |
| rozmarin | rozma**reen** | rosemary |
| salvie | **sal**vyeh | sage |
| sare | **sareh** | salt |
| scorţişoară | scortsee**shwar**er | cinnamon |
| sovîrv | so**virv** | oregano |
| şofran | sho**fran** | saffron |
| tarhon | **tar**hon | tarragon |
| usturoi | oostoo**roy** | garlic |
| vanilie | vanee**lee**-eh | vanilla |

## Cheese  *Brînză*

Cheese is a very important constituent of Romanian cuisine, and it is eaten daily by most people. Although it is not the custom to finish meals with cheese, you'll often find it served at breakfast or as a main meal with polenta.

The most popular type of cheese is Romanian feta, although there are many other varieties.

| | | |
|---|---|---|
| **brînză afumată** | **brin**zer afoo**mat**er | smoked cheese |
| **brînză topită** | **brin**zer to**pee**ter | processed cheese |
| **brînză de vaci** | **brin**zer deh vach<sup>y</sup> | cottage cheese |
| **caşcaval** | cashca**val** | a type of cheddar |
| **şvaiţer** | **shvay**tser | a type of Swiss cheese with holes |
| **caş** (cash) | | An unsalted feta cheese made from ewe's milk. |
| **telemea** (telemeh-a) | | *Caş* that has been stored in salted brine. |
| **urdă** (oorder) | | A soft unfermented cheese made from ewe's milk. |

## Fruit and nuts  *Fructe şi nuci*

| | | |
|---|---|---|
| Do you have any fresh fruit? | **Aveţi fructe proaspete?** | avets<sup>y</sup> **frooc**teh **prwas**peteh |
| I'd like a (fresh) fruit cocktail. | **Aş vrea un cocteil de fructe (proaspete).** | ash vreh-a oon coc**tayl** deh **frooc**teh (**prwas**peteh) |
| **afine** | a**fee**neh | blueberries |
| **agrişe** | a**gree**sheh | gooseberries |
| **alune de pădure** | a**loo**neh deh per**doo**reh | hazelnuts |
| **ananas** | a**na**nas | pineapple |
| **arahidă** | ara**hee**der | peanuts |
| **banană** | ba**na**ner | banana |
| **caise** | ca**ee**seh | apricots |
| **căpşuni** | cerp**shoon**<sup>y</sup> | strawberries |
| **castane** | cas**ta**neh | chestnuts |
| **cireşe** | chee**re**sheh | cherries |
| **coacăze negre** | **cwa**cerzeh **ne**greh | blackcurrants |
| **curmale** | coor**ma**leh | dates |
| **fructe uscate** | **frooc**teh oos**ca**teh | dried fruit |

| | | |
|---|---|---|
| **grepfrut** | **grep**froot | grapefruit |
| **gutui** | goo**tooy** | quince |
| **lămîie** | ler**miyeh** | lemon |
| **lămîie verde** | la**miyeh verdeh** | lime |
| **mandarine** | manda**reeneh** | tangerine |
| **măr** | merr | apple |
| **migdale** | meeg**daleh** | almonds |
| **nectarină** | necta**reener** | nectarine |
| **nucă de cocos** | **noo**cer deh **cocos** | coconut |
| **nuci** | nooch<sup>y</sup> | walnuts |
| **pară** | **parer** | pear |
| **pepene galben** | **pepeneh galben** | melon |
| **pepene roşu** | **pepeneh roshoo** | watermelon |
| **piersică** | **pyerseecer** | peach |
| **portocală** | porto**caler** | orange |
| **prune** | **prooneh** | plums |
| **prune uscate** | **prooneh ooscateh** | prunes |
| **smeură** | sme<sup>oo</sup>rer | raspberries |
| **smochine** | smo**keeneh** | figs |
| **stafide** | sta**feedeh** | raisins |
| **struguri** | **stroo**goor<sup>y</sup> | grapes |

## Desserts—Pastries *Deserturi—Patiserie*

Romanian cakes or tortes are generally made from sponge moistened in light syrup and layered with various fillings including butter cream or whipped cream flavoured with vanilla, chocolate and nuts. Smaller versions of these are called *prăjituri*. At Easter and Christmas, Romanians like to eat *cozonac*, which resembles Italian panetone.

| | | |
|---|---|---|
| I'd like a dessert, please. | **Aş vrea un desert, vă rog.** | ash vreh-**a** oon de**sert** ver rog |
| What do you recommend? | **Ce recomandaţi?** | cheh recoman**dats**<sup>y</sup> |
| Something light, please. | **Ceva uşor, vă rog.** | cheva oo**shor** ver rog |
| Just a small portion. | **O porţie mică numai.** | o **portsee**-eh **mee**cer **noo**migh |
| **bezele** | **bezeleh** | small meringues |
| **budincă de brînză de vaci** | **boodeen**cer deh **brin**zer deh vach<sup>y</sup> | sweetened cheese souffle |
| **chec** | kec | rectangular sponge cake |

| | | |
|---|---|---|
| **clătite** | cler**teet**eh | pancakes |
| **clătite cu brînză** | cler**teet**eh coo **brin**zer | pancakes filled with sweetened cheese mixed with egg |
| **cremşnit** | **crems**hneet | millefeuille (napoleon) |
| **dulceaţa** | **doo**chatser | preserved whole fruits |
| **fursecuri** | **foor**secoor$^y$ | small biscuits or tea cakes |
| **îngheţată** | in**get**sater | ice cream |
| **pandişpan** | pan**deesh**pan | sponge cake |
| **plăcintă** | pler**cheen**ter | flaky pastry pie |
| **prăjitură** | prerzhee**toor**er | an individual torte |
| **salată de fructe** | sa**lat**er deh **frooc**teh | fruit salad |
| **spumă de fragi** | **spoo**mer deh fraj$^y$ | wild strawberry mousse |
| **ştrudel cu mere** | **shtroo**del coo **mer**eh | apple strudel |
| **tartă cu fructe** | **tar**ter coo **frooc**teh | small round fruit tart |
| **tort** | tort | large layer cake |
| **tort de bezea** | tort deh bezeh-**a** | layered cream meringue |
| **tort de nuci** | tort deh nooch$^y$ | walnut layer cake |
| **tort Joffre** | tort zhofr | rich chocolate cake |

**baclava**
(baclava)

A flaky pastry pie from Turkey, filled with nuts and sweetened with syrup.

**cozonac**
(cozonac)

A large sweet loaf made with yeast, eggs and milk flavoured with nuts, raisins, poppy seeds or Turkish delight. This dessert is traditionally eaten at Easter and Christmas.

**lapte de pasăre**
(lapteh deh paserreh)

'Floating islands': egg whites beaten with sugar until stiff and served floating on a custard sauce.

**papanaşi**
(papanash$^y$)

A traditional dessert made from cottage cheese mixed with eggs and sugar, then formed into flattened rounds and fried or boiled. They are usually served with sweet cream or jam.

**pască**
(pascer)

An Easter treat consisting of yeast dough cases containing a variety of fillings, including chocolate cream and soft cheese mixed with egg, sugar and raisins.

**savarină**
(savareener)

A round sponge cake moistened in syrup and filled with whipped cream.

EATING OUT

## Drinks *Băuturi*

### Beer *Bere*

The standard national measure is the *halbă*, roughly equivalent to half a litre. The name derives from the large glass mug in which beer is generally served.

Apart from national brands of beer, commonly sold in 1/2-litre bottles, many types of foreign beer are available in cans, but you'll find the national brands cheaper and worth a try. Look out for *Bucegi*, a potent 12% lager, or *Azuga*, another popular beer.

| | | |
|---|---|---|
| What would you like to drink? | **Ce doriți să beți?** | cheh doreets<sup>y</sup> ser bets<sup>y</sup> |
| I'd like a beer, please. | **Aş vrea o bere, vă rog.** | ash vreh-a o bereh ver rog |
| Have a beer! | **Ia o bere!** | ya o bereh |
| A bottle of lager, please. | **O sticlă de bere blondă vă rog.** | o steecler deh bereh blonder, ver rog |
| A half litre of ale/dark beer, please. | **O halbă de bere neagră, vă rog.** | oh halber deh bereh neh-agrer ver rog |
| **bere blondă** | bereh blonder | pale ale/lager |
| **bere neagră** | bereh neh-agrer | brown ale |

### Wine *Vin*

Romania produces many wines of worldwide renown. From the North of Moldova comes the famous wine of *Cotnari*. Further south there are other well-known vineyards—Panciu, Nicoreşti, Coteşti, Jariştea and Odobeşti—producing varieties such as Pinot Gris, Riesling and Fetească.

In Wallachia the vine cultures of Dealu Mare, Valea Călugărească, Urlaţi, Tohani and Pietroasele are equally famed, with two varieties particularly appreciated: *Tămîioasa* of *Pietroasele* and the *Busuioaca* of *Valea Călugărească*. Sweet wines come from the vineyards of Murfatlar and Babadag, and in Transylvania the wines from the Tîrnave vineyards are also widely enjoyed.

Wine is commonly mixed with soda water to make *un şpriţ*, a refreshing meal-time drink. As Romania produces such a great variety of white and red wines, imported wines are virtually non-existent.

| | | |
|---|---|---|
| May I have the wine list? | **Puteţi să-mi daţi lista de vinuri?** | pootets<sup>y</sup> serm<sup>y</sup> dats<sup>y</sup> **lee**sta deh **vee**noor<sup>y</sup> |
| I'd like a... of red wine/white wine. | **Aş vrea o... de vin roşu/vin alb.** | ash vreh-a o... deh veen **ro**shoo/veen alb |
| a bottle | **o sticlă** | o **stee**cler |
| half a bottle | **jumătate de sticlă** | joomer**ta**teh deh **stee**cler |
| a carafe | **o carafă** | o ca**ra**fer |
| a small carafe | **o carafă mică** | o ca**ra**fer **mee**cer |
| a glass | **un pahar** | oon pa**har** |
| How much is a bottle of champagne? | **Cît costă o sticlă de şampanie?** | cìt **cos**ter o **stee**cler deh sham**pan**yeh |
| Bring me another bottle/glass of..., please. | **Mai aduceţi-mi o sticlă/un pahar de..., vă rog.** | migh adoo**chet**seem<sup>y</sup> o **stee**cler/oon pa**har** deh... ver rog |
| Where does this wine come from? | **De unde provine acest vin?** | deh **oon**deh pro**vee**neh a**chest** veen |

| | | |
|---|---|---|
| red | **roşu** | **ro**shoo |
| white | **alb** | alb |
| rosé | **rozé** | **ro**zeh |
| sweet | **dulce** | **dool**cheh |
| dry | **sec** | sec |
| medium dry | **demi-sec** | **de**mee-sec |
| sparkling | **spumos** | spoo**mos** |
| chilled | **rece** | **re**cheh |
| at room temperature | **la temperatura camerei** | la tempera**too**ra **ca**meray |

## Other alcoholic drinks  *Alte băuturi alcoolice*

Other national drinks include *ţuică*, a plum brandy, *vişinată*, a liquor made from cherry syrup and white spirit, and vodka. A refreshing drink, often sold by itinerant street-sellers from barrels, is *braga*, a sweet, low alcohol, bread beer.

| I'd like a/an... | Aş vrea... | ashy vreh-a |
|---|---|---|
| aperitif | un aperitiv | oon apereeteev |
| cognac | un coniac | oon conyac |
| gin | un gin | oon jeen |
| liqueur | un lichior | oon leekyor |
| rum | un rom | oon rom |
| vermouth | un vermut | oon vermoot |
| vodka | o vodcă | o vodcer |
| whisky | un whisky | oon weesky |
| neat (straight) | simplu | seemploo |
| on the rocks | cu cuburi de ghiaţă | coo cooboor$^y$ deh gyatser |
| with a little water | cu puţină apă | coo pootseener aper |
| Give me a large gin and tonic, please. | Daţi-mi o măsură mare de gin şi apă tonică, vă rog. | datseem$^y$ o mersoorer mareh deh jeen shee aper toneecer ver rog |
| Just a dash of soda, please. | Puţin sifon, vă rog. | pootseen seefon ver rog |

## Nonalcoholic drinks  *Băuturi nealcoolice*

Fruit juices and well-known brands of canned soft drinks are readily available, especially in Bucharest and other major towns. Mineral water (*apă minerală*), bottled, at one of over 100 Romanian spas, is widely drunk, even though it is safe to drink tap water.

| apple juice | suc de mere | sooc deh mereh |
|---|---|---|
| fruit juice | suc de fructe | sooc deh froocteh |
| grapefruit juice | suc de grepfrut | sooc deh grepfroot |
| herb tea | ceai de plante medicinale | chay deh planteh medeecheenaleh |
| lemon juice | suc de lămîie | sooc deh lermiyeh |
| lemonade | limonadă | leemonader |
| milk | lapte | lapteh |
| mineral water | apă minerală | aper meeneraler |
|   fizzy (carbonated) |   apă gazoasă |   aper gazwaser |
|   still |   apă simplă |   aper seempler |
| orange juice | suc de portocale | sooc deh portocaleh |
| orangeade | oranjadă | oranzhader |
| tomato juice | suc de roşii | sooc deh roshee |
| tonic water | apă tonică | aper toneecer |

| | | |
|---|---|---|
| **cvas/socadă** | cvas/socader | elderflower cordial |
| **lapte acru** | lapteh acroo | drinking yoghurt |
| **sirop** | | Home-made syrup made from various fruits, |
| (seerop) | | for example raspberries or cherries, and |
| | | drunk diluted with water. |

## Hot beverages *Băuturi calde*

Romanians drink Turkish coffee although the trend is changing to instant coffee. Tea is generally not consumed in public places but many people drink lemon or herbal teas at home.

| | | |
|---|---|---|
| I'd like a/an... | **Aş vrea...** | ash vreh-a o/oon |
| (hot) chocolate | **un lapte cald cu cacao** | oon lapteh cald coo cacao |
| coffee | **o cafea** | o cafeh-a |
| with cream | **cu frişcă** | coo freeshcer |
| with milk | **cu lapte** | coo lapteh |
| black | **neagră** | neh-agrer |
| decaffeinated | **decofeinată** | decofeh-eenater |
| Turkish coffee | **turcească** | toorchashcer |
| espresso coffee | **espresso** | espresso |
| mokka | **moca** | moca |
| tea | **un ceai** | oon chay |
| cup of tea | **o cana de ceai** | o caner deh chay |
| with milk/lemon | **cu lapte/cu lămîie** | coo lapteh/coo lermiyeh |
| iced tea | **ceai cu ghiaţă** | chay coo gyatser |

## Complaints *Reclamaţii*

| | | |
|---|---|---|
| There's a plate/glass missing. | **Lipseşte o farfurie/un pahar.** | leepseshteh o farfooree-eh/oon pahar |
| I don't have a knife/fork/spoon. | **Nu am cuţit/furculiţă/lingură.** | noo am cootseet/foorcooleetser/leengoorer |
| That's not what I ordered. | **Aceasta nu este ce am comandat.** | achasta noo yesteh cheh am comandat |
| I asked for... | **Am comandat...** | am comandat |
| There must be some mistake. | **Cred că este o greşeala.** | cred cer yesteh o greshaler |
| May I change this? | **Pot schimba aceasta?** | pot scheemba achasta |
| I asked for a small portion (for the child). | **Am comandat o porţie mică (pentru copil).** | am comandat o portsyeh meecer (pentroo copeel) |

| The meat is... | Carnea este... | carneh-a yesteh |
| overdone | prea prăjită | preh-a prerzheeter |
| underdone | nu este prăjită bine | noo yesteh prerzheeter beeneh |
| too rare | prea crudă | preh-a crooder |
| too tough | prea tare | preh-a tareh |
| This is too... | Aceasta este prea... | achasta yesteh preh-a |
| bitter/salty/sweet | amară/sărată/dulce | amarer/serrater/doolcheh |
| I don't like this. | Nu-mi place aceasta. | noom<sup>y</sup> placheh achasta |
| The food is cold. | Mâncarea este rece. | mincareh-a yesteh recheh |
| This isn't fresh. | Aceasta nu este proaspătă. | achasta noo yesteh prwasperter |
| What's taking you so long? | De ce durează așa de mult? | de cheh doorazer asha deh moolt |
| Have you forgotten our drinks? | Ați uitat băuturile noastre? | ats<sup>y</sup> ooytat ber-ootooreeleh nwastreh |
| The wine doesn't taste right. | Nu e bun vinul. | noo yeh boon veenool |
| This isn't clean. | Acesta nu este curat. | achesta noo yesteh coorat |
| Would you ask the head waiter to come over? | Vreți să chemați pe ospătarul șef să vină aici? | vrets<sup>y</sup> ser kemats<sup>y</sup> peh ospertarool shef ser veener aeech<sup>y</sup> |

## The bill (check) *Nota de plată*

It is customary to leave a tip if the service has been good. Most restaurants expect payment in cash but some large hotels have restaurants that will accept credit cards.

| I'd like to pay. | Aș vrea să plătesc. | ash vreh-a ser plertesc |
| We'd like to pay separately. | Vrem să plătim separat. | vrem ser plerteem separat |
| I think there's a mistake in this bill. | Cred că este o greșeală în nota de plată. | cred cer yesteh o greshaler in nota deh plater |
| What's this amount for? | Ce reprezintă suma aceasta? | cheh reprezeenter sooma achasta |
| Is service included? | Serviciul este inclus? | serveechyool yesteh eencloos |

| Is everything included? | **Totul este inclus?** | totool yesteh eencloos |
| Do you accept traveller's cheques? | **Acceptaţi cecuri de voiaj?** | accheptats_y checoor_y deh vo-yazh |
| Can I pay with this credit card? | **Pot plăti cu această carte de credit?** | pot plertee coo achaster carteh deh credeet |
| Please round it up to... | **Rotunjiţi suma la...** | rotoonzheets_y sooma la |
| Keep the change. | **Păstraţi restul.** | perstrats_y restool |
| That was delicious. | **Mîncarea a fost delicioasă.** | mincareh-a a fost deleechywaser |
| We enjoyed it, thank you. | **Ne-a plăcut foarte mult, mulţumesc.** | na plercoot fwarteh moolt mooltsoomesc |

---

**SERVICIUL ESTE INCLUS**
SERVICE INCLUDED

---

### Snacks—Picnic *Gustări—Picnic*

| Give me two of these and one of those. | **Daţi-mi, va rog, doua de acestea şi una de aceea.** | datseem_y ver rog do-wer deh achesteh-a shee oona deh acheya |
| to the left/right | **din stînga/din dreapta** | deen stinga/deen drapta |
| above/below | **de deasupra/de dedesubt** | deh dasoopra/deh dedesoobt |
| It's to take away. | **De luat acasa.** | deh lwat acaser |
| I'd like a piece of cake. | **Aş vrea o prăjitură.** | ash vreh-a o prerzheetoorer |
| fried sausage | **cîrnat prăjit** | cirnat prerzheet |
| omelette | **omletă** | omleter |
| open sandwich | **sendvici** | sendveech_y |
| with ham | **cu şuncă** | coo shooncer |
| with cheese | **cu brînză** | coo brinzer |
| potato salad | **salată de cartofi** | salater deh cartof_y |
| sandwich | **sendvici** | sendveech_y |

Here's a basic list of food and drink that might come in useful when shopping for a picnic.

| apples | **mere** | mereh |
| bananas | **banane** | bananeh |
| biscuits (Br.) | **biscuiţi** | beescooeets_y |

TIPPING, see inside back-cover

| | | |
|---|---|---|
| beer | **bere** | be**reh** |
| bread | **pîine** | **pi**yneh |
| butter | **unt** | oont |
| cheese | **brînză** | **brin**zer |
| chips (Am.) | **cartofi prăjiţi** | car**tof**<sup>y</sup> prer**zheets**<sup>y</sup> |
| chocolate bar | **ciocolată** | chyoco**later** |
| coffee | **cafea** | ca**feh-a** |
| cold cuts | **salamuri** | sala**moor**<sup>y</sup> |
| cookies | **fursecuri** | foorse**coor**<sup>y</sup> |
| crisps | **cartofi prăjiţi** | car**tof**<sup>y</sup> prer**zheets**<sup>y</sup> |
| eggs | **ouă** | **o**-wer |
| gherkins (pickles) | **castraveciori muraţi** | castrave**chyor**<sup>y</sup> moo**rats**<sup>y</sup> |
| grapes | **struguri** | stroo**goor**<sup>y</sup> |
| ice cream | **îngheţată** | inge**tsater** |
| milk | **lapte** | **lap**teh |
| mustard | **muştar** | moosh**tar** |
| oranges | **portocale** | porto**caleh** |
| pepper | **piper** | pee**per** |
| roll | **chiflă** | **cheef**ler |
| salt | **sare** | **sa**reh |
| sausage | **cîrnat** | cîr**nat** |
| soft drink | **băuturi răcoritoare** | ber-oo**toor**<sup>y</sup> rercoree**twa**reh |
| sugar | **zahăr** | za**herr** |
| tea bags | **pliculeţe de ceai** | plee**cool**etseh deh chay |
| yoghurt | **iaurt** | ya**oort** |

You may find also these a tasty addition to your picnic:

| | | |
|---|---|---|
| **covrigi** | covreej<sup>y</sup> | pretzels |
| **crenvurşti** | crenvoorsht<sup>y</sup> | hot dog sausage |
| **croissant** | crwasant | French croissant |
| **gogoşi** | go**gosh**<sup>y</sup> | doughnuts |
| **napolitane** | napolee**ta**neh | wafers with filling |
| **pateuri cu brînză** | pate**oor**<sup>y</sup> coo **brin**zer | puff pastries filled with cheese |
| **pateuri cu carne** | pate**oor**<sup>y</sup> coo **car**neh | puff pastries filled with meat |
| **pizza** | **peet**sa | pizza |

TIPPING, see inside back-cover

# Travelling around

## Plane *Avion*

The only airline that provides a direct daily service to Romania is TAROM, the national airline, although Lufthansa, Swiss Air and Austrian Airlines operate flights to Bucharest.

Almost all major towns have an airport. The Timişoara airport operates international flights to Austria and Germany. However, the national airports are small and become very busy during peak season. Every town has a TAROM booking agency and you should have no difficulty purchasing a flight ticket.

| | | |
|---|---|---|
| Is there a flight to Constanţa? | **Există un zbor pentru Constanţa?** | egzeester oon zbor pentroo constantsa |
| Is it a direct flight? | **Este direct?** | yesteh deerect |
| When's the next flight to Cluj? | **La ce oră este urmatorul zbor pentru Cluj?** | la cheh orer yesteh oormertoorool zbor pentroo cloozh |
| Is there a connection to Timişoara? | **Există o legătură cu Timişoara?** | egzeester o legertoorer coo teemeshwara |
| I'd like to book a ticket to Oradea. | **Aş vrea să rezerv un bilet pentru Oradea.** | ash vreh-a ser rezerv oon beelet pentroo oradeh-a |
| single (one-way) | **dus, numai** | doos, noomigh |
| return (round trip) | **dus-întors** | doos-intors |
| business class | **"business class"** | business class |
| aisle seat | **un loc spre culoar** | oon loc spreh coolwar |
| window seat | **un loc la fereastră** | oon loc la ferastrer |
| What time do we take off? | **La ce oră decolează avionul?** | la cheh orer decolazer aveeoonool |
| What time should I check in? | **La ce ora trebuie să înregistrez bagajele?** | la cheh orer trebooyeh ser inrejeestrez bagazheleh |
| Is there a bus to the airport? | **Este un autobuz care merge la aeroport?** | yesteh oon aootobooz careh merjeh la a-eroport |
| What's the flight number? | **Care este numărul de zbor?** | careh yesteh noomerrool deh zbor |

| | | |
|---|---|---|
| What time do we arrive? | **La ce oră ajungem?** | la cheh orer azhoonjem |
| I'd like to … my reservation. | **Aş vrea să … rezervarea.** | ash vreh-a ser … rezervareh-a |
| cancel | **anulez** | anoolez |
| change | **schimb** | skeemb |
| confirm | **confirm** | confeerm |

| | |
|---|---|
| **SOSIRI**<br>ARRIVAL | **PLECARI**<br>DEPARTURE |

**Train** *Tren*

Romanian National Railways (SNCFR) have a well-developed rail network and provide a good service at a reasonable price. However, Romanian trains are slow by Western European standards.

The three main types of train service are as follows.

| | |
|---|---|
| **rapide**<br>(rapeedeh) | These express trains offer the fastest service. They stop only at major towns and seats must be reserved in advance. |
| **accelerat**<br>(acchelerat) | Direct trains; you should reserve your seat as these trains are very popular. |
| **tren de persoane**<br>(tren deh perswaneh) | These are normally local trains, which provide the slowest method of rail travel. They are not advisable for long journeys, but can be ideal for enjoying some picturesque scenery in the Carpathian mountains. |

First and second class tickets are available on all trains. It is advisable to book your seat in advance; reservations (*loc rezervat*) are obligatory on rapide trains. Sleeping berths and couchettes on *rapide* trains should also be booked in advance. Facilities are rather basic: there is no running water, soap or toilet paper in the WC, and dining cars frequently run out of supplies.

However, trains do run on time and connections are good. The main train station in Bucharest is *Gara de Nord*, and there are generally between four and five trains per day for any major destination.

Tickets can be purchased from railway stations and travel agencies. There are no reductions for students, children or disabled travellers, although pensioners can get concessions. Romanian trains are not equipped for wheelchairs.

## To the railway station *La gară*

| | | |
|---|---|---|
| Where's the railway station? | **Unde este gara?** | oondeh yesteh gara |
| Taxi! | **Taxi!** | taxee |
| Take me to the... | **Vreau să merg la...** | vra°° ser merg la |
| main railway station | **gară** | garer |
| What's the fare? | **Cît costă?** | cit coster |

| | |
|---|---|
| **INTRARE** | ENTRANCE |
| **IEŞIRE** | EXIT |
| **SPRE PEROANE** | TO THE PLATFORMS |
| **BIROU DE INFORMATII** | INFORMATION |

## Where's the...? *Unde este...?*

| | | |
|---|---|---|
| Where is/are (the)...? | **Unde se află...?** | oondeh seh afler |
| bar | **barul** | barool |
| booking office | **agenţia de voiaj** | ajentseea deh voyazh |
| currency exchange office | **biroul de schimb valutar** | beero-ool deh skeemb valootar |
| left-luggage office (baggage check) | **biroul de bagaje** | beero-ool deh bagazheh |
| lost property (lost and found) office | **biroul de obiecte pierdute** | beero-ool deh obyecteh pyerdooteh |
| newsstand | **chioşcul de ziare** | kyoshcool deh zyareh |
| platform 7 | **linia şapte** | leenya shapteh |
| reservations office | **biroul de rezervări** | beero-ool deh rezerverrᵞ |
| restaurant | **restaurantul** | resta°°rantool |
| snack bar | **chioşcul cu gustări** | kyoshcool coo goosterrᵞ |
| ticket office | **casa de bilete** | casa deh beeleteh |
| waiting room | **sala de aşteptare** | sala deh ashteptareh |
| Where are the toilets? | **Unde sînt toaletele?** | oondeh sint to-aleteleh |

TAXI, see page 21

68

## Inquiries *Biroul de informaţii*

| When is the... train to Suceava? | **La ce ora pleacă... tren spre Suceava?** | la cheh orer pleh-acer... tren spreh soochava |
| first/last/next | **primul/ultimul/ urmatorul** | preemool/oolteemool/ oormertoro ool |
| What time does the train to Bacău leave? | **La ce oră pleacă trenul de Bacău?** | la cheh orer pleh-acer trenool deh bacoh |
| What's the fare to Bucharest? | **Cît costă biletul pînă la Bucureşti?** | cit coster beeletool piner la boocooresht[y] |
| Is it a through train? | **Este un tren direct?** | yesteh oon tren deerect |
| Is there a connection to...? | **Este o legatură cu...?** | yesteh o legertoorer coo... |
| Do I have to change trains? | **Trebuie să schimb trenul?** | trebooyeh ser skeemb trenool |
| Is there enough time to change? | **Am destul timp să schimb trenul?** | am destool teemp ser skeemb trenool |
| Is the train running on time? | **Merge în timp trenul?** | merjeh in teemp trenool |
| What time does the train arrive in Ploieşti? | **La ce oră ajunge trenul în Ploieşti?** | la cheh orer azhoonjeh trenool in ployesht[y] |
| Is there a dining car/ sleeping car on the train? | **Trenul acesta are vagon restaurant/ vagon de dormit?** | trenool achesta areh vagon resta[oo]rant/vagon deh dormeet |
| Does the train stop in Sinaia? | **Trenul acesta opreşte în Sinaia?** | trenool achesta opreshteh in seenaya |
| Which platform does the train to Cluj leave from? | **De la ce peron pleacă trenul de Cluj?** | deh la cheh peron pleh-acer trenool deh cloozh |
| Which platform does the train from Iaşi arrive at? | **La ce peron vine trenul de Iaşi?** | la cheh peron veeneh trenool deh yash[y] |
| I'd like a time-table. | **Aş vrea un mers al trenurilor.** | ash vreh-a oon mers al trenooreelor |

| | |
|---|---|
| **Trebuie să schimbaţi la ...** | You have to change at ... |
| **Schimbaţi la ... şi luaţi un tren local.** | Change at ... and get a local train. |
| **Peronul şapte este ...** | Platform 7 is ... |
| **acolo/la etaj** | over there/upstairs |
| **la stînga/la dreapta** | on the left/on the right |
| **Aveţi un tren spre ... la ...** | There's a train to ... at ... |
| **Trenul dumneavoastră o să plece de la linia opt.** | Your train will leave from platform 8. |
| **Trenul are o întîrziere de ... minute.** | There will be a delay of ... minutes. |
| **Clasa întîi la capul trenului/la mijlocul trenului/la coada trenului.** | First class at the front/in the middle/at the rear. |

### Tickets *Bilete*

| | | |
|---|---|---|
| I'd like a ticket to Bucharest. | **Vreau un bilet pentru Bucureşti.** | vra°° oon bee**let** pentroo boocoo**resht**ʸ |
| single (one-way) | **dus** | doos |
| return (round trip) | **dus-întors** | doos-în**tors** |
| first/second class | **clasa întîi/clasa a doua** | **clasa întiy/clasa a dowa** |
| half price | **jumătate de preţ** | zhoo**mertateh** deh prets |

### Reservation *Rezervări*

| | | |
|---|---|---|
| I'd like to reserve a ... | **Aş vrea să rezerv un ...** | ash vreh-**a** ser re**zerv** oon |
| seat (by the window) | **loc (lîngă fereastră)** | loc (**linger** ferastrer) |
| berth | **cuşetă** | coosheter |
|   upper |   **patul de sus** |   patool deh soos |
|   middle |   **patul de la mijloc** |   patool deh la **meezh**loc |
|   lower |   **patul de jos** |   patool deh zhos |
| berth in the sleeping car | **cuşeta la vagonul de dormit** | coosheter la vagonool deh dormeet |

## All aboard *In vagoane*

| | | |
|---|---|---|
| Is this the right platform for the train to Sibiu? | Acesta este peronul pentru trenul de Sibiu? | achesta yesteh peronool pentroo trenool deh seebee°° |
| Is this the right train to Predeal? | Trenul acesta merge la Predeal? | trenool achesta merjeh la predeh-al |
| Excuse me. Could I get past? | Pardon, vă rog. Vreţi să-mi faceţi loc? | pardon ver rog. vretsy sermy fachetsy loc |
| Is this seat taken? | Este liber locul acesta? | yesteh leeber locool achesta |

| FUMĂTORI | NEFUMĂTORI |
|---|---|
| SMOKER | NONSMOKER |

| | | |
|---|---|---|
| I think that's my seat. | Cred că acesta este locul meu. | cred cer achesta yesteh locool me°° |
| Would you let me know before we get to Ploiesti? | Vreţi să mă anunţaţi, vă rog, cînd ajungem la Ploieşti? | vretsy ser mer anoontsatsy ver rog cind azhoonjem la ployeshty |
| What station is this? | Ce staţie este aici? | cheh statsyeh yesteh aeechy |
| How long does the train stop here? | Cît timp stă trenul în gara aceasta? | cit teemp ster trenool in gara achasta |
| When do we arrive in Bucharest? | Cînd ajungem la Bucureşti? | cind azhoonjem la boocooreshty |

## Sleeping car *Vagon de dormit*

Couchettes and sleepers need to be booked well in advance and Western standards should not be expected. Rates vary according to distance.

| | | |
|---|---|---|
| Are there any free compartments in the sleeping car? | Sînt locuri libere la vagonul de dormit? | sint locoory leebereh la vagonool deh dormeet |
| Where's the sleeping car? | Unde este vagonul de dormit? | oondeh yesteh vagonool deh dormeet |
| Where's my berth? | Unde este cuşetă mea? | oondeh yesteh coosheter meh-a |
| I'd like a lower berth. | Aş vrea o cuşetă mai jos. | ash vreh-a o coosheter migh zhos |

| Would you make up our berths? | **Vreţi să ne faceţi patul, vă rog?** | vrets<sup>y</sup> ser neh fachets<sup>y</sup> patool ver rog |
| Would you wake me at 7 o'clock? | **Puteţi să mă sculaţi la ora şapte, vă rog?** | pootets<sup>y</sup> ser mer scoolats<sup>y</sup> la ora shapteh ver rog |

## Eating *La masă*

All *rapide* and *accelerate* trains have dining cars (*vagon restaurant*). However, the food is not always of the highest quality and Romanians tend to use the restaurant for drinking.

| Where's the dining-car? | **Unde este vagonul restaurant?** | oondeh yesteh vagonool resta°°rant |

## Baggage—Porters *Bagaje—Hamali*

| Porter! | **Alo! Hamal!** | alo, hamal |
| Can you help me with my luggage? | **Vreţi să mă ajutaţi şi pe mine cu bagajele, vă rog?** | vrets<sup>y</sup> ser mer azhootats<sup>y</sup> shee peh meeneh coo bagazheleh ver rog |
| Where are the luggage trolleys (carts)? | **Unde sînt cărucioarele de bagaje?** | oondeh sint cerroochywareleh deh bagazheh |
| Where are the luggage lockers? | **Unde sînt cabinele de bagaje?** | oondeh sint cabeeneleh deh bagazheh |
| Where's the left-luggage office (baggage check)? | **Unde este biroul de bagaje?** | oondeh yesteh beero-ool deh bagazheh |
| I'd like to leave my luggage, please. | **Aş vrea să las bagajele, vă rog.** | ash vreh-a ser las bagazheleh ver rog |
| I'd like to register (check) my luggage. | **Aş vrea să fac înregistrarea bagajelor.** | ash vreh-a ser fac inrejeestrareh-a bagazhelor |

> **ÎNREGISTRAREA BAGAJELOR**
> REGISTERING (CHECKING) BAGGAGE

## Underground (subway) *Metroul*

Bucharest is the only city in Romania with an underground network. There are three main lines and trains run very frequently. Fares are inexpensive, and the monthly ticket provides an economical way of travelling around.

PORTERS, see also page 18

72

| Where's the nearest underground station? | **Este vreo stație de metrou prin apropiere?** | yesteh vro statsyeh deh metro°° preen apropyereh |
| Does this train go to...? | **Acest tren merge la...?** | achest tren merjeh la |
| Where do I change for...? | **Unde trebuie să schimb pentru...?** | oondeh trebooyeh ser skeemb pentroo |
| Is the next station...? | **Prima stație este...?** | preema statsyeh yesteh |
| Which line should I take to...? | **Ce tren trebuie să iau pentru...?** | cheh tren trebooyeh ser ya°° pentroo |

### Coach (long-distance bus) *Autocarul*

Every town has a coach station. However, there are very few long-distance bus services and coach travel is slow, uncomfortable and frequently unreliable.

| When's the next coach to...? | **La ce oră pleacă urmatorul autocar spre...?** | la cheh orer pleh-acer oormertorool a°°tocar spreh |
| Does this coach stop at...? | **Autocarul acesta se oprește la...?** | a°°tocarool achesta seh opreshteh la |
| How long does the journey (trip) take? | **Cît durează călătoria?** | cît doorazer cerlertoreea |

### Bus—Tram (streetcar) *Autobuz—Tramvai*

Buses, trolleybuses and trams do not have conductors. You must buy your ticket before your journey from a kiosk belonging to RATB or ITB, the local transport institutions. On entering the bus, tram or trolleybus, you should validate your ticket in the punch machine. The penalty for travelling without a ticket is a heavy on-the-spot fine. Since a flat fare is charged regardless of distance, it is advisable to purchase a book of tickets (*carnet de bilete*).

| I'd like a booklet of tickets. | **Aș vrea un carnet de bilete.** | ash vreh-a oon carnet deh beeleteh |

| | | |
|---|---|---|
| Which tram (streetcar) goes to the town centre? | **Ce tramvai merge în centru?** | cheh tram**vigh** mer**j**eh in **chen**troo |
| Where can I get a bus to the opera? | **De unde pot lua un autobuz pentru operă?** | deh **oon**deh pot lwa oon a°°to**booz** pen**troo op**erer |
| Which bus do I take to Palatul Cotroceni? | **Ce autobuz merge la Palatul Cotroceni?** | cheh a°°to**booz** mer**j**eh la pala**tool** cotro**chen**ᵛ |
| Where's the bus stop? | **Unde este stația de autobuz?** | **oon**deh **yes**teh **stat**sya deh a°°to**booz** |
| When is the ... bus to Palatul Cotroceni? | **La ce oră vine ... autobuzul care merge la Palatul Cotroceni?** | la cheh **or**er **vee**neh ... a°°to**boo**zool **car**eh mer**j**eh la pala**tool** cotro**chen**ᵛ |
| first/last/next | **primul/ultimul/ următorul** | **pree**mool/**ool**teemool/ oormer**to**rool |
| How much is the fare to...? | **Cît costă pîna la ...?** | cît **cos**ter **pi**ner la |
| Do I have to change buses? | **Trebuie să schimb autobuzul?** | tre**boo**yeh ser skeemb a°°to**boo**zool |
| How many bus stops are there to ...? | **Cîte stații sînt pîna la ...?** | **cit**eh **stat**see sint **pi**ner la |
| Will you tell me when to get off? | **Puteți să-mi spuneți cînd să cobor?** | poo**tets**ᵛ serm**ᵛ spoo**nets**ᵛ cind ser co**bor** |
| I want to get off at Piața Unirii. | **Aș vrea să cobor la Piața Unirii.** | ash vreh-a ser co**bor** la **pyat**sa oo**nee**ree |

| | |
|---|---|
| **STAȚIA DE AUTOBUZ** | BUS STOP |
| **STAȚIE FACULTATIVA** | REQUEST STOP |

## Boat service *Debarcader*

Cruises on the Danube (*Dunărea*) and boat trips in the Danube Delta (*Delta Dunării*) can be booked through the National Tourist Office (ONT).

| | | |
|---|---|---|
| When does the next boat for ... leave? | **La ce oră pleacă urmatoarea barcă ...?** | la cheh **or**er pleh-**ac**er oormert**war**eh-a **bar**cer |

| Where's the embarkation point? | Unde se face îmbarcarea? | oondeh seh facheh imbarcareh-a |
| How long does the crossing take? | Cît timp durează traversarea? | cît teemp doorazer traversareh-a |
| Which port(s) do we stop at? | La ce port(uri) vă opriți? | la cheh port(oorᵛ) ver opreetsᵛ |
| I'd like to take a cruise/ tour of the harbour. | Aş vrea să fac o croazieră în jurul portului. | ash vreh-a ser fac o cro-azyerer în zhoorool portoolooy |
| boat | barcă | barcer |
| cabin | cabină | cabeener |
| single/double | de o persoană/de două persoane | deh o perswaner/deh do-wer perswaneh |
| deck | punte | poonteh |
| ferry | bac | bac |
| hydrofoil | nava cu aripi portante | naver coo areepᵛ portanteh |
| life belt/boat | colac de salvare/ barcă de salvare | colac deh salvareh/barcer deh salvareh |
| port | port | port |
| reclining seat | scaun rabatabil | scaᵒᵒn rabatabeel |
| river cruise | croazieră pe fluviu | cro-azyerer peh floovyᵒᵒ |
| ship | vapor | vapor |
| steamer | vapor cu abur | vapor coo aboor |

## Other means of transport  *Alte mijloace de transport*

Although people occasionally hitchhike in Romania, bear in mind that compared to the West the cars are smaller and there are less of them on the road. It is not advisable for women to hitchhike alone.

| to hitchhike | a face autostopul | a facheh aᵒᵒtostopool |
| to walk | a merge pe jos | a merjeh peh zhos |
| cable car | teleferic | telefereec |
| helicopter | elicopter | eleecopter |
| moped | motoretă | motoreter |
| motorbike/scooter | motocicletă/scuter | motocheecleter/scooter |

## Bicycle hire  *Închirieri de biciclete*

| I'd like to hire a... bicycle. | Aş vrea să închiriez o bicicletă ... | ash vreh-a ser înkeeree-ez o beecheecleter |
| 5-gear | cinci viteze | cheenchᵛ veetezeh |
| mountain | munte | moonteh |

## Car *Autoturismul*

Most roads are not very wide but the major routes are reasonably well maintained. There are no motorways except for a short toll motorway between Bucharest and Piteşti. Traffic regulations are similar to any Western European country, with priority given to vehicles coming from the right at main junctions. It is customary to give a short signal on your horn when overtaking.

Driving at night is not advised as roads are poorly lit and cyclists and horse carts frequently travel without adequate lights. The wearing of seatbelts, though not compulsory, is advised, and drinking with any alcohol in the bloodstream is prohibited.

Petrol stations are less numerous than in the West, but are generally marked on maps. In major towns unleaded petrol may be available, though this cannot be obtained in country areas. There are no roadside phone facilities in case of accident.

| | | |
|---|---|---|
| Where's the nearest (self-service) filling station? | **Unde este cea mai apropiată staţie Peco (cu autoservire) prin apropiere?** | oondeh **yes**teh cha migh apropy**ater stats**yeh **peco** (coo a<sup>oo</sup>toser**vee**reh) preen apropy**ereh** |
| Fill it up, please. | **Faceţi plinul, vă rog.** | fa**chets**ʸ **plee**nool ver rog |
| Give me... litres of petrol (gasoline). | **Puneţi... litri de benzină.** | poo**nets**ʸ ... **leet**rʸ deh ben**zee**ner |
| super (premium)/ regular/unleaded/ diesel | **super/normală/ fără plumb/ motorină** | **soo**per/nor**mal**er/ **fer**rer ploomb/ moto**ree**ner |
| Please check the... | **Vă rog să verificaţi...** | ver rog ser vereefee**cats**ʸ |
| battery | **bateria** | bate**ree**a |
| brake fluid | **lichidul de frînă** | lee**kee**dool deh **fri**ner |
| oil/water | **uleiul/apa** | oo**ley**ool/**a**pa |
| Would you check the tyre pressure? | **Vă rog să verificaţi presiunea roţilor.** | ver rog ser vereefee**cats**ʸ presyoo**neh**-a **ro**tseelor |
| 1.6 front, 1.8 rear. | **l,6 în faţă, l,8 în spate.** | l,6 in **fat**ser l,8 in **spa**teh |
| Please check the spare tyre, too. | **Vă rog, verificaţi şi roata de rezervă.** | ver rog vereefee**cats**ʸ shee **rwa**ta deh re**zer**ver |

CAR HIRE, see page 20

| Can you mend this puncture (fix this flat)? | **Puteţi vulcaniza roata aceasta?** | pootets<sup>y</sup> voolcaneeza rwata achasta |
| Would you change the... please? | **Vreţi să schimbaţi... vă rog?** | vrets<sup>y</sup> ser skeembats<sup>y</sup>... ver rog |
| bulb | **becul** | becool |
| fan belt | **cureaua de la ventilator** | coorawa deh la venteelator |
| spark(ing) plugs | **bujiile** | boozhee-eeleh |
| tyre | **roata** | rwata |
| wipers | **ştergătoarele** | shtergertwareleh |
| Would you clean the windscreen (windshield)? | **Vreţi să spălaţi parbrizul, vă rog?** | vrets<sup>y</sup> ser sperlats<sup>y</sup> parbreezool ver rog |

## Asking the way—Street directions *Cum să găsim drumul*

| Can you tell me the way to...? | **Puteţi să-mi spuneţi care este drumul spre...?** | pootets<sup>y</sup> serm<sup>y</sup> spoonets<sup>y</sup> careh yesteh droomool spreh |
| In which direction is...? | **În ce direcţie se află...?** | in cheh deerectsyeh seh afler |
| How do I get to...? | **Cum ajung la...?** | coom azhoong la |
| Are we on the right road for...? | **Sîntem pe drumul bun pentru...?** | sintem peh droomool boon pentroo |
| How far is the next village? | **Cît de departe este satul următor?** | cît deh departeh yesteh satool oormertor |
| How far is it to... from here? | **Ce distanţă este pînă la... de aici?** | cheh deestantser yesteh piner la... deh aeech<sup>y</sup> |
| Is there a motorway (expressway)? | **Există autostradă?** | egzeester a<sup>oo</sup>tostrader |
| How long does it take by car/on foot? | **Cît timp ia cu maşina/pe jos?** | cît teemp ya coo masheena/peh zhos |
| Can you tell me where... is? | **Puteţi să-mi spuneţi unde este...?** | pootets<sup>y</sup> serm<sup>y</sup> spoonets<sup>y</sup> oondeh yesteh |
| How can I find this place/address? | **Unde este acest loc/Unde este această adresă?** | oondeh yesteh achest loc/ oondeh yesteh achaster adreser |
| Where's this? | **Unde este aceasta?** | oondeh yesteh achasta |
| Can you show me on the map where I am? | **Puteţi să-mi arătaţi pe hartă unde sînt?** | pootets<sup>y</sup> serm<sup>y</sup> arertats<sup>y</sup> peh harter oondeh sint |
| Where are the nearest public toilets? | **Unde este o toaletă publică prin apropiere?** | oondeh yesteh oh to-aleter poobleecer preen apropyereh |

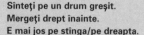

| | |
|---|---|
| **Sînteţi pe un drum greşit.** | You're on the wrong road. |
| **Mergeţi drept înainte.** | Go straight ahead. |
| **E mai jos pe stînga/pe dreapta.** | It's down there on the left/right. |
| **vis-a-vis/în spate...** | opposite/behind... |
| **lîngă/după...** | next to/after... |
| **nord/sud** | north/south |
| **est/vest** | east/west |
| **Mergeţi pînă la prima/a doua intersecţie.** | Go to the first/second crossroads (intersection). |
| **Luaţi-o la stînga la semafoare.** | Turn left at the traffic lights. |
| **Luaţi-o la dreapta la colţul următor.** | Turn right at the next corner. |
| **Mergeţi pe strada...** | Take the... road. |
| **Este o stradă cu sens unic.** | It's a one-way street. |
| **Trebuie să vă întoarceţi la...** | You have to go back to... |
| **Urmaţi semnele pentru Constanţa.** | Follow signs for Constanţa. |

## Parking *Parcare*

Parking places are attended by a fee collector; there are no disks or parking meters. In Bucharest your vehicle may be clamped if parked in a no-parking zone.

| | | |
|---|---|---|
| Where can I park? | **Unde se poate parca?** | oondeh seh pwateh parca |
| Is there a car park nearby? | **Există un teren de parcare prin apropiere?** | egzeester oon teren deh parcareh preen apropyereh |
| May I park here? | **Pot să parchez aici?** | pot ser parkez aeech$^y$ |
| How long can I park here? | **Cît timp pot să parchez aici?** | cit teemp pot ser parkez aeech$^y$ |
| What's the charge per hour? | **Cît costă pe oră?** | cit coster peh orer |
| Do you have some change? | **Aveţi nişte mărunt?** | avets$^y$ neeshteh merroont |

## Breakdown—Road assistance *Pană de motor—Asistenţă rutieră*

If you have a breakdown call the nearest *Auto Servis*. If your car needs to be towed, dial 927 for the Romanian Automobile Club (ACR—*Automobil Clubul Roman*).

| | | |
|---|---|---|
| Where's the nearest garage? | **Este vreun Servis prin apropiere?** | yesteh vroon servees preen apropyereh |
| My car has broken down. | **Maşina mea are o pană de motor.** | masheena meh-a areh o paner deh motor |
| Where can I make a phone call? | **De unde pot da un telefon?** | deh oondeh pot da oon telefon |
| I've had a break-down at... | **Sînt în pană la...** | sint in paner la |
| Can you send a mechanic? | **Puteţi să trimiteţi un mecanic?** | pootetsʸ ser treemeetetsʸ oon mecaneec |
| My car won't start. | **Motorul nu porneşte.** | motorool noo porneshteh |
| The battery is dead. | **Bateria este consu-mată.** | batereea yesteh consoomater |
| I've run out of petrol (gasoline). | **Am rămas în pană de benzină.** | am rermas in paner deh benzeener |
| I have a flat tyre. | **Am o roată dezum-flată.** | am o rwater dezoomflater |
| The engine is over-heating. | **Motorul se încălzeşte prea tare.** | motorool seh încerlzeshteh preh-a tareh |
| There's something wrong with the... | **E o defecţiune la...** | yeh o defectsyooneh la |
| brakes | **frîne** | frineh |
| carburettor | **carburator** | carboorator |
| exhaust pipe | **ţeava de eşapa-ment** | tsava deh eshapament |
| radiator | **radiator** | radeeator |
| wheel | **roată** | rwater |
| Can you send a break-down van (tow truck)? | **Puteţi trimite o maşină de depa-nare?** | pootetsʸ treemeeteh o masheener deh depanareh |
| How long will you be? | **Cît o să dureze?** | cit o ser doorezeh |
| Can you give me an estimate? | **Puteţi să-mi spu-neţi cît costă cu aproximaţie?** | pootetsʸ sermʸ spoonetsʸ cit coster coo aproxeematsyeh |

## Accident—Police  *Accident—Poliţie*

| Please call the police. | **Vă rog chemaţi poliţia.** | ver rog ke**mats**ʸ po**leets**ya |
|---|---|---|
| There's been an accident. It's about 2 km from ... | **A fost un accident la vreo 2km de ...** | a fost oon acchee**dent** la vro 2km deh |
| Where's there a telephone? | **Unde se găseşte un telefon?** | **oon**deh seh ger**sesh**teh oon tele**fon** |
| Call a doctor/an ambulance quickly. | **Chemaţi un doctor/o salvare imediat.** | ke**mats**ʸ oon **doc**tor/o sal**var**eh eeme**dyat** |
| There are people injured. | **Sînt oameni răniţi.** | sint **wa**menʸ rer**neets**ʸ |
| Here's my driving licence. | **Poftim carnetul meu de conducere.** | pof**teem** carne**tool** me°° deh con**doo**chereh |
| What's your name and address? | **Cum vă numiţi şi unde locuiţi?** | coom ver noo**meets**ʸ shee **oon**deh loco**oeets**ʸ |
| What's your insurance company? | **Care este compania dumneavoastră de asigurări?** | **careh yes**teh compa**neea** doomnav**was**trer deh aseegoo**rerr**ʸ |

## Road signs  *Semne de circulaţie*

| | |
|---|---|
| **ANIMALE** | Animals |
| **ATENTIE** | Caution |
| **ATENTIE SCOALA** | Caution school |
| **CADERI DE PIETRE** | Falling rocks |
| **CEDEAZĂ TRECEREA** | Give way |
| **COBORIRE PERICULOASA** | Dangerous descent |
| **CURBA DEOSEBIT DE PERICULOASA** | Dangerous bend |
| **DEPĂŞIREA INTERZISĂ** | No overtaking |
| **DIVERSIUNE** | Diversion |
| **DRUM CU DENIVELARI** | Uneven road surface |
| **INTOARCEREA INTERZISĂ** | No turning |
| **LIMITĂ DE VITEZĂ** | Speed limit |
| **PARCARE INTERZISĂ** | No parking |
| **POLEI** | Icy road |
| **REDUCETI VITEZĂ** | Slow down |
| **SANTIER IN LUCRU** | Road works ahead |
| **SENS GIRATORIU** | Roundabout |
| **SENS UNIC** | One way |
| **TINETI DREAPTA** | Keep right |
| **TRAFIC INTERZIS** | No traffic allowed |
| **TRECERE PIETONI** | Pedestrian crossing |

NUMBERS, see page 147

# Sightseeing

| Where's the tourist office? | Unde se află oficiul de turism? | oondeh seh afler ofeechyool deh tooreesm |
| What are the main points of interest? | Care sînt obiectivele turistice importante? | careh sint obyecteeveleh tooreesteecheh eemportanteh |
| We're here for... | Sîntem aici numai pentru... | sintem aeechᵛ noomigh pentroo |
| only a few hours | cîteva ore | cìteva oreh |
| a day | o zi | o zee |
| a week | o săptămînă | o serpterminer |
| Can you recommend a sightseeing tour/ an excursion? | Ne puteţi recomanda un traseu prin împrejurimi/o excursie? | neh pootetsᵛ recomanda oon traseᵒᵒ preen imprezhooreemᵛ/ o excoorsyeh |
| Where do we leave from? | De unde se pleacă? | deh oondeh seh pleh-acer |
| Will the bus pick us up at the hotel? | Vine autobuzul să ne ia de la hotel? | veeneh aᵒᵒtoboozool ser neh ya deh la hotel |
| How much does the tour cost? | Cît costă aceastä excursie? | cìt coster achaster excoorsyeh |
| What time does the tour start? | La ce oră începe excursia? | la cheh orer ìnchepeh excòorsya |
| Is lunch included? | Masa de prînz este inclusă în biletul de excursie? | masa deh prinz yesteh eenclooser in beeletool deh excoorsyeh |
| What time do we get back? | La ce oră ne întoarcem? | la cheh orer neh ìntwarchem |
| Do we have free time in...? | Avem timp liber în...? | avem teemp leeber in |
| Is there an English-speaking guide? | Aveţi un ghid care vorbeşte englezeşte? | avetsᵛ oon geed careh vorbeshteh englezeshteh |
| I'd like to hire a private guide for... | Aş vrea să angajez un ghid particular pentru... | ash vreh-a ser angazhez oon geed parteecoolar pentroo |
| half a day | jumătate de zi | zhoomertateh deh zee |
| a day · | o zi | o zee |

| Where is/Where are the ...? | Unde este/sînt ...? | oondeh yesteh/sint |
|---|---|---|
| abbey | mînăstirea | minersteereh-a |
| art gallery | galeria de artă | galereea deh arter |
| birth place | casa memorială | casa memoryaler |
| botanical gardens | grădina botanică | grerdeena botaneecer |
| building | clădirea | clerdeereh-a |
| business district | zona băncilor | zona berncheelor |
| castle | castelul | castelool |
| cathedral | catedrala | catedrala |
| cave | peştera | peshtera |
| cemetery | cimitirul | cheemeeteerool |
| citadel | cetatea | chtateh-a |
| city centre | centrul oraşului | chentrool orashoolooy |
| civic centre | centrul civic | chentrool cheeveec |
| chapel | capela | capela |
| church | biserica | beesereeca |
| concert hall | sala de concerte | sala deh concherteh |
| convent | mînăstirea | minersteereh-a |
| court house | tribunalul | treeboonalool |
| downtown area | centrul | chentrool |
| embankment | cheiul | keyool |
| exhibition | expoziţia | expozeetsya |
| factory | uzina | oozeena |
| fair | tîrgul | tirgool |
| flea market | talciocul | talchyocool |
| fortress | cetatea | chetateh-a |
| fountain | fîntîna | fintina |
| gardens | grădina | grerdeena |
| harbour | portul | portool |
| lake | lac | lac |
| library | biblioteca | beebleeoteca |
| market | piaţa | pyatsa |
| memorial | monumentul comemorativ | monoomentool comemorateev |
| monastery | mînăstirea | minersteereh-a |
| monument | monumentul | monoomentool |
| museum | muzeul | moozeool |
| old town | oraşul vechi | orashool vek<sup>y</sup> |
| opera house | opera | opera |
| palace | palatul | palatool |
| park | parcul | parcool |
| parliament building | clădirea parlamen-tului | clerdeereh-a parlamentoolooy |
| planetarium | planetarul | planetarool |
| royal palace | palatul regal | palatool regal |

| ruins | **ruinele** | rooeeneleh |
| shopping area | **centrul comercial** | chentrool comerchyal |
| square | **piaţa** | pyatsa |
| stadium | **stadionul** | stadyonool |
| statue | **statuia** | statooya |
| stock exchange | **bursa** | boorsa |
| theatre | **teatrul** | teh-atrool |
| tomb | **mormîntul** | mormintool |
| tower | **turnul** | toornool |
| town hall | **primărie** | preemerreea |
| triumphal arch | **arcul de triumf** | arcool deh treeoomf |
| university | **universitatea** | ooneeverseetateh-a |
| zoo | **grădina zoologică** | grerdeena zoolojeecer |

## Admission *Intrare*

| Is... open on Sundays? | **Este... deschis duminica?** | yesteh... deskees doomeeneeca |
| What are the opening hours? | **La ce oră deschideţi?** | la cheh orer deskeedets$^y$ |
| When does it close? | **La ce ora închideţi?** | la cheh orer inkeedets$^y$ |
| How much is the entrance fee? | **Cît costă intrarea?** | cît coster eentrareh-a |
| Is there any reduction for (the)...? | **Aveţi reduceri pentru...?** | avets$^y$ redoocher$^y$ pentroo |
| children | **copii** | copee |
| disabled | **persoane invalide** | perswaneh eenvaleedeh |
| groups | **grupuri** | groopoor$^y$ |
| pensioners | **pensionari** | pensyonar$^y$ |
| students | **studenţi** | stoodents$^y$ |
| Do you have a guidebook (in English)? | **Aveţi un ghid în englezeşte?** | avets$^y$ oon geed in englezeshteh |
| Can I buy a catalogue? | **Pot cumpăra oon catalog?** | pot coomperra oon catalog |
| Is it all right to take pictures? | **Este permis să fac poze?** | yesteh permees ser fac pozeh |
| Is there easy access for the disabled? | **Există acces pentru persoane invalide?** | egzeester acches pentroo perswaneh eenvaleedeh |
| Are there facilities/ activities for children? | **Există amenajări/ jocuri pentru copii?** | egzeester amenazherr$^y$/ zhocoor$^y$ pentroo copee |

| **INTRARE GRATUITA** | ADMISSION FREE |
| **FOTOGRAFIEREA INTERZISĂ** | NO CAMERAS ALLOWED |

### Who—What—When? *Cine—Ce—Cînd?*

| | | |
|---|---|---|
| What's that building? | Ce clădire este aceea? | cheh clerdeereh yeseh acheya |
| Who was the...? | Cine a fost...? | cheeneh a fost |
| architect | arhitectul | arheetectool |
| artist | artistul | arteestool |
| painter | pictorul | peectorool |
| sculptor | sculptorul | scoolptorool |
| Who built it? | Cine a construit-o? | cheeneh a construoeeto |
| Who painted that picture? | Cine a pictat acel tablou? | cheeneh a peectat achel tablou°° |
| When did he live? | Cînd a trăit? | cind a trer-eet |
| When was it built? | Cînd a fost construit? | cind a fost construoeet |
| Where's the house where... lived? | Unde este casa în care a locuit...? | oondeh yesteh casa in careh a locooeet |
| We're interested in... | Interesează... | eenteresazer |
| antiques | antichitațile | anteekeetertseeleh |
| archaeology | arheologia | arheolojeea |
| art | arta | arta |
| botany | botanica | botaneeca |
| ceramics | ceramica | cherameeca |
| coins | numismatica | noomeesmateeca |
| fine arts | artele frumoase | arteleh froomwaseh |
| furniture | mobila stil | mobeela steel |
| geology | geologia | jeolojeea |
| handicrafts | artizanatul | arteezanatool |
| history | istoria | eestorya |
| medicine | medicina | medeecheena |
| music | muzica | moozeeca |
| natural history | știintele naturale | shtee-eentseleh natooraleh |
| ornithology | ornitologia | orneetolojeea |
| painting | pictura | peectoora |
| pottery | olăritul | olerreetool |
| religion | religia | releejya |
| sculpture | sculptura | scoolptoora |
| zoology | zoologia | zoolojeea |
| Where's the... department? | Unde se află departamentul de...? | oondeh seh afler departamentool deh |

| It's... | Este... | **yes**teh |
|---------|---------|------------|
| amazing | **uluitor** | oolooee**tor** |
| awful | **groaznic** | **grwaz**neec |
| beautiful | **frumos** | froo**mos** |
| gloomy | **sumbru** | **soom**broo |
| impressive | **impresionant** | eempresyo**nant** |
| interesting | **interesant** | eente**resant** |
| magnificent | **magnific** | mag**nee**feec |
| pretty | **drăguț** | drer**goots** |
| strange | **straniu** | **stran**yoo |
| superb | **superb** | soo**perb** |
| terrifying | **îngrozitor** | ingrozee**tor** |
| tremendous | **nemaipomenit** | neh-**migh**pome**neet** |
| ugly | **urît** | oo**rit** |

## Churches—Religious services *Biserici—Slujbe religioase*

The Orthodox religion is the national religion in Romania, though others are also practised.

| Is there a... near here? | Există o... prin apropiere? | eg**zees**ter o... preen apro**pye**reh |
|---------|---------|------------|
| Catholic church | **biserică catolică** | bee**se**reecer cato**lee**cer |
| Orthodox church | **biserică ortodoxă** | bee**se**reecer orto**dox**er |
| Protestant church | **biserică protestantă** | bee**se**reecer protes**tan**ter |
| mosque | **moschee** | mos**key**eh |
| synagogue | **sinagogă** | seena**go**ger |
| What time is...? | **La ce ora este...?** | la cheh **o**rer **yes**teh |
| mass/the service | **slujba** | **sloozh**ba |
| Where can I find a... who speaks English? | **Unde pot găsi un... care vorbește englezește?** | **oon**deh pot ger**see** oon... careh vor**besh**teh engle**zesh**teh |
| priest/minister/ rabbi | **preot/pastor/rabin** | **preh**-ot/**pas**tor/**ra**been |
| I'd like to visit the church. | **Aș vrea să vizitez biserica.** | ash vreh-**a** ser veezee**tez** bee**se**reeca |
| I'd like to go to confession. | **Aș vrea să merg să mă spovedesc.** | ash vreh-**a** ser merg ser mer spove**desc** |

## In the countryside *La ţară*

| | | |
|---|---|---|
| Is there a scenic route to ...? | **Este vreun traseu turistic spre ...?** | yesteh vroon trase°° tooreesteec spreh |
| How far is it to ...? | **Este departe pînă la ...?** | yesteh departeh piner la |
| Can we walk there? | **Putem merge pînă acolo?** | pootem merjeh piner acolo |
| How high is that mountain? | **Ce înălţime are muntele acela?** | cheh inerltseemeh areh moonteleh achela |
| What kind of ... is that? | **Ce fel de ... este acesta?** | cheh fel deh ... yesteh achesta |
| animal | **animal** | aneemal |
| bird | **pasăre** | paserreh |
| flower | **floare** | flwareh |
| tree | **copac** | copac |

## Landmarks *Puncte de reper*

| | | |
|---|---|---|
| bridge | **pod** | pod |
| cliff | **stîncă** | stincer |
| farm | **fermă** | fermer |
| field | **cîmp** | cimp |
| footpath | **potecă** | potecer |
| forest | **pădure** | perdooreh |
| garden | **grădină** | grerdeener |
| hill | **deal** | deh-al |
| house | **casă** | caser |
| lake | **lac** | lac |
| meadow | **pajişte** | pazheeshteh |
| mountain | **munte** | moonteh |
| (mountain) pass | **trecătoare** | trecertwareh |
| path | **potecă** | potecer |
| peak | **vîrf** | virf |
| pond | **iaz** | yaz |
| river | **riu** | ri°° |
| road | **drum** | droom |
| sea | **mare** | mareh |
| spring | **izvor** | eezvor |
| valley | **vale** | valeh |
| village | **sat** | sat |
| vineyard | **vie** | vee-eh |
| wall | **zid** | zeed |
| waterfall | **cascadă** | cascader |
| wood | **pădure** | perdooreh |

ASKING THE WAY, see page 76

# Relaxing

### Cinema (movies)—Theatre  *Cinema—Teatru*

Going to the cinema is a popular pastime in Romania. Both national films and subtitled foreign films are regularly screened. You can find out what's on from the local newspapers.

| | | |
|---|---|---|
| What's on at the cinema tonight? | **Ce film rulează la cinema deseară?** | cheh feelm rooleh-azer la cheenema desarer |
| What's playing at the... Theatre? | **Ce piesă se joacă la Teatrul...** | cheh pyeser seh zhwacer la teh-atrool |
| What sort of play is it? | **Ce fel de piesă este?** | cheh fel deh pyeser yesteh |
| Who's it by? | **De cine este?** | deh cheeneh yesteh |
| Can you recommend (a)...? | **Puteţi recomanda...?** | pootets<sup>y</sup> recomanda |
| good film | **un film bun** | oon feelm boon |
| comedy | **o comedie** | o comedee-eh |
| musical | **o comedie muzicală** | o comedee-eh moozeecaler |
| Where's that new film directed by... being shown? | **Unde rulează filmul acela regizat de...** | oondeh rooleh-azer feelmool achela rejeezat deh |
| Who's in it? | **Cine joacă?** | cheeneh zhwacer |
| Who's playing the lead? | **Cine joacă rolul principal?** | cheeneh zhwacer rolool preencheepal |
| Who's the director? | **Cine a regizat filmul?** | cheeneh a rejeezat feelmool |
| At which theatre is that new play by... being performed? | **La ce teatru se joacă noua piesă a lui...?** | la cheh teh-atroo seh zhwacer nowa pyeser a loo<sup>y</sup> |
| What time does it begin? | **La ce oră începe?** | la cheh orer inchepeh |
| Are there any seats for tonight? | **Sînt locuri pentru deseară?** | sint locoor<sup>y</sup> pentroo desarer |

| How much are the seats? | **Cît costă un bilet?** | cit **cost**er oon bee**let** |
| I'd like to reserve 2 seats for the show on Friday evening. | **Aş vrea să rezerv 2 locuri pentru spectacolul de vineri seara.** | ash vreh-**a** ser re**zerv** 2 lo**coor**ᵞ pen**troo** spectaco**lool** deh **veen**erᵞ **sara** |
| Can I have a ticket for the matinée on Tuesday? | **Aveţi un bilet pentru marţi la matineu.** | avets**ᵞ** oon bee**let** pen**troo** marts**ᵞ** la **mateene**°° |
| I'd like a seat in the stalls (orchestra). | **Aş vrea un loc în stal.** | ash vreh-**a** oon loc **in** stal |
| Not too far back. | **Nu prea în spate.** | noo preh-a in **spateh** |
| Somewhere in the middle. | **Undeva pe la mij-loc.** | oonde**va** peh la **meezh**loc |
| How much are the seats in the circle (mezzanine)? | **Cît costă biletele la balcon?** | cit **cost**er bee**let**eleh la **balcon** |
| May I have a programme, please? | **Pot avea un program, vă rog?** | pot aveh-**a** oon pro**gram** ver rog |
| Where's the cloakroom? | **Unde este garde-roba?** | **oon**deh **yest**eh garde**roba** |

---

| **Regret, nu mai sînt bilete.** | I'm sorry, we're sold out. |
| **Mai sînt doar cîteva bilete la balcon.** | There are only a few seats left in the circle (mezzanine). |
| **Biletul, vă rog?** | May I see your ticket? |
| **Acesta este locul dumneavoastră.** | This is your seat. |

## Opera—Ballet—Concert *Operă—Balet—Concert*

| Can you recommend a(n)...? | **Puteţi reco-manda...?** | poo**tets**ᵞ recoman**da** |
| ballet | **un balet** | oon ba**let** |
| concert | **un concert** | oon con**chert** |
| opera | **o operă** | o **oper**er |
| operetta | **o operetă** | o **oper**eter |

DAYS OF THE WEEK, see page 151

| Where's the opera house/the concert hall? | **Unde este Operă/ sala de concerte?** | oondeh yesteh operer/sala deh concherteh |
| What's on at the opera tonight? | **Ce se joacă la operă deseară?** | cheh seh zhwacer la operer desarer |
| Who's singing/ dancing? | **Cine cîntă/dan- sează?** | cheeneh cinter/dansazer |
| Which orchestra is playing? | **Ce orchestră cîntă?** | cheh orkestrer cinter |
| What are they playing? | **Ce cîntă?** | cheh cinter |
| Who's the conductor/ soloist? | **Cine dirijează/Cine este solist?** | cheeneh deereezhazer/ cheeneh yesteh soleest |

### Nightclubs *Cluburi de noapte*

| Can you recommend a good nightclub? | **Puteţi să recoman- daţi un club de noapte bun?** | pootets<sup>y</sup> ser recomandats<sup>y</sup> oon cloob deh nwapteh boon |
| Is there a floor show? | **Este un spectacol în mijlocul pub- licului?** | yesteh oon spectacol in meezhlocool poobleecoolooy |
| What time does the show start? | **La ce oră începe spectacolul?** | la cheh orer inchepeh spectacolool |
| Is evening dress required? | **Se cere toaletă de seară?** | se chereh to-aleter deh sarer |

### Discos *Discoteci*

| Where can we go dancing? | **Unde putem merge să dansăm?** | oondeh pootem merjeh ser danserm |
| Is there a discotheque in town? | **Exista o discotecă în oraş?** | egzeester o deescotecer in orash |
| Would you like to dance? | **Vreţi să dansăti?** | vrets<sup>y</sup> ser dansats<sup>y</sup> |

### Sports *Sport*

Romanians love both outdoor and indoor sports. Football is the most popular and every city has its own team. Handball, bas- ketball, tennis and rugby also have a good following. Winter sports are widely enjoyed, and there are well-equipped ski resorts at Sinaia, Predeal, Poiana and Braşov. For information about sporting events, contact the National Tourist Office or buy the local sports paper *Sportul*.

| | | |
|---|---|---|
| Is there a football (soccer) match anywhere this Saturday? | **Este vreun meci de fotbal pe undeva simbăta asta?** | **yes**teh vroon mech[v] deh fotbal peh oond**eva** si mberta asta |
| Which teams are playing? | **Ce echipe joacă?** | cheh e**keeph** zhwa**cer** |
| Can you get me a ticket? | **Puteţi să-mi luaţi şi mie un bilet?** | poo**tets**[v] serm[v] lwats[v] shee mee-eh oon bee**let** |

| | | |
|---|---|---|
| basketball | **baschet** | **basket** |
| boxing | **box** | box |
| car racing | **raliu** | **rale**°° |
| cycling | **ciclism** | chee**cleesm** |
| football (soccer) | **fotbal** | **fotbal** |
| horse racing | **curse de cai** | **coor**seh deh cay |
| (horse-back) riding | **călărie** | cerler**ree**-eh |
| mountaineering | **alpinism** | alpee**neesm** |
| skiing | **ski** | skee |
| swimming | **a înota** | a î**nota** |
| tennis | **tenis** | te**nees** |
| volleyball | **voleibal** | **voley**bal |

| | | |
|---|---|---|
| I'd like to see a boxing match. | **Aş vrea să văd un meci de box.** | ash vreh-**a** ser verd oon mech[v] deh box |
| What's the admission charge? | **Cît costă biletul de intrare?** | cit **cos**ter beele**tool** deh een**trareh** |
| Where's the nearest golf course? | **Unde este terenul de golf cel mai apropiat?** | **oon**deh **yes**teh tere**nool** deh golf chel migh apro**pyat** |
| Where are the tennis courts? | **Unde se află terenurile de tenis?** | **oon**deh seh **af**ler tereno**oreeleh** deh te**nees** |
| What's the charge per...? | **Cît costă pe...?** | cit **cos**ter peh |
| day/round/hour | **zi/meci/ora** | zee/mech[v]/**orer** |
| Can I hire (rent) rackets? | **Pot să închiriez rachete de tenis?** | pot ser înkee**ree**-ez ra**keteh** deh te**nees** |
| Where's the race course (track)? | **Unde este hipodromul?** | **oon**deh **yes**teh heepo**dro**mool |

| Is there any good fishing/hunting around here? | **Există un loc bun de pescuit/vînat prin împrejurimi?** | egzeester oon loc boon deh pescooeet/vinat preen imprezhooreem<sup>y</sup> |
| Do I need a permit? | **Am nevoie de permis?** | am nevoyeh deh permees |
| Where can I get one? | **De unde pot obține un permis?** | deh oondeh pot obtseeneh oon permees |
| Can one swim in the lake/river? | **E permis înotul în lac/rîu?** | yeh permees inotool in lac/ri<sup>oo</sup> |
| Is there a swimming pool here? | **Există o piscină aici?** | egzeester o peescheener aeech<sup>y</sup> |
| Is it open-air or indoor? | **Este piscină în aer liber sau bazin acoperit?** | yesteh peescheener in aer leeber sa<sup>oo</sup> bazeen acopereet |
| Is it heated? | **Apa bazinului este incalzită?** | apa bazeenoolooy yesteh incerlzeeter |
| What's the temperature of the water? | **Ce temperatură are apa?** | cheh temperatoorer areh apa |
| Is there a sandy beach? | **Există o plajă cu nisip?** | egzeester o plazher coo neeseep |

## On the beach  *La plajă*

The Black Sea resorts are very popular for their smooth sandy beaches and beautiful hot weather during summer months. Mamaia, the 'pearl' of the Black Sea, offers the sandiest beach.

| Is it dangerous to swim here? | **Înotul aici este periculos?** | inotool aeech<sup>y</sup> yesteh pereecooloos |
| Is there a lifeguard? | **Există salvamar?** | egzeester salvamar |
| Is it safe for children? | **Este lipsit de pericol pentru copii?** | yesteh leepseet deh pereecol pentroo copee |
| The sea is very calm. | **Marea este foarte liniștită.** | mareh-a yesteh fwarteh leeneeshteeter |
| There are some big waves. | **Sînt niște valuri mari.** | sint neeshteh valoor<sup>y</sup> mar<sup>y</sup> |
| Are there any dangerous currents? | **Sînt curenți periculoși?** | sint coorents<sup>y</sup> pereecoolosh<sup>y</sup> |
| I want to hire (rent) a/an/ some ... | **Vreau să închiriez ...** | vra<sup>oo</sup> ser inkeeree-ez |
| bathing hut (cabana) | **o cabină** | o cabeener |
| deck chair | **un șezlong** | oon shezlong |
| motorboat | **o barcă cu motor** | o barcer coo motor |
| rowing-boat | **o barcă cu rame** | o barcer coo rameh |

| sailing boat | **o barcă cu pînză** | o barcer coo **pi**nzer |
| skin-diving equipment | **un echipament de plonjat** | oon ekeepament deh plon**zh**at |
| sunshade (umbrella) | **o umbrelă de soare** | o oombreler deh swareh |
| surfboard | **un acuaplan/o planşă de surf** | oon acwa**plan**/o **plan**sher deh surf |
| water-skis | **nişte skiuri nautice** | **nee**shteh **skee**oor^y naooteecheh |
| windsurfer | **o planşă de wind-surf** | o **plan**sher deh **weend**surf |

> **PLAJA PARTICULARA** — PRIVATE BEACH
> **ÎNOTUL INTERZIS** — NO SWIMMING

## Winter sports *Sporturi de iarnă*

| Is there a skating rink near here? | **Există un patinuar prin apropiere?** | egzeester oon pateenwar preen apropyereh |
| I'd like to ski. | **Aş vrea să schiez.** | ash vreh-**a** ser skee-ez |
| Are there any ski runs for...? | **Sînt piste de schi pentru...?** | sint **pee**steh deh skee **pen**troo |
| beginners | **începători** | incheper**tor**^y |
| average skiers | **schiori de nivel mediu** | skeeor^y deh nee**vel** medyoo |
| good skiers | **schiori buni** | skeeor^y boon^y |
| Can I take skiing lessons? | **Pot să iau lecţii de schiat?** | pot ser ya^oo **lect**see deh **skee**at |
| Are there any ski lifts? | **Există teleski?** | egzeester tele**skee** |
| I want to hire... | **Vreau să închiriez...** | vra^oo ser inkeereey-**ez**... |
| poles | **o prăjină** | o prerzhee**ner** |
| skates | **nişte patine** | **nee**shteh pa**teen**eh |
| ski boots | **nişte ghete de schi** | **nee**shteh **get**eh deh skee |
| skiing equipment | **un echipament de schi** | oon ekeepament deh skee |
| skis | **nişte schiuri** | **nee**shteh **skee**oor^y |

# Making friends

## Introductions *Prezentări*

Romanians have a reputation for being outgoing and friendly, and you should have no problem making friends. However, it is regarded as impolite if you address someone you don't know very well using the informal *tu*. This privilege is reserved for relatives, close friends and young people of a similar age and professional standing. You should use the formal *dumneavoastră* until your acquaintance makes it clear that he or she wants you to use the more familiar form of address.

| | | |
|---|---|---|
| May I introduce...? | **Daţi-mi voie să vă prezint pe...?** | **dat**seem$^y$ **vo**yeh ser ver pre**zeent** peh |
| Mihai, this is... | **Mihai, ţi-l prezint pe...** | mee**hay** tseel pre**zeent** peh |
| My name is... | **Mă numesc...** | mer noo**mesc** |
| Pleased to meet you! | **Încîntat de cunoştinţă!** | incîntat deh coonosh**teent**ser |
| What's your name? | **Cum vă numiţi?** | coom ver noo**meets**$^y$ |
| How are you? | **Ce mai faceţi?** | cheh migh **fachets**$^y$ |
| Fine, thanks. And you? | **Bine, mulţumesc. Şi dumneavoastră?** | **bee**neh mooltsoo**mesc**. shee doomna**vwas**trer |

## Follow up *Pentru a sparge gheaţa*

| | | |
|---|---|---|
| How long have you been here? | **De cîtă vreme sînteţi aici?** | deh **cit**er **vre**meh **sin**tets$^y$ **aeech**$^y$ |
| We've been here a week. | **Sîntem aici de o săptămînă.** | **sin**tem **aeech**$^y$ deh o serpter**mi**ner |
| Is this your first visit? | **Aceasta este prima vizită?** | a**chas**ta **yes**teh **preema vee**eeter |
| No, we came here last year. | **Nu, am fost aici şi anul trecut.** | noo am fost **aeech**$^y$ shee **a**nool tre**coot** |
| Are you enjoying your stay? | **Vă place aici?** | ver **pla**cheh **aeech**$^y$ |
| Yes, I like it very much. | **Da, îmi place foarte mult.** | da im$^y$ **pla**cheh **fwar**teh moolt |

| | | |
|---|---|---|
| I like the scenery a lot. | Îmi place peisajul foarte mult. | im<sup>y</sup> placheh paysazhool fwarteh moolt |
| What do you think of the country/people? | Ce părere ai despre ţară/oameni? | cheh perrereh igh despreh tsarer/wamen<sup>y</sup> |
| Where do you come from? | De unde veniţi? | deh oondeh veneets<sup>y</sup> |
| I'm from... | Vin din... | veen deen |
| What nationality are you? | Ce naţionalitate aveţi? | cheh natsyonaleetateh avets<sup>y</sup> |
| I'm... | Sînt... | sint |
| American | american | amereecan |
| British | britanic | breetaneec |
| Canadian | canadian | canadyan |
| English | englez | englez |
| Irish | irlandez | eerlandez |
| Where are you staying? | Unde locuiţi? | oondeh locooeets<sup>y</sup> |
| Are you on your own? | Sînteţi singur? | sintets<sup>y</sup> seengoor |
| I'm with my... | Sînt cu... | sint coo |
| wife | soţia mea | sotseea meh-a |
| husband | soţul meu | sotsool me<sup>oo</sup> |
| family | familia mea | fameelya meh-a |
| children | copii mei | copee may |
| parents | părinţii mei | perreentsee may |
| boyfriend/girlfriend | prietenul meu/ prietena mea | pree-etenool me<sup>oo</sup>/pree-etena meh-a |

| | | |
|---|---|---|
| father/mother | tata/mama | tata/mama |
| son/daughter | băiat/fată | beryat/fater |
| brother/sister | frate/soră | frateh/sorer |
| uncle/aunt | unchi/mătuşă | oonkee/mertoosher |
| nephew/niece | nepot/nepoată | nepot/nepwater |
| cousin | văr | verr |

| | | |
|---|---|---|
| Are you married/ single? | Sînteţi căsătorit/ necăsătorit? | sintets<sup>y</sup> cersertoreet/ necersertoreet |
| Do you have children? | Aveţi copii? | avets<sup>y</sup> copee |
| What do you do? | Cu ce vă ocupaţi? | coo cheh ver ocoopats<sup>y</sup> |
| I'm a student. | Sînt student. | sint stoodent |

COUNTRIES, see page 146

| What are you studying? | **Ce studiați?** | cheh stoo**dyats**ʸ |
| I'm here on a business trip/on holiday. | **Sînt aici în interes de serviciu/în vacanță.** | sint **aeech**ʸ in eenter**es** deh ser**vee**chyoo/in va**can**tser |
| Do you travel a lot? | **Călătoriți mult?** | cerlerto**reets**ʸ moolt |
| Do you play cards/ chess? | **Jucați cărți/șah?** | zhoo**cats**ʸ certs**ʸ**/shah |

## The weather  *Vreme*

| What a lovely day! | **Ce zi frumoasă!** | cheh zee froom**waser** |
| What awful weather! | **Ce vreme urîtă!** | cheh **vre**meh oo**ri**ter |
| Isn't it cold/ hot today? | **Nu-i așa că e frig/ cald afară?** | nooy **asha** cer yeh freeg/ cald a**fa**rer |
| Is it usually as warm as this? | **E de obicei așa de cald?** | yeh deh obee**chay asha** deh cald |
| Do you think it's going to... tomorrow? | **Credeți că va fi... mîine?** | **credets**ʸ cer va fee... **miy**neh |
| be a nice day | **frumos** | froo**mos** |
| rain | **ploaie** | **plwa**yeh |
| snow | **zăpadă** | **zer**pader |
| What's the weather forecast? | **Ce vreme se pre-vede?** | cheh **vre**meh seh pre**ve**deh |

| cloud | **nori** | nor**ʸ** |
| fog | **ceață** | **chat**ser |
| frost | **ger** | jer |
| ice | **gheață** | **gya**tser |
| lightning | **fulgere** | **fool**jereh |
| moon | **lună** | **loo**ner |
| rain | **ploaie** | **plwa**yeh |
| sky | **cer** | cher |
| snow | **zăpadă** | **zer**pader |
| star | **stea** | steh-**a** |
| sun | **soare** | **swa**reh |
| thunder | **tunet** | **too**net |
| thunderstorm | **furtună** | foor**too**ner |
| wind | **vînt** | vint |

## Invitations *Invitaţii*

| Would you like to have dinner with us on…? | Vreţi să veniţi să luăm masa de seară împreună …? | vrets[y] ser veneets[y] ser lwerm masa deh sarer impreooner |
| Would you like to have dinner with us on…? | | |
| May I invite you to lunch? | Vreţi să luaţi masa de prînz cu mine? | vrets[y] ser lwats[y] masa deh prinz coo meeneh |
| Can you come round for a drink this evening? | Puteţi veni să bem ceva deseară? | pootets[y] venee ser bem cheva desarer |
| There's a party. Are you coming? | Dau o petrecere. Puteţi veni? | da[oo] oh petrechereh. pootets[y] venee |
| That's very kind of you. | Sînteţi foarte amabil. | sintets[y] fwarteh amabeel |
| Great. I'd love to come. | Da, cu multă plăcere. | da coo moolter plerchereh |
| What time shall we come? | La ce oră trebuie să venim? | la cheh orer trebooyeh ser veneem |
| May I bring a friend? | Pot să aduc un prieten? | pot ser adooc oon preeeten |
| I'm afraid we have to leave now. | Regret, trebuie să plecam. | regret trebooyeh ser plecerm |
| Next time you must come to visit us. | E rîndul dumneavoastră să ne vizitaţi. | yeh rindool doomnavwastrer ser neh veezeetats[y] |
| Thanks for the evening. It was great. | Mulţumesc pentru invitaţie. Ne-am simţit foarte bine. | mooltsoomesc pentroo eenveetatsyeh. neh-am seemtseet fwarteh beeneh |

## Dating *Întîlniri*

| Do you mind if I smoke? | Vă deranjează dacă fumez? | ver deranzhazer dacer foomez |
| Would you like a cigarette? | Doriţi o ţigară? | doreets[y] o tseegarer |
| Do you have a light, please? | Aveţi un foc, vă rog? | avets[y] oon foc ver rog |
| Why are you laughing? | De ce rîdeţi? | de cheh ridets[y] |
| Is my Romanian that bad? | Vorbesc aşa de rău româneşte? | vorbesc asha deh roh romineshteh |
| Do you mind if I sit here? | Pot sta aici? | pot sta aeech[y] |

DAYS OF THE WEEK, see page 151

| | | |
|---|---|---|
| Can I get you a drink? | Ce doriţi să beţi? | cheh doreets\* ser bets\* |
| Are you waiting for someone? | Aşteptaţi pe cineva? | ashteptats\* peh cheeneva |
| Are you free this evening? | Sînteţi liber deseară? | sintets\* leeber desarer |
| Would you like to go out with me tonight? | Putem ieşi împreună deseară? | pootem yeshee impreooner desarer |
| Would you like to go dancing? | Aţi vrea să mergem să dansăm? | ats\* vreh-a ser merjem ser danserm |
| I know a good discotheque. | Stiu o discotecă bună. | shtee°° o deescotecer booner |
| Shall we go to the cinema (movies)? | Vreţi să mergem la cinema? | vrets\* ser merjem la cheenema |
| Would you like to go for a drive? | Vreţi să ne plimbăm cu maşina? | vrets\* ser neh pleemberm coo masheena |
| Where shall we meet? | Unde ne întîlnim? | oondeh neh intilneem |
| I'll pick you up at your hotel. | O să vin să vă iau de la hotel. | o ser veen ser ver ya°° deh la hotel |
| I'll call for you at 8. | O să vin la ora 8. | o ser veen la ora 8 |
| May I take you home? | Vă pot conduce acasă? | ver pot condoocheh acaser |
| Can I see you again tomorrow? | Ne putem întîlni din nou mîine? | neh pootem intilnee deen no°° miyneh |
| I hope we'll meet again. | Sper să ne întîlnim din nou. | sper ser neh intilneem deen no°° |

... and you might answer:

| | | |
|---|---|---|
| I'd love to, thank you. | Mulţumesc, cu plăcere. | mooltsoomesc coo plerchereh |
| Thank you, but I'm busy. | Mulţumesc, sînt ocupat/ocupată. | mooltsoomesc sint ocoopat/ocoopater |
| No, I'm not interested, thank you. | Mulţumesc, nu mă interesează. | mooltsoomesc noo mer eenteresazer |
| Leave me alone, please! | Lasă-mă în pace, te rog! | laser-mer in pacheh teh rog |
| Thank you, it's been a wonderful evening. | Mulţumesc, a fost o seară minunată. | mooltsoomesc a fost o seh-arer meenoonater |
| I've enjoyed myself. | M-am distrat foarte bine. | mam deestrat fwarteh beeneh |

# Shopping Guide

This shopping guide is designed to help you find what you want with ease, accuracy and speed. It features:

1. A list of all major shops, stores and services (p. 98).
2. Some general expressions required when shopping to allow you to be specific and selective (p. 100).
3. Full details of the shops and services most likely to concern you. Here you'll find advice, alphabetical lists of items and conversion charts listed under the headings below.

## Shops, stores and services *Magazine şi servicii*

Opening hours vary. As a general rule, state-owned shops are open from 8am until 6pm, while privately owned shops remain in business from 9am until 6pm, although some stay open round the clock. Department stores are open from l0am until 7pm. A few shops stay open on Saturdays but all are closed on Sundays. Bakeries are closed from noon on Friday until Monday morning, so be sure to stock up for the weekend as you won't be able to buy bread elsewhere.

Romanians usually buy fresh fruit, vegetables and herbs from open-air markets, *piaţa*, which can be found all over Bucharest and other cities.

| | | |
|---|---|---|
| Where's the nearest …? | **Unde este prin apropiere …?** | oondeh yesteh preen apropyereh |
| antique shop | **un magazin de antichităţi** | oon magazeen deh anteekeeterts<sup>y</sup> |
| art gallery | **o galerie de artă** | o galeree-eh deh arter |
| baker's | **o brutărie** | o brooter-ree-eh |
| bank | **o bancă** | o bancer |
| barber's | **o frizerie** | o freezeh-ree-eh |
| beauty salon | **un salon de cosmetică** | oon salon deh cosmeteecer |
| bookshop | **o librărie** | o leebrer-ree-eh |
| butcher's | **o măcelărie** | o mercheler-ree-eh |
| camera shop | **un magazin foto** | oon magazeen foto |
| chemist's | **o farmacie** | o farmachee-eh |
| dairy | **un magazin de brînzeturi şi lapte** | oon magazeen deh brînzetoor<sup>y</sup> shee lapteh |
| delicatessen | **un magazin de delicatese** | oon magazeen deh deleecateseh |
| dentist | **un cabinet dentar** | oon cabeenet dentar |
| department store | **un magazin universal** | oon magazeen ooneeversal |
| drugstore | **o farmacie** | o farmachee-eh |
| dry cleaner's | **o curăţătorie** | o coorertsertoree-eh |
| electrical goods shop | **un magazin de aparatură electrică** | oon magazeen deh aparatoorer electreecer |
| fishmonger's | **o pescărie** | o pescer-ree-eh |
| florist's | **o florărie** | o florer-ree-eh |
| furrier's | **o blănărie** | o blerner-ree-eh |
| greengrocer's | **un aprozar** | oon aprozar |

LAUNDRY, see page 29/HAIRDRESSER'S, see page 30

| grocer's | o băcănie | o bercer**nee**-eh |
| hairdresser's (ladies/men) | o coafor/o frizerie | o cwa**for**/o freezeh-**ree**-eh |
| hospital | un spital | oon spee**tal** |
| ironmonger's | o fierărie | o fee-ehrer-**ree**-eh |
| jeweller's | un magazin de bijuterii | oon maga**zeen** deh beezhooter**ee** |
| launderette | o spălătorie Nufă-rul | o sperlerto-**ree**-eh noo**fer**rool |
| laundry | o spălătorie | o sperlerto-**ree**-eh |
| library | o bibliotecă | o beeblyo**te**cer |
| market | o piață | o **pyat**ser |
| newsagent's | un chioșc de ziare | oon **kyoshc** deh **zya**reh |
| newsstand | un chioșc de ziare | oon **kyoshc** deh **zya**reh |
| optician | un optician | oon optee**chyan** |
| pastry shop | o plăcintărie | o plercheenter-**ree**-eh |
| photographer | un atelier de foto-grafiat | oon ate**lyer** deh fotografee**at** |
| police station | un post de poliție | oon post deh po**leet**see-eh |
| post office | o poșta | o **posh**ta |
| second-hand bookshop | un anticariat | oon anteeca**ryat** |
| second-hand shop | o consignație | o conseeg**nats**yeh |
| shoemaker's (repairs) | o cizmărie | o cheezmer-**ree**-eh |
| shoe shop | un magazin de încălțăminte | oon maga**zeen** deh incerltser**meen**teh |
| shopping centre | un centru comer-cial | oon **chen**troo comer**chyal** |
| souvenir shop | un magazin de suveniruri | oon maga**zeen** deh sooveneeroor$^y$ |
| stationer's | o papetărie | o papeter-**ree**-eh |
| supermarket | un magazin ali-mentar | oon maga**zeen** aleemen**tar** |
| sweet shop | un magazin de dul-ciuri | oon maga**zeen** deh **dool**chyoor$^y$ |
| tailor's | o croitorie | o croeeto**ree**-eh |
| telegraph office | o birou PTT | o bee**roh** peh-teh-teh |
| tobacconist's | o tutungerie | o tootoonjeh-**ree**-eh |
| toy shop | un magazin de jucării | oon maga**zeen** deh zhoocer-**ree** |
| travel agency | o agenție de voiaj | o ajent**see**-eh deh vo**yazh** |
| vegetable store | un aprozar | oon apro**zar** |
| veterinarian | un veterinar | oon vetere**nar** |
| watchmaker's | o ceasornicărie | o chasorneecer-**ree**-eh |
| wine merchant | un magazin de vinuri | oon maga**zeen** deh **vee**noor$^y$ |

**General expressions** *Expresii de uz general*

### Where? *Unde?*

| | | |
|---|---|---|
| Where's there a good ...? | Unde este un/o ... de bună calitate? | oondeh yesteh oon/o ... deh booner caleetateh |
| Where can I find a ...? | Unde se găseşte un/o ...? | oondeh seh gerseshteh oon/o |
| Where's the main shopping area? | Unde este centrul comercial princi-pal? | oondeh yesteh chentrool comerchyal preencheepal |
| Is it far from here? | Este departe de aici? | yesteh departeh deh aeech<sup>y</sup> |
| How do I get there? | Cum se ajunge acolo? | coom seh azhoonjeh acolo |

| SOLDURI | SALE |
|---|---|

### Service *Servicii*

| | | |
|---|---|---|
| Can you help me? | Puteţi să mă aju-taţi? | pootets<sup>y</sup> ser mer azhootats<sup>y</sup> |
| I'm just looking. | Mă uit doar. | mer ooyt dwar |
| Do you sell ...? | Vindeti ...? | veendets<sup>y</sup> |
| I'd like to buy ... | Aş vrea să cumpăr ... | ash vreh-a ser coomperr |
| I'd like ... | Aş vrea ... | ash vreh-a |
| Can you show me some ...? | Puteţi să-mi arătaţi nişte ...? | pootets<sup>y</sup> serm<sup>y</sup> arertats<sup>y</sup> neeshteh |
| Do you have any ...? | Aveţi ... ? | avets<sup>y</sup> |
| Where's the ... department? | Unde este raionul de ... | oondeh yesteh rayonool deh ... |
| Where is the lift (elevator)/escalator? | Unde este liftul/ escalatorul? | oondeh yesteh leeftool/ escalatorool |

| INTRARE | ENTRANCE |
|---|---|
| IEŞIRE | EXIT |
| IEŞIRE DE INCENDIU | EMERGENCY EXIT |
| INVENTAR | CLOSED FOR STOCKTAKING |

### That one *Acela*

| | | |
|---|---|---|
| Can you show me ...? | **Puteţi să-mi arătaţi ...** | pootets<sup>y</sup> serm<sup>y</sup> arertats<sup>y</sup> |
| this/that | **acesta/acela** | achesta/achela |
| the one in the window | **cel din vitrină** | chel deen veetreener |

### Defining the article *Descrierea obiectului*

| | | |
|---|---|---|
| I'd like a ... one. | **Aş vrea una ...** | ash vreh-a oona |
| big | **mare** | mareh |
| cheap | **ieftină** | yefteener |
| dark | **închisă la culoare** | inkeeser la coolwareh |
| good | **bună** | booner |
| heavy | **grea** | greh-a |
| large | **largă** | larger |
| light (weight) | **uşoară** | ooshwarer |
| light (colour) | **deschisă la culoare** | deskeeser la coolwareh |
| oval | **ovală** | ovaler |
| rectangular | **rectangulară** | rectangoolarer |
| round | **rotundă** | rotoonder |
| small | **mică** | meecer |
| square | **pătrată** | pertrater |
| sturdy | **durabilă** | doorabeeler |
| I don't want anything too expensive. | **Nu vreau nimic prea scump.** | noo vra<sup>oo</sup> neemeec preh-a scoomp |

### Preference *Preferinţe*

| | | |
|---|---|---|
| Can you show me some others? | **Puteţi să-mi arătaţi şi altele?** | pootets<sup>y</sup> serm<sup>y</sup> arertats<sup>y</sup> shee alteleh |
| Don't you have anything ...? | **Nu aveţi nimic ... ?** | noo avets<sup>y</sup> neemeec |
| cheaper/better | **mai ieftin/mai bun** | migh yefteen/migh boon |
| larger/smaller | **mai mare/mai mic** | migh mareh/migh meec |

### How much *Cît costă*

| | | |
|---|---|---|
| How much is this? | **Cît costă aceasta?** | cît coster achasta |
| How much are they? | **Cît costă acestea?** | cît coster achesteh-a |
| I don't understand. | **Nu înţeleg.** | noo inteleg |
| Please write it down. | **Vă rog scrieţi aceasta.** | ver rog scree-ets<sup>y</sup> achasta |

COLOURS, see page 112

| | | |
|---|---|---|
| I don't want to spend more than ... lei. | **Nu vreau să cheltuiesc mai mult de ... lei.** | noo vra°° ser keltooyesc migh moolt deh ... lay |

### Decision *Decizii*

| | | |
|---|---|---|
| It's not quite what I want. | **Nu este chiar ce vreau eu.** | noo yesteh kyar cheh vra°° ye°° |
| No, I don't like it. | **Nu-mi place.** | noom<sup>y</sup> placheh |
| I'll take it. | **Il cumpăr.** | il **coom**perr |

### Ordering *A face o comandă*

| | | |
|---|---|---|
| Can you order it for me? | **Il puteţi comanda?** | il pootets<sup>y</sup> coman**da** |
| How long will it take? | **Cît timp va dura?** | cît teemp va doo**ra** |

### Delivery *Livrarea*

| | | |
|---|---|---|
| I'll take it with me. | **Il iau cu mine.** | il ya°° coo **mee**neh |
| Deliver it to the ... Hotel. | **Livraţi-l la Hotelul ...** | leevrat**seel** la hoteloo**l** |
| Please send it to this address. | **Vă rog să-l livraţi la această adresă.** | ver rog serl leevrats<sup>y</sup> la achaster adreser |
| Will I have any difficulty with the customs? | **Credeţi că pot avea dificultaţi la vamă?** | credets<sup>y</sup> cer pot aveh-a deefeecoolterts<sup>y</sup> la vamer |

### Paying *Plata*

| | | |
|---|---|---|
| How much is it? | **Cît costă?** | cît **cos**ter |
| Can I pay by traveller's cheque? | **Pot plăti cu cec de călătorie?** | pot pler**tee** coo chec deh cerlertoree-eh |
| Do you accept dollars/pounds? | **Primiţi dolari/lire sterline?** | preemeets<sup>y</sup> dolar<sup>y</sup>/leereh sterleeneh |
| Do you accept credit cards? | **Acceptaţi cărţi de credit?** | ac-cheptats<sup>y</sup> certs<sup>y</sup> deh credeet |
| Do I have to pay the VAT (sales tax)? | **Trebuie să plătesc TVA?** | trebooyeh ser plertesc tehveh-a |
| I think there's a mistake in the bill. | **Cred că este o greşeală în nota de plată.** | cred cer yesteh o greshaler în nota deh plater |

### Anything else? *Mai doriţi ceva?*

| No, thanks, that's all. | **Nu, mulţumesc, asta-i tot.** | noo mooltsoo**mesc** astay tot |
| Yes, I'd like ... | **Da, aş vrea ...** | da ash vreh-**a** |
| Can you show me ...? | **Puteţi să-mi arătaţi ... ?** | pootets<sup>y</sup> serm<sup>y</sup> arertats<sup>y</sup> |
| May I have a bag, please? | **Puteţi să-mi daţi o pungă, vă rog?** | pootets<sup>y</sup> serm<sup>y</sup> dats<sup>y</sup> o **poong**er ver rog |
| Could you wrap it up for me, please? | **Vreţi să-l împache-taţi, vă rog?** | vrets<sup>y</sup> serl impake**tats**<sup>y</sup> ver rog |
| May I have a receipt? | **Puteţi să-mi daţi, vă rog, o chitanţa?** | pootets<sup>y</sup> serm<sup>y</sup> dats<sup>y</sup> ver rog o kee**tant**ser |

### Dissatisfied? *Nemulţumit?*

| Can you exchange this, please? | **Puteţi să-mi schim-baţi aceasta, vă rog?** | pootets<sup>y</sup> serm<sup>y</sup> skeem**bats**<sup>y</sup> a**chas**ta ver rog |
| I want to return this. | **Vreau să înapoiez aceasta.** | vra<sup>oo</sup> ser inapo**yez** a**chas**ta |
| I'd like a refund. Here's the receipt. | **Aş vrea plata îna-poi. Poftiţi chi-tanţa.** | ash vreh-**a** plata inapoy. pof**teets**<sup>y</sup> keetantsa |

---

| Cu ce vă pot ajuta? | Can I help you? |
| Ce doriţi? | What would you like? |
| Ce ... doriţi? | What ... would you like? |
| culoare/măsura/calitate | colour/shape/quality |
| Regret, dar nu mai avem. | I'm sorry, we don't have any. |
| S-a terminat stocul. | We're out of stock. |
| Vreţi să-l vi-l comandăm? | Shall we order it for you? |
| Il luaţi cu dumneavoastră sau vreţi să vi-l expediem noi? | Will you take it with you or shall we send it? |
| Mai doriţi ceva? | Anything else? |
| Aceasta face ... lei, vă rog. | That's ... lei, please. |
| Casa este acolo. | The cash desk is over there. |

## Bookshop—Stationer's *Librărie—Papetărie*

There are plenty of kiosks selling national newspapers. However, foreign newspapers can be found only in big hotels in Bucharest.

| | | |
|---|---|---|
| Where's the nearest ...? | Există prin apropiere ...? | egzeester preen apropyereh |
| bookshop | o librărie | o leebrer-**ree**-eh |
| stationer's | o papetărie | o papeter-**ree**-eh |
| newsstand | un chioşc de ziare | oon kyoshc deh **zy**areh |
| Where can I buy an English-language newspaper? | Unde pot cumpăra un ziar în limba engleză? | **oon**deh pot coomperra oon zyar in **leem**ba englezer |
| Where's the guide-book section? | Unde este raionul de ghiduri? | **oon**deh **yes**teh rayonool deh **gee**door^y |
| Where do you keep the English books? | Unde ţineţi cărţile englezeşti? | **oon**deh **tsee**nets^y **cerr**tseeleh englezesht^y |
| Have you any of ... 's books in English? | Aveţi vreo carte de ... în engleză? | avets^y vro **car**teh deh ... in englezer |
| Do you have second-hand books? | Aveţi cărţi la mîna a doua? | avets^y certs^y la mina a do-wa |
| I want to buy a/an/some ... | Vreau să cumpăr ... | vra°° ser **coom**perr |
| address book | o agendă de adrese | o a**jen**der deh a**dre**seh |
| adhesive tape | nişte scoci | **neesh**teh scoch^y |
| ball-point pen | un pix cu pastă | oon peex coo **pas**ter |
| book | o carte | o **car**teh |
| calendar | un calendar | oon calen**dar** |
| carbon paper | nişte hîrtie indigou | **neesh**teh hir**tee**-eh eendee**goh** |
| crayons | nişte creioane | **neesh**teh crey**wa**neh |
| dictionary | un dicţionar | oon deects**yo**nar |
| Romanian-English | Roman-Englez | romin-englez |
| pocket | de buzunar | deh boozoo**nar** |
| drawing pins | nişte pioneze | **neesh**teh peeo**ne**zeh |
| envelopes | nişte plicuri | **neesh**teh **plee**coor^y |
| eraser | o gumă | o **goo**mer |
| exercise book | un caiet | oon **ca**yet |
| felt-tip pen | o carioca | o car**yo**ca |
| fountain pen | un stilou cu cerneală | oon stee**loh**°° coo cher**na**ler |
| glue | nişte lipici | **neesh**teh lee**peech**^y |
| grammar book | o carte de gramatică | o **car**teh deh grama**teec**er |

| | | |
|---|---|---|
| guidebook | **un ghid** | oon geed |
| ink | **niște cerneală** | neeshteh chernaler |
| black/red/blue | **neagră/roșie/ albastră** | neh-agrer/roshee-eh/ albastrer |
| (adhesive) labels | **niște etichete (colante)** | neeshteh eteeketeh (colanteh) |
| magazine | **revistă** | reveester |
| map | **o hartă** | o harter |
| street map | **o hartă a strǎzilor** | o harter a strerzeelor |
| road map of ... | **o hartă a drumu- rilor naționale** | o harta a droomooreelor natsyonaleh |
| mechanical pencil | **un creion mecanic** | oon creyon mecaneec |
| newspaper | **un ziar** | oon zyar |
| American/English | **american/engle- zesc** | amereecan/englezesc |
| notebook | **un carnet** | oon carnet |
| note paper | **niște hîrtie de scris** | neeshteh hirtee-eh deh screes |
| paintbox | **o cutie de culori** | o cootee-eh deh coolor$^y$ |
| paper | **niște hîrtie** | neeshteh hirtee-eh |
| paperback | **o carte** | o carteh |
| paperclips | **niște agrafe pentru hîrtie** | neeshteh agrafeh pentroo hirtee-eh |
| paper napkins | **niște șervețele de hîrtie** | neeshteh shervetseleh deh hirtee-eh |
| paste | **niște clei** | neeshteh clay |
| pen | **un stilou** | oon steelo$^{oo}$ |
| pencil | **un creion** | oon creyon |
| pencil sharpener | **o ascuțitoare** | o ascootseetwareh |
| playing cards | **niște cărți de joc** | neeshteh certs$^y$ deh zhoc |
| pocket calculator | **calculator de buzu- nar** | calcoolator deh boozoonar |
| postcard | **o vedere** | o vedereh |
| propelling pencil | **un creion mecanic** | oon creyon mecaneec |
| refill (for a pen) | **o rezervă de stilou** | o rezerver deh steelo$^{oo}$ |
| rubber | **o gumă** | o goomer |
| ruler | **o linie** | o leenyeh |
| stapler | **un capsator** | oon capsator |
| staples | **niște capse pentru capsator** | neeshteh capseh pentroo capsator |
| string | **niște sfoară** | neeshteh sfwarer |
| thumbtacks | **niște pioneze** | neeshteh pyonezeh |
| travel guide | **un ghid turistic** | oon geed tooreesteec |
| typewriter ribbon | **o panglică pentru mașină de scris** | o pangleecer pentroo masheener deh screes |
| writing pad | **un bloc notes** | oon bloc notes |

## Camping and sports equipment *Camping şi echipament de sport*

| I'd like (to hire) a(n)/some ... | Aş vrea (să închiriez) ... | ash vreh-a (ser inkeree-ez) |
|---|---|---|
| air bed (mattress) | o saltea pneumatică | o salteh-a pne°°mateecer |
| backpack | un rucsac | oon roocsac |
| beach towel | un prosop de plajă | oon prosop deh plazher |
| butane gas | o butelie de gaz | o bootelyeh deh gaz |
| campbed | un pat de camping | oon pat deh kempeeng |
| (folding) chair | un scaun (pliant) | oon sca°°n (pleeant) |
| charcoal | cărbune pentru grătar | cerrbooneh pentroo grertar |
| compass | o busolă | o boosoler |
| cool box | o geantă frigorifică | o janter freegoreefeecer |
| deck chair | un şezlong | oon shezlong |
| fishing tackle | nişte unelte de pescuit | neeshteh oonelteh deh pescoo°eet |
| flashlight | o lanternă | o lanterner |
| groundsheet | o folie de muşama pentru cort | o folyeh deh mushama pentroo cort |
| hammock | un hamac | oon hamac |
| insect spray (killer) | un insecticid | oon eensecteecheed |
| kerosene | gaz | gaz |
| lamp | o lampă | o lamper |
| lantern | un felinar | oon feleenar |
| mallet | un ciocan | oon chyocan |
| matches | nişte chibrituri | neeshteh keebreetoor^y |
| (foam rubber) mattress | o saltea (de burete de cauciuc) | o salteh-a (deh booreteh deh ca°°chyooc) |
| mosquito net | o plasă de ţinţari | o plaser deh tsintsar^y |
| paraffin | parafină | parafeener |
| picnic basket | un coş pentru picnic | oon cosh pentroo peecneec |
| pump | o pompă | o pomper |
| rope | o frînghie | o fringee-eh |
| rucksack | un rucsac | oon roocsac |
| skin-diving equipment | echipament de plonjat | ekeepament deh plonzhat |
| sleeping bag | un sac de dormit | oon sac deh dormeet |
| (folding) table | o masă pliantă | o maser pleeanter |
| tent | un cort | oon cort |
| tent pegs | nişte cîrlige de cort | neeshteh cirleejeh deh cort |
| tent pole | un stîlp de cort | oon stilp deh cort |
| torch | o lanternă | o lanterner |
| water flask | un termos | oon termos |

CAMPING, see page 32

## Chemist's (drugstore) *Farmacie*

Cosmetics and toiletries can be purchased at a *drogherie* or in the cosmetic department of large stores, while medicine and cotton wool can be bought at a *farmacie*. Some privately owned pharmacies also stock a good range of imported medicine and personal care products.

### General expressions *Expresii de uz general*

| | | |
|---|---|---|
| Where's the nearest (all-night) chemist's? | **Unde se află o farmacie (non stop) prin apropiere?** | oondeh seh afler o farmachee-eh (non stop) preen apropyereh |
| What time does the chemist's open/close? | **La ce oră se deschide/închide farmacia?** | la cheh orer deskeedeh/ïnkeedeh farmachee-a |

### 1—Pharmaceutical *Expresii pentru uz farmaceutic*

| | | |
|---|---|---|
| I'd like something for ... | **Aş vrea ceva pentru ...** | ash vreh-a cheva pentroo |
| a cold/a cough | **răceală/tuse** | rercheh-aler/tooseh |
| hay fever | **alergie la polen** | alerjee-eh la polen |
| insect bites | **înţepături de insecte** | intsepertoor[y] deh eensecteh |
| sunburn | **arsuri de soare** | arsoor[y] deh swareh |
| travel/altitude sickness | **rău de călătorie/rău de înalţime** | roh deh cerlertoree-eh/roh deh ïnerltseemeh |
| an upset stomach | **stomac deranjat** | stomac deranzhat |
| Can you prepare this prescription for me? | **Puteţi să-mi preparaţi această reţetă?** | pootets[y] serm[y] preparats[y] achaster retseter |
| Can I get it without a prescription? | **Pot cumpăra aceasta fără reţetă?** | pot coomperra achasta ferrer retseter |
| Shall I wait? | **Pot să aştept?** | pot ser ashtept |
| Can I have a/an/some ...? | **Puteţi să-mi daţi ...?** | pootets[y] serm[y] dats[y] |
| adhesive plaster | **nişte leucoplast** | neeshteh le[oo]coplast |
| analgesic | **un calmant** | oon calmant |
| antiseptic cream | **o cremă antiseptică** | o cremer anteesepteecer |
| aspirin | **nişte aspirină** | neeshteh aspeereener |
| bandage | **un bandaj** | oon bandazh |
| elastic bandage | **un bandaj elastic** | oon bandazh elasteec |

DOCTOR see page 137

| | | |
|---|---|---|
| Band-Aids® | niște pansamente | neeshteh pansamenteh |
| condoms | niște prezervativ | neeshteh prezervateev |
| contraceptives | niște anticoncepționale | neeshteh anteeconcheptsyonaleh |
| corn plasters | niște leucoplast pentru bătături | neeshteh le°°coplast pentroo bertertoorʸ |
| cotton wool (absorbent cotton) | niște vată | neeshteh vater |
| cough drops | niște picături de tuse | neeshteh peecertoorʸ deh tooseh |
| disinfectant | un desinfectant | oon dezeenfectant |
| ear drops | niște picături pentru urechi | neeshteh peecertoorʸ pentroo oorekʸ |
| eye drops | niște picături pentru ochi | neeshteh peecertoorʸ pentroo okʸ |
| first-aid kit | o trusă de prim ajutor | o trooser deh preem azhootor |
| gauze | niște tifon | neeshteh teefon |
| insect repellent/ spray | un spray contra insectelor | oon spray contra eensectelor |
| iodine | niște iod | neeshteh yod |
| laxative | niște laxative | neeshteh laxateeveh |
| mouthwash | o apă de gură | o aper deh goorer |
| nose drops | niște picături de nas | neeshteh peecertoorʸ deh nas |
| sanitary towels (napkins) | niște tampoane externe | neeshteh tampwaneh externeh |
| sleeping pills | niște somnifere | neeshteh somneefeh-reh |
| suppositories | niște supozitoare | neeshteh soopozeetwareh |
| ... tablets | niște pastile ... | neeshteh pasteeleh |
| tampons | niște tampoane interne | neeshteh tampwaneh eenterneh |
| thermometer | un termometru | oon termometroo |
| throat lozenges | niște pastile pentru dureri de gît | neeshteh pasteeleh pentroo doorerʸ deh git |
| tranquillizers | niște tranchilizante | neeshteh trankeeleeezanteh |
| vitamin pills | niște vitamine (tablete) | neeshteh veetameeneh (tableteh) |

| | |
|---|---|
| **OTRAVA** | POISON |
| **NUMAI PENTRU UZ EXTERN** | FOR EXTERNAL USE ONLY |

DOCTOR, see page 137

## 2—Toiletry *Parfumerie*

| I'd like a/an/some ... | Aş vrea ... | ash vreh-a |
|---|---|---|
| after-shave lotion | o loţiune după ras | o lotsyooneh dooper ras |
| astringent | o loţiune astrin-gentă | o lotsyooneh astreenjenter |
| bath salts | nişte săruri de baie | neeshteh ser-roorʸ deh bayeh |
| blusher (rouge) | o ruj de obraz | o roozh deh obraz |
| bubble bath | o spumă de baie | o spoomer deh bayeh |
| cream | o cremă | o cremer |
| cleansing cream | un lapte demachiant | oon lapteh demakeeant |
| foundation cream | un fond de ten | oon fond deh ten |
| moisturizing cream | o cremă hidra-tantă | o cremer heedratanter |
| deodorant | un deodorant | oon deodorant |
| eyeliner | un creion de ple-oape | oon creyon deh plewapeh |
| eye shadow | un fard de pleoape | oon fard deh plewapeh |
| face powder | o pudră de obraz | o poodrer deh obraz |
| lipsalve | un strugurel de buze | oon stroogoorel deh boozeh |
| lipstick | un ruj de buze | oon roozh deh boozeh |
| make-up remover pads | nişte tampoane pentru dema-chiat | neeshteh tampwaneh pentroo demakyat |
| mascara | un rimel | oon reemel |
| nail brush | o periuţă de unghii | o peryootser deh oongee |
| nail file | o pilă de unghii | o peeler deh oongee |
| nail polish | o ojă de unghii | o ozher deh oongee |
| nail polish remover | o acetonă | o achetoner |
| nail scissors | o forfecuţă de unghii | o forfecootser deh oongee |
| perfume | un parfum | oon parfoom |
| powder | o pudră | o poodrer |
| powder puff | un puf de pudră | oon poof deh poodrer |
| razor | un aparat de ras | oon aparat deh ras |
| razor blades | nişte lame | neeshteh lameh |
| rouge | un ruj de obraz | oon roozh deh obraz |
| safety pins | nişte ace de sig-uranţă | neeshteh acheh deh seegoorantser |
| shaving brush | un pămătuf de ras | oon permertoof deh ras |
| shaving cream | o cremă de ras | o cremer deh ras |
| soap | un săpun | oon serpoon |

110

| sponge | un burete | oon booreteh |
| sun-tan cream | o cremă de bronzat | o cremer deh bronzat |
| sun-tan oil | un ulei de bronzat | oon oolay deh bronzat |
| talcum powder | o pudră de talc | o poodrer deh talc |
| tissues | niște batiste de hîr-tie | neeshteh bateesteh deh hirtee-eh |
| toilet paper | niște hîrtie igienică | neeshteh hirtee-eh eejyeneecer |
| toilet water | o apă de toaletă | o aper deh to-aleter |
| toothbrush | o perie de dinți | o peree-eh deh deents<sup>y</sup> |
| toothpaste | o pastă de dinți | o paster deh deents<sup>y</sup> |
| towel | un prosop | oon prosop |
| tweezers | o pensetă | o penseter |

## For your hair *Pentru păr*

| bobby pins | agrafe | agrafeh |
| colour shampoo | un șampon col-orant | oon shampon colorant |
| comb | un piepten | oon pyepten |
| curlers | bigudiuri | beegoodeeoor<sup>y</sup> |
| dry shampoo | un șampon | oon shampon |
| dye | o vopsea | o vopseh-a |
| hairbrush | o perie de păr | o peree-eh deh perr |
| hair gel | un gel de păr | oon jel deh perr |
| hairgrips | clame | clameh |
| hair lotion | o loțiune de păr | o lotsyooneh deh perr |
| hairpins | ace de păr | acheh deh perr |
| hair spray | un fixativ de par | oon feexateev deh perr |
| setting lotion | o loțiune de fixat | o lotsyooneh deh feexat |
| shampoo for dry/greasy (oily) hair | un șampon pentru păr uscat/gras | oon shampon pentroo perr ooscat/gras |
| tint | o vopsea | o vopseh-a |
| wig | o perucă | o peroocer |

## For the baby *Pentru copil*

| baby food | alimente pentru sugari | aleementeh pentroo soogar<sup>y</sup> |
| dummy (pacifier) | o suzetă | o soozeter |
| feeding bottle | un biberon | oon beeberon |
| nappies (diapers) | scutece de unică folosință | scootecheh deh ooneecer foloseentser |

## Clothing *Îmbrăcăminte*

If you want to buy something specific, prepare yourself in advance. Look at the list of clothing on page 115. Get some idea of the colour, material and size you want. They're all listed on the next few pages.

### General *Fraze de uz general*

| I'd like ... | Aş vrea ... | ash vreh-a |
|---|---|---|
| I'd like ... for a ten-year-old boy/girl. | Aş vrea ... pentru un băiat/o fată de zece ani. | ash vreh-a ... pentroo oon beryat/oh fater deh zecheh anʸ |
| I'd like something like this. | Aş vrea ceva ca aceasta. | ash vreh-a cheva ca achasta |
| I like the one in the window. | Imi place cel din vitrină. | imʸ placheh chel deen veetreener |
| How much is that per metre? | Cît costă un metru din aceasta? | cit coster oon metroo deen achasta |

| 1 centimetre (cm) = 0.39 in. | 1 inch = 2.54 cm |
|---|---|
| 1 metre (m) = 39.37 in. | 1 foot = 30.5 cm |
| 10 metres = 32.81 ft. | 1 yard = 0.91 m. |

### Colour *Culoarea*

| I'd like something in ... | Aş vrea ceva in ... | ash vreh-a cheva in |
|---|---|---|
| I'd like a darker/lighter shade. | Aş vrea o culoare mai închisă/mai deschisă. | ash vreh-a o coolwareh migh inkeeser/migh deskeeser |
| I'd like something to match this. | Aş vrea ceva să se potrivească cu aceasta. | ash vreh-a cheva ser se potreeveh-ascer coo achasta |
| I don't like the colour. | Nu-mi place culoarea. | noomʸ placheh coolwarea |

| beige | **bej** | bezh |
| black | **negru** | **ne**groo |
| blue | **albastru** | al**bas**troo |
| brown | **maro** | **ma**ro |
| fawn | **gălbui** | ger**lbooy** |
| golden | **auriu** | a°°ree°° |
| green | **verde** | **verd**eh |
| grey | **gri** | gree |
| mauve | **mov** | mov |
| orange | **portocaliu** | portoca**lee**°° |
| pink | **roz** | roz |
| purple | **purpuriu** | poor**pooree**°° |
| red | **roşu** | ro**shoo** |
| scarlet | **stacojiu** | staco**zhe**°° |
| silver | **argintiu** | argeen**tee**°° |
| turquoise | **turcoaz** | toor**cwaz** |
| white | **alb** | alb |
| yellow | **galben** | **gal**ben |
| light ... | **deschis** | des**kees** |
| dark ... | **închis** | in**kees** |

| **simplă** | **cu dungi** | **cu buline** | **în carouri** | **cu imprimeu** |
| (**seem**pler) | (coo doonj'') | (coo **boo**leeneh) | (in caro-oor'') | (coo eem**preeme**°°) |

## Fabric *Pînzeturi*

| Do you have anything in ...? | **Aveţi ceva din ...?** | a**vets**'' **che**va deen |
| Is that ...? | **Aceasta este ...?** | a**chas**ta **yes**teh |
| handmade | **făcut de mînă** | fer**coot** deh **mi**ner |
| imported | **din import** | deen eem**port** |
| made here | **făcută aici** | fer**coo**ter a**eech**'' |
| I'd like something thinner. | **Aş vrea ceva mai subţire.** | ash vreh-a **che**va migh soobt**see**reh |
| Do you have anything of better quality? | **Aveţi ceva de calitate mai bună?** | a**vets**'' **che**va deh calee**tat**eh migh **boo**ner |
| What's it made of? | **Din ce este facută?** | deen cheh **yes**teh fer**coo**ter |

| cambric | batist | bateest |
| camel-hair | păr de cămilă | perr deh cermeeler |
| chiffon | şifon | sheefon |
| corduroy | velur | veloor |
| cotton | bumbac | boombac |
| crepe | crep | crep |
| denim | doc | doc |
| felt | fetru | fetroo |
| flannel | flanelă | flaneler |
| gabardine | gabardină | gabardeener |
| lace | dantelă | danteler |
| leather | piele | pyeleh |
| linen | in | een |
| poplin | poplin | popleen |
| satin | satin | sateen |
| silk | mătase | mertaseh |
| suede | piele de căprioară | pyeleh deh cerpreewarer |
| towelling | bumbac flauşat | boombac fla°°shat |
| velvet | catifea | cateefeh-a |
| velveteen | bumbac pluşat | boombac plooshat |
| wool | lînă | liner |
| worsted | lînă toarsă | liner twarser |

| Is it ...? | Este ...? | yesteh |
| pure cotton/wool | de bumbac/lînă pură | deh boombac/liner poorer |
| synthetic | material sintetic | materyal seenteteec |
| colourfast | nu iese la spălat | noo yeseh la sperlat |
| crease (wrinkle) resistant | nu se şifonează | noo seh sheefoneh-azer |
| Is it hand washable/ machine washable? | Se spală de mînă/la maşină? | seh spaler deh miner/la masheener |
| Will it shrink? | Va intra la apă? | va eentra la aper |

### Size *Măsura*

| I take size 38. | Port măsura 38. | port mersoora 38 |
| Could you measure me? | Puteţi să-mi luaţi măsura? | pootetsʸ sermʸ lwatsʸ mersoora |
| I don't know the Romanian sizes. | Nu cunosc măsurile româneşti. | noo coonosc mersooreeleh romineshtʸ |

Sizes can vary somewhat from one manufacturer to another, so be sure to try on shoes and clothing before you buy.

NUMBERS, see page 147

Magazine

## Women *Femei*

| | Dresses/Suits | | | | | |
|---|---|---|---|---|---|---|
| American | 8 | 10 | 12 | 14 | 16 | 18 |
| British | 10 | 12 | 14 | 16 | 18 | 20 |
| Continental | 36 | 38 | 40 | 42 | 44 | 46 |

| | Stockings | | | | | | Shoes | | | |
|---|---|---|---|---|---|---|---|---|---|---|
| American | $8\frac{1}{2}$ | 9 | $9\frac{1}{2}$ | 10 | $10\frac{1}{2}$ | | 6 | 7 | 8 | 9 |
| British | | | | | | | $4\frac{1}{2}$ | $5\frac{1}{2}$ | $6\frac{1}{2}$ | $7\frac{1}{2}$ |
| Continental | 0 | 1 | 2 | 3 | 4 | 5 | 37 | 38 | 40 | 41 |

## Men *Bărbaţi*

| | Suits/overcoats | | | | | | Shirts | | | |
|---|---|---|---|---|---|---|---|---|---|---|
| American British | 36 | 38 | 40 | 42 | 44 | 46 | 15 | 16 | 17 | 18 |
| Continental | 46 | 48 | 50 | 52 | 54 | 56 | 38 | 40 | 42 | 44 |

| | Shoes | | | | | | | | |
|---|---|---|---|---|---|---|---|---|---|
| American British | 5 | 6 | 7 | 8 | $8\frac{1}{2}$ | 9 | $9\frac{1}{2}$ | 10 | 11 |
| Continental | 38 | 39 | 40 | 41 | 42 | 43 | 44 | 44 | 45 |

| | | |
|---|---|---|
| small (S) | **mic** | meec |
| medium (M) | **mediu** | medyoo |
| large (L) | **mare** | mareh |
| extra large (XL) | **extralarg** | extralarg |
| larger/smaller | **mai mare/mai mic** | migh mareh/migh meec |

### A good fit? *O masură potrivită?*

| | | |
|---|---|---|
| Can I try it on? | **Pot să-l probez?** | pot serl probez |
| Where's the fitting room? | **Unde este cabina de probă?** | oondeh yesteh cabeena deh prober |
| Is there a mirror? | **Aveţi o oglindă?** | avetsᵛ o ogleender |
| It fits very well. | **Îmi vine foarte bine.** | imᵛ veeneh fwarteh beeneh |
| It doesn't fit. | **Nu-mi vine bine.** | noomᵛ veeneh beeneh |
| It's too ... | **Este prea ...** | yesteh preh-a |
| short/long | **scurt/lung** | scoort/loong |
| tight/loose | **strîmt/larg** | strimt/larg |
| How long will it take to alter? | **Cît durează modificarea?** | cît dooreh-azer modeefeecareh-a |

NUMBERS, see page 147

## Clothes and accessories *Haine şi accesorii*

| I would like a/an/some ... | Aş vrea ... | ash vreh-a |
|---|---|---|
| anorak | un hanorac | oon hano**rac** |
| bathing cap | o cască de înot | o **cas**cer deh **i**not |
| bathing suit | un costum de baie | oon cos**toom** deh **ba**yeh |
| bathrobe | un halat de baie | oon ha**lat** deh **ba**yeh |
| blouse | o bluză | o **bloo**zer |
| boxer shorts | chiloţi bărbăteşti | kee**lots**ᵧ berber**tesht**ᵧ |
| bow tie | un papion | oon papee-**on** |
| bra | un sutien | oon soo**tyen** |
| braces | nişte bretele | **neesh**teh bre**te**leh |
| cap | o şapcă | o **shap**cer |
| cardigan | o jachetă | o zha**ke**ter |
| coat | o haină | o **hay**ner |
| dress | o rochie | o **ro**kee-eh |
| with long sleeves | cu mîneci lungi | coo **mi**nech ᵧ **loonj** ᵧ |
| with short sleeves | cu mîneci scurte | coo **mi**nech ᵧ **scoor**teh |
| sleeveless | fără mîneci | **fer**rer **mi**nechy |
| dressing gown | un capot | oon **ca**pot |
| evening dress (woman's) | o rochie de seară | o **ro**kee-eh deh **seh**-arer |
| girdle | o centură | o chen**too**rer |
| gloves | nişte mănuşi | **neesh**teh mer**noosh** ᵧ |
| handbag | o geantă | o jeh-**an**ter |
| handkerchief | o batistă | o ba**tee**ster |
| hat | o pălărie | o perler-**ree**-eh |
| jacket | o jachetă | o zha**ke**ter |
| jeans | nişte blugi | **neesh**teh **blooj** ᵧ |
| jersey | un jerseu | oon zher**se**°° |
| jumper (Br.) | un pulover | oon **poo**lover |
| kneesocks | nişte soşete lungi | **neesh**teh sho**se**teh **loonj** ᵧ |
| nightdress | o pijama | o **peezha**ma |
| overalls | o salopetă | o salo**pe**ter |
| pair of ... | o pereche de ... | o pe**re**keh deh ... |
| panties | chiloţi | kee**lots** ᵧ |
| pants (Am.) | pantaloni | panta**lon** ᵧ |
| panty girdle | o burtieră | o boor**tye**rer |
| panty hose | ciorapi cu chilot | chyo**rap** ᵧ coo **kee**lot |
| pullover | un pulovăr | oon **poo**loverr |
| polo (turtle)-neck | cu guler pe gît | coo **goo**ler peh git |
| round-neck | cu guler în jurul gîtului | coo **goo**ler in **zhoo**rool **gi**toolooy |
| V-neck | cu guler în formă de V | coo **goo**ler in **for**mer deh veh |

| with long/short sleeves | cu mîneci lungi/scurte | coo mînech^y loonj^y/ scoorteh |
| without sleeves | fără mîneci | ferrer mînech^y |
| pyjamas | o pijama | o peezhama |
| raincoat | o haină de ploaie | o hayner deh plwayeh |
| scarf | un fular | oon foolar |
| shirt | o cămaşă | o cermasher |
| shorts | şort | short |
| skirt | o fustă | o fooster |
| slip | un jupon | oon zhoopon |
| socks | nişte şosete | neeshteh shoseteh |
| stockings | nişte ciorapi lungi | neeshteh chyorap^y loonj^y |
| suit (man's) | un costum bărbă-tesc | oon costoom berrbertesc |
| suit (woman's) | un costum de damă | oon costoom deh damer |
| suspenders (Am.) | nişte bretele | neeshteh breteleh |
| sweater | un pulover | oon poolover |
| sweatshirt | o bluză de trening din bumbac | o bloozer deh treneeng deen boombac |
| swimming trunks | un costum de baie/ un slip | oon costoom deh bayeh/ oon sleep |
| swimsuit | un costum de înot | oon costoom deh înot |
| T-shirt | o cămaşă | o cermasher |
| tie | o cravată | o cravater |
| tights | nişte dresuri | neeshteh dresoor^y |
| tracksuit | un trening | oon treneeng |
| trousers | nişte pantaloni | neeshteh pantalon^y |
| umbrella | o umbrelă | o oombreler |
| underpants | nişte chiloţi | neeshteh keelots^y |
| undershirt | un maiou | oon mayo°° |
| vest (Am.) | o vestă | o vester |
| vest (Br.) | un maiou | oon mayo°° |
| waistcoat | o vestă | o vester |

| belt | curea | cooreh-a |
| buckle | cataramă | cataramer |
| button | nasture | nastooreh |
| collar | guler | gooler |
| cuff links | butoni de manşetă | booton^y deh mansheter |
| pocket | buzunar | boozoonar |
| press stud (snap fastener) | capsă | capser |
| zip (zipper) | fermoar | fermwar |

## Shoes *Pantofi*

| | | |
|---|---|---|
| I'd like a pair of ... | **Aş vrea o pereche de ...** | ash vreh-a o perekeh deh |
| boots | **cizme** | cheezmeh |
| moccasins | **mocasini** | mocaseen<sup>y</sup> |
| plimsolls (sneakers) | **tenişi** | teneesh<sup>y</sup> |
| sandals | **sandale** | sandaleh |
| shoes | **pantofi** | pantof<sup>y</sup> |
| flat | **plaţi** | plats<sup>y</sup> |
| with a heel | **cu tocuri** | coo tocoor<sup>y</sup> |
| with leather soles | **cu talpă de piele** | coo talper deh pyeleh |
| with rubber soles | **cu talpă de cauciuc** | coo talper deh caoochyooc |
| slippers | **papuci** | papooch<sup>y</sup> |
| These are too ... | **Aceştia sînt ...** | acheshtya sint |
| narrow/wide | **strimţi/largi** | strimts<sup>y</sup>/larj<sup>y</sup> |
| big/small | **mari/mici** | mar<sup>y</sup>/meech<sup>y</sup> |
| Do you have a larger/ smaller size? | **Aveţi o măsură mai mare/mică?** | avets<sup>y</sup> o mersoorer migh mareh/meecer |
| Do you have the same in black? | **Aveţi acelaşi model pe negru?** | avets<sup>y</sup> achelash<sup>y</sup> model peh negroo |
| cloth | **pînză** | pinzer |
| leather | **piele** | pyeleh |
| rubber | **cauciuc** | caoochyooc |
| suede | **piele de căprioară** | pyeleh deh cerpreewarer |
| Is it real leather? | **Este piele veritabilă?** | yesteh pyeleh vereetabeeler |
| I need some shoe polish/shoelaces. | **Am nevoie de nişte cremă de pantofi/şireturi.** | am nevoyeh deh neeshteh cremer deh pantof<sup>y</sup>/sheeretoor<sup>y</sup> |

Shoes worn out? Here's the key to getting them fixed again:

| | | |
|---|---|---|
| Can you repair these shoes? | **Puteţi repara aceşti pantofi?** | pootets<sup>y</sup> repara achesht<sup>y</sup> pantof<sup>y</sup> |
| Can you stitch this? | **Puteţi coase aceasta?** | pootets<sup>y</sup> cwaseh achasta |
| I want new soles and heels. | **Vreau pingele şi călciie noi.** | vra<sup>oo</sup> peenjeleh shee cerlciyeh noy |
| When will they be ready? | **Cînd vor fi gata?** | cind vor fee gata |

NUMBERS, see page 147/COLOURS, see page 112

## Electrical appliances *Aparatură electrică*

Voltage in Romania is 220 AC. Plugs are the common European two-pin type. Adaptors are unobtainable in Romania, so you should bring one with you.

| What's the voltage? | Ce voltaj este pe reţea? | cheh voltazh yesteh peh retseh-a |
| Do you have a battery for this? | Aveţi o baterie pentru aceasta? | avets<sup>y</sup> oh bateree-eh pentroo achasta |
| This is broken. Can you repair it? | Aceasta este defectă. O puteţi repara? | achasta yesteh defecter. o pootets<sup>y</sup> repara |
| Can you show me how it works? | Puteţi să-mi arătaţi cum funcţionează? | pootets<sup>y</sup> serm<sup>y</sup> arertats<sup>y</sup> coom foonctsyoneh-azer |
| I'd like (to hire) a video cassette. | Aş vrea să închiriez o casetă video. | ash vreh-a ser inkeeree-ez o caseter veedeo |
| I'd like a/an/ some ... | Aş vrea ... | ash vreh-a |
| adaptor | un adaptor | oon adaptor |
| amplifier | un amplificator | oon ampleefeecator |
| bulb | un bec | oon bec |
| CD player | un 'compact disc player' | oon compact deesc player |
| clock-radio | un radio-ceas | oon radyo-chas |
| electric toothbrush | o perie de dinţi electrică | o peree-eh deh deents<sup>y</sup> electreecer |
| extension lead (cord) | un prelungitor | oon preloonjeetor |
| hair dryer | un uscător de păr | oon ooscertor deh perr |
| headphones | nişte căşti audio | neeshteh cersht<sup>y</sup> aoodeeo |
| (travelling) iron | un fier de călcat (de voiaj) | oon fyer deh cerlcat (deh voyazh) |
| lamp | o lampă | o lamper |
| plug | un ştecher | oon shteker |
| portable ... | ... portabil | portabeel |
| radio | un radio | oon radyo |
| car radio | un radio de maşină | oon radyo deh masheener |
| (cassette) recorder | un casetofon | oon casetofon |
| record player | un pick-up | oon 'pick-up' |
| shaver | un aparat de ras | oon aparat deh ras |
| speakers | nişte difuzoare | neeshteh deefoozwareh |
| (colour) television | un televizor (color) | oon televeezor (color) |
| transformer | un transformator | oon transformator |
| video-recorder | un aparat video | oon aparat veedeo |

## Grocery *Băcănie*

| I'd like some bread, please. | Aș vrea niște pîine, vă rog. | ash vreh-**a** neeshteh p**i**yneh ver rog |
| What sort of cheese do you have? | Ce fel de brînză aveți? | cheh fel deh **brin**zer avets$^y$ |
| A piece of ... | O bucată de ... | o boo**ca**ter deh |
| that one | aceea | a**cheh**-a |
| the one on the shelf | cea de pe raft | cheh-a deh peh raft |
| I'll have one of those, please. | Vreau una dintr-acelea, vă rog. | vra$^{oo}$ **oo**na deen-tra**cheh**leh-a ver rog |
| May I help myself? | Pot să mă servesc? | pot ser mer ser**vesc** |
| I'd like ... | Aș vrea ... | ash vreh-**a** |
| a kilo of apples | un kilogram de mere | oon keelo**gram** deh **me**reh |
| half a kilo of tomatoes | o jumătate kilogram de roșii | o zhoomer**ta**teh keelo**gram** deh ro**shee** |
| 100 grams of butter | o sută de grame de unt | o **su**ter deh **gra**meh deh oont |
| a litre of milk | un litru de lapte | oon **lee**troo deh **lap**teh |
| half a dozen eggs | șase ouă | **sha**seh o-wer |
| 4 slices of ham | patru felii de șuncă | **pa**troo fe**lee** deh **shoon**cer |
| a packet of tea | un pachet de ceai | oon pa**ket** de chay |
| a jar of jam | un borcan de gem | oon bor**can** deh jem |
| a tin (can) of peaches | o cutie de piersici | o **coo**tee-eh deh **pyer**seech$^y$ |
| a tube of mustard | un tub de muștar | oon toob deh **moosh**tar |
| a box of chocolates | o cutie de ciocolată | o **coo**tee-eh deh chyoco**la**ter |

| 1 kilogram or kilo (kg.) = 1000 grams (g.) | |
|---|---|
| 100 g. = 3.5 oz. | ½ kg. = 1.1 lb. |
| 200 g. = 7.0 oz. | 1 kg. = 2.2 lb. |
| 1 oz. = 28.35 g. | |
| 1 lb. = 453.60 g. | |

| 1 litre (l.) = 0.88 imp. quarts = 1.06 U.S. quarts | |
|---|---|
| 1 imp. quart = 1.14 l. | 1 U.S. quart = 0.95 l. |
| 1 imp. gallon = 4.55 l. | 1 U.S. gallon = 3.8 l. |

FOOD, see also page 63

## Household articles *Articole de menaj*

| | | |
|---|---|---|
| aluminiumfoil | **folie de aluminiu** | folyeh deh aloomeenyoo |
| bottle opener | **deschizător de sticle** | deskeezertor deh steecleh |
| bucket | **găleată** | gerleh-ater |
| can/tin opener | **deschizător de conserve** | deskeezertor deh conserveh |
| candles | **luminări** | loominerr$^y$ |
| clothes pegs (pins) | **cîrlige de rufe** | cîrleejeh deh roofeh |
| corkscrew | **tirbușon** | teerbooshon |
| frying pan | **tigaie** | teegayeh |
| matches | **chibrituri** | keebreetoor$^y$ |
| paper napkins | **șervețele de hîrtie** | shervetseleh deh hîrtee-eh |
| plastic bags | **pungi de plastic** | poonj$^y$ deh plasteec |
| saucepan | **cratiță** | crateetser |
| tea towel | **șervet de bucătărie** | shervet deh boocerter-ree-eh |
| vacuum flask | **termos** | termos |
| washing powder | **detergent de rufe** | deterjent deh roofeh |
| washing-up liquid | **detergent de vase** | deterjent deh vaseh |

## Tools *Scule*

| | | |
|---|---|---|
| hammer | **ciocan** | chyocan |
| nails | **cuie** | cooyeh |
| penknife | **briceag** | breechag |
| pliers | **clește** | cleshteh |
| scissors | **foarfece** | fwarfecheh |
| screws | **șuruburi** | shoorooboor$^y$ |
| screwdriver | **șurubelniță** | shooroobelneetser |
| spanner | **cheie de piulițe** | keyeh deh pyooleetseh |

### Crockery *Veselă*

| | | |
|---|---|---|
| cups | **cești** | chesht$^y$ |
| mugs | **căni** | cern$^y$ |
| plates | **farfurii** | farfooree |
| saucers | **farfurioare** | farfoorywareh |
| tumblers | **pahar** | pahar |

### Cutlery (flatware) *Tacîmuri*

| | | |
|---|---|---|
| forks | **furculițe** | foorcooleetseh |
| knives | **cuțite** | cootseeteh |
| spoons | **linguri** | leengoor$^y$ |
| teaspoons | **lingurițe** | leengooreetseh |

## Jeweller's—Watchmaker's *Bijuterie—Ceasornicărie*

| | | |
|---|---|---|
| Could I see that, please? | **Pot să văd acela, vă rog?** | pot ser verd a**che**la ver rog |
| Do you have anything in gold? | **Aveți ceva din aur?** | a**vets**ʸ cheva deen aᵒᵒr |
| How many carats is this? | **Cîte carate are acesta?** | **ci**teh ca**ra**teh areh a**ches**ta |
| Is this real silver? | **Este argint veritabil?** | **yes**teh ar**jeent** veree**ta**beel |
| Can you repair this watch? | **Puteți repara acest ceas?** | poo**tets**ʸ repara a**chest** chas |
| I'd like a/an/some ... | **Aș vrea ...** | ash vreh-**a** |
| alarm clock | **un ceas deșteptător** | oon chas deshtepter**tor** |
| bangle | **o brățară** | o brert**sa**rer |
| battery | **o baterie** | o bate**ree**-eh |
| bracelet | **o brățară** | o brert**sa**rer |
|   chain bracelet | **o brățară lănțișor** | o brert**sa**rer lernt**see**shor |
|   charm bracelet | **o brățară cu talismanuri** | o brert**sa**rer coo tal**ees**ma**noor**ʸ |
| brooch | **o broșă** | o bro**sher** |
| chain | **un lanț** | oon lants |
| charm | **talisman** | tal**ees**man |
| cigarette case | **o tabacheră** | o taba**ke**rer |
| cigarette lighter | **o brichetă** | o bree**ke**ter |
| clip | **o clamă** | o **cla**mer |
| clock | **un ceas** | oon chas |
| cross | **o cruce** | o **croo**cheh |
| cuckoo clock | **un ceas cu cuc** | oon chas coo cooc |
| cuff links | **butoni de manșetă** | boo**ton**ʸ deh man**she**ter |
| cutlery | **niște tacîmuri** | **neesh**teh tac**ee**moor**ʸ |
| earrings | **niște cercei** | **neesh**teh cher**chay** |
| gem | **o piatră prețioasă** | o **pya**trer pretsee**wa**ser |
| jewel box | **cutie pentru bijuterii** | coo**tee**-eh **pen**troo beejoo**te**ree |
| mechanical pencil | **un creion mecanic** | oon creyon me**ca**neec |
| music box | **o cutie muzicală** | o coo**tee**-eh moozee**ca**ler |
| necklace | **un colier** | oon co**lyer** |
| pendant | **un pandantiv** | oon pandan**teev** |
| pin | **un ac** | oon ac |
| pocket watch | **un ceas de buzunar** | oon chas deh boozoo**nar** |
| powder compact | **o pudră compactă** | o **poo**drer com**pac**ter |
| propelling pencil | **un creion mecanic** | oon cre**yon** me**ca**neec |

| ring | un inel | oon eenel |
|---|---|---|
| engagement ring | un inel de logodnă | oon eenel deh logodner |
| signet ring | un inel cu sigiliu | oon eenel coo seejeelyoo |
| wedding ring | o verighetă | o vereegeter |
| rosary | un rozar | oon rozar |
| silverware | obiecte de argint | obyecteh deh arjeent |
| tie clip | o clamă de cravată | o clamer deh cravater |
| tie pin | un ac de cravată | oon ac deh cravater |
| watch | un ceas | oon chas |
| automatic | automat | a°°tomat |
| digital | digital | deejeetal |
| quartz | cu cuarţ | coo cwarts |
| with a second hand | cu secundar | coo secoondar |
| waterproof | antiacvatic | antee-acvateec |
| watchstrap | o curea de ceas | o cooreh-a de chas |
| wristwatch | un ceas de mînă | oon chas deh miner |

| amber | chihlimbar | keeh-leembar |
|---|---|---|
| amethyst | ametist | ameteest |
| chromium | crom | crom |
| copper | cupru | cooproo |
| coral | coral | coral |
| crystal | cristal | creestal |
| cut glass | sticlă şlefuită | steecler shlefooeeter |
| diamond | diamant | deeamant |
| emerald | smarald | smarald |
| enamel | email | emaeel |
| gold | aur | a°°r |
| gold plate | aurit | a°°reet |
| ivory | fildeş | feeldesh |
| jade | jad | zhad |
| onyx | onix | oneex |
| pearl | perlă | perler |
| pewter | aliaj pe bază de cositor | alee-azh peh bazer deh coseetor |
| platinum | platină | plateener |
| ruby | rubin | roobeen |
| sapphire | safir | safeer |
| silver | argint | arjeent |
| silver plate | argintat | arjeentat |
| stainless steel | inox | eenox |
| topaz | topaz | topaz |
| turquoise | turcuaz | toorcwaz |

### Optician *Optician*

| | | |
|---|---|---|
| I've broken my glasses. | **Mi-am spart ochelarii.** | myam spart okelaree |
| Can you repair them for me? | **Puteţi să mi-i reparaţi?** | pootets<sup>y</sup> ser mee reparats<sup>y</sup> |
| When will they be ready? | **Cînd vor fi gata?** | cind vor fee gata |
| Can you change the lenses? | **Puteţi schimba lentilele?** | pootets<sup>y</sup> skeemba lenteeleleh |
| I'd like tinted lenses. | **Aş vrea lentile fumurii.** | ash vreh-a lenteeleh foomooree |
| The frame is broken. | **Rama este ruptă.** | rama yesteh roopter |
| I'd like a spectacle case. | **Aş vrea un port-ochelari.** | ash vreh-a oon port-okelar<sup>y</sup> |
| I'd like to have my eyesight checked. | **Aş vrea un control al vederii.** | ash vreh-a oon control al vederee |
| I'm short-sighted/long-sighted. | **Sînt miop/prezbit.** | sint meeop/prezbeet |
| I'd like some contact lenses. | **Aş vrea lentile de contact.** | ash vreh-a lenteeleh deh contact |
| I've lost one of my contact lenses. | **Am pierdut o lentilă de contact.** | am pyerdoot o lenteeler deh contact |
| Could you give me another one? | **Puteţi să-mi daţi alta?** | pootets<sup>y</sup> serm<sup>y</sup> dats<sup>y</sup> alta |
| I have hard/soft lenses. | **Am lentile dure/flexibile.** | am lenteeleh dooreh/flexeebeeleh |
| Do you have any contact-lens fluid? | **Aveţi lichid pentru lentile de contact?** | avets<sup>y</sup> leekeed pentroo lenteeleh deh contact |
| I'd like to buy a pair of sunglasses. | **Aş vrea să cumpăr o pereche de ochelari de soare.** | ash vreh-a ser coomperr o perekeh deh okelar<sup>y</sup> deh swareh |
| May I look in a mirror? | **Pot să mă uit într-o oglindă?** | pot ser mer ooyt intro ogleender |
| I'd like to buy a pair of binoculars. | **Aş vrea să cumpăr un binoclu.** | ash vreh-a ser coomperr oon beenocloo |

124

## Photography *Fotografie*

| I'd like a(n) ... camera. | **Aş vrea un aparat de fotografiat ...** | ash vreh-a oon aparat deh fotografeeat |
| automatic | **automat** | a<sup>oo</sup>tomat |
| inexpensive | **nu prea scump** | noo preh-a scoomp |
| simple | **simplu** | seemploo |
| Can you show me some ..., please? | **Puteţi să-mi ară-taţi, vă rog, nişte ...?** | poote**ts**ʸ serm**ʸ** arer**tats**ʸ ver rog **neesh**teh |
| cine (movie) cameras | **aparate de filmat** | aparateh deh **feel**mat |
| video cameras | **camere video** | camereh veedeo |
| I'd like to have some passport photos taken. | **Aş vrea să fac nişte poze de paşaport.** | ash vreh-a ser fac **neesh**teh **po**zeh deh pasha**port** |

## Film *Film*

| I'd like a film for this camera. | **Aş vrea un film pentru aparatul acesta.** | ash vreh-a oon feelm **pen**troo apara**tool** a**ches**ta |
| black and white | **alb-negru** | alb-**negroo** |
| colour | **color** | color |
| colour negative | **negativ color** | nega**teev** color |
| colour slide | **diapozitiv color** | deeapo**zee**teev color |
| cartridge | **încărcător de film** | incer**cer**tor deh feelm |
| disc film | **disc de film** | deesc deh feelm |
| roll film | **bobină de film** | bo**bee**ner deh feelm |
| video cassette | **casetă video** | ca**se**ter **vee**deo |
| 24/36 exposures | **24/36 expuneri** | 24/36 ex**poo**nerʸ |
| this size | **mărimea aceasta** | mer**ree**meh-a a**ches**ta |
| this ASA/DIN number | **numărul acesta de ASA/DIN** | **noo**merrool a**ches**ta deh ASA/DIN |
| artificial light type | **pentru lumină artif-icială** | **pen**troo loo**mee**ner arteefee**chy**aler |
| daylight type | **pentru lumină de zi** | **pen**troo loo**mee**ner deh zee |
| fast (high-speed) | **de viteză ultrara-pidă** | deh vee**te**zer ooltrara**pee**der |
| fine grain | **film cu sensibilitate mare** | feelm coo senseebeelee**ta**teh **ma**reh |

## Processing *Developat*

| | | |
|---|---|---|
| How much do you charge for processing? | **Cît costă developa-tul?** | cit **coster** developa**tool** |
| I'd like ... prints of each negative. | **Aş vrea ... poze pentru fiecare negativ.** | ash vreh-**a** ... **po**zeh pen**troo** fye**ca**reh nega**teev** |
| with a matt finish | **cu faţă mată** | coo **fa**tser **ma**ter |
| with a glossy finish | **cu faţă lucioasă** | coo **fa**tser loo**chy**wa**ser** |
| Will you enlarge this, please? | **Puteţi să măriţi aceasta, vă rog?** | poo**tets**ʸ ser mer**reets**ʸ a**chas**ta ver rog |
| When will the photos be ready? | **Cînd vor fi gata pozele?** | cind vor fee **ga**ta **po**zeleh |

## Accessories and repairs *Accesorii şi reparaţii*

| | | |
|---|---|---|
| I'd like a/an/some ... | **Aş vrea ...** | ash vreh-**a** |
| batteries | **nişte baterii** | **neesh**teh bate**ree** |
| camera case | **un port-aparat** | oon port-apa**rat** |
| (electronic) flash | **un blitz (electronic)** | oon bleets (electro**neec**) |
| filter | **un filtru** | oon **feel**troo |
| for black and white | **pentru film alb-negru** | pen**troo** feelm alb-**ne**groo |
| for colour | **pentru film color** | pen**troo** feelm color |
| lens | **un obiectiv** | oon obyec**teev** |
| telephoto lens | **un teleobiectiv** | oon teleobyec**teev** |
| wide-angle lens | **un obiectiv sup-erangular** | oon obyec**teev** sooperango**olar** |
| lens cap | **capacul obiectivu-lui** | capa**cool** obyec**teev**voo**looy** |
| Can you repair this camera? | **Puteţi repara acest aparat de fotogra-fiat?** | poo**tets**ʸ repa**ra** a**chest** apa**rat** deh fotogra**feeat** |
| The film is jammed. | **Filmul este blocat.** | **feel**mool **yes**teh blo**cat** |
| There's something wrong with the ... | **Ceva este în nereg-ulă cu ...** | che**va** **yes**teh in nere**gool**er coo |
| exposure counter | **dispozitivul de numărătoare** | deespozee**teev**ool deh noomerer**ta**reh |
| film winder | **maneta de rulat fil-mul** | ma**ne**ta deh roo**lat** **feel**mool |
| flash attachment | **legăturile de blitz** | leger**too**reeleh deh bleets |
| lens | **obiectiv** | obyec**teev** |
| light meter | **celula fotoelectrică** | che**loo**la fotoe**lec**treecer |
| rangefinder | **telemetru** | tele**me**troo |
| shutter | **obturator** | obtoo**ra**tor |

NUMBERS, see page 147

## Tobacconist's *Tutungerie*

Most shops, kiosks and minimarkets sell Romanian and imported cigarettes.

| | | |
|---|---|---|
| A packet of cigarettes, please. | Un pachet de ţigări, vă rog. | oon pa**ket** deh tseegerr<sup>y</sup> ver rog |
| Do you have any American/English cigarettes? | Aveţi ţigări americane/englezeşti? | a**vets**<sup>y</sup> tsee**gerr**<sup>y</sup> amereecaneh/engle**zesht**<sup>y</sup> |
| I'd like a carton. | Aş vrea un cartuş. | ash vreh-**a** oon car**toosh** |
| Give me a/some ..., please. | Daţi-mi ..., vă rog. | **da**tseem<sup>y</sup> ... ver rog |
| candy | nişte dropsuri | **neesh**teh **drop**soor<sup>y</sup> |
| chewing gum | nişte gumă de mestecat | **neesh**teh **goo**mer deh **mes**tecat |
| chewing tobacco | nişte tutun de mestecat | **neesh**teh too**toon** deh **mes**tecat |
| chocolate | nişte ciocolată | **neesh**teh chyoco**later** |
| cigarette case | o tabacheră | o taba**kerer** |
| cigarette holder | un port-ţigaret | oon port-tsee**garet** |
| cigarettes | nişte ţigări | **neesh**teh tsee**gerr**<sup>y</sup> |
| filter-tipped/ | cu filtru/fără | coo **feel**troo/**ferrer** |
| without filter | filtru | **feel**troo |
| light/dark tobacco | blonde/brune | **blon**deh/**broo**neh |
| mild/strong | slabe/tari | **sla**beh/**ta**ree |
| menthol | mentolate | mento**la**teh |
| king-size | superlungi | **soo**per**loonj**<sup>y</sup> |
| cigars | trabuc | tra**booc** |
| lighter | o brichetă | o bree**keter** |
| lighter fluid/gas | nişte gaz de brichetă | **neesh**teh gaz de bree**keter** |
| matches | nişte chibrituri | **neesh**teh kee**bree**toor<sup>y</sup> |
| pipe | o pipa | o **pee**per |
| pipe cleaners | nişte instrumente pentru pipă | **neesh**teh een**stroo**menteh **pen**troo **pee**per |
| pipe tobacco | nişte tutun de pipă | **neesh**teh too**toon** deh **pee**per |
| pipe tool | un dispozitiv de curăţat pipă | oon deespo**zee**teev deh **coo**rert**sat pee**per |
| postcard | o vedere | o ve**de**reh |
| snuff | nişte tutun de prizat | **neesh**teh too**toon** deh pree**zat** |
| stamps | nişte timbre | **neesh**teh **teem**breh |
| sweets | nişte dulciuri | **neesh**teh **dool**chyoor<sup>y</sup> |
| wick | o meşă | o **me**sher |

## Miscellaneous *Diverse*

### Souvenirs *Suveniruri*

Shops called *artizanat* sell typical Romanian souvenirs including finely embroidered tunics, blouses, napkins, tablecloths and headscarves. You'll also find traditional woollen carpets handwoven with intricate geometric patterns, hand-painted Easter eggs, decorative pottery and beautifully carved wooden utensils.

If you are interested in *objets d'art*, including icons on wood or glass, look for the shops belonging to the Artists' Union called *Fondul plastic*. There are many good contemporary art shops in Bucharest, notably Dominus (at the National Theatre).

Catalogues of medieval art make excellent souvenirs of Romania, as do records or CDs of Romanian folk and classical music. And don't forget to take home a bottle or two of Romanian plum brandy (*ţuica*).

| art book | **album de artă** | alboom deh arter |
|---|---|---|
| carpet | **carpetă/covor** | carpeter/covor |
| ceramics | **ceramică** | cherameeker |
| embroidered headscarf | **maramă** | maramer |
| embroidered tablecloth | **faţă de masă brodată** | fatser der maser brodater |
| folk music | **muzică populară** | mooziker popularer |
| icon | **icoană** | eekwaner |
| painting | **tablou/pictură** | tablo°°/pictoorer |
| pottery | **olărit** | oler-reet |
| tapestry | **tapiserie** | tapeeseree-eh |
| wooden utensil | **unelte de lemn** | oonelteh deh lemn |

### Records—Cassettes *Discuri—Casete*

| I'd like a ... | **Aş vrea ...** | ash vreh-a |
|---|---|---|
| cassette | **o casetă** | caseter |
| video cassette | **o video casetă** | veedeo caseter |
| compact disc | **un compact disc** | oon compact deesc |

NUMBERS, see page 147

| L.P.(33 rpm) | disc LP | disc el-pee |
| single | disc single | disc singel |

| Do you have any records by ...? | Aveţi discuri de ... | avets⁄ deescoor⁄ deh |
| Can I listen to this record? | Pot asculta discul acesta? | pot ascoolta deescool achesta |
| chamber music | muzică de cameră | moozeecer deh camerer |
| classical music | muzică clasică | moozeecer claseecer |
| folk music | muzică populară | moozeecer popoolarer |
| folk song | cîntec popular | cîntec popoolar |
| instrumental music | muzică instrumen-tală | moozeecer eenstroomentaler |
| jazz | jazz | jazz |
| light music | muzică uşoară | moozeecer ooshwarer |
| orchestral music | muzică simfonică | moozeecer seemfonicer |
| pop music | muzică pop | moozeecer pop |

## Toys *Jucării*

| I'd like a toy/game ... | As vrea o juca-rie/un joc ... | ash vreh-a o zhoocer-ree-eh/oon zhoc |
| for a boy | pentru un băiat | pentroo oon beryat |
| for a 5-year-old girl | pentru o fetiţă de 5 ani | pentroo o feteetser deh 5 an⁄ |
| (beach) ball | o minge (de plajă) | o meenjeh (deh plazher) |
| bucket and spade (pail and shovel) | o galetică şi lopăţică | o gerletseecer shee lopertseecer |
| building blocks (bricks) | nişte cuburi | neeshteh cooboor⁄ |
| chess set | un joc de şah | oon zhoc deh shah |
| colouring book | o carte de colorat | o carteh deh colorat |
| doll | o păpuşă | o perpoosher |
| electronic game | un joc electronic | oon zhoc electroneec |
| playing cards | nişte cărţi de joc | neeshteh cerrts⁄ deh zhoc |
| roller skates | nişte patine cu rotile | neeshteh pateeneh coo roteeleh |
| snorkel | un tub de scafan-dru | oon toob deh scafandroo |
| teddy bear | un ursuleţ | oon oorsoolets |
| toy car | o maşină jucărie | o masheener zhoocer-ree-eh |

NUMBERS, see page 147

# Your money: banks—currency

The Romanian unit of currency is the *leu*—le°° (plural: *lei*), divided into 100 *bani*—**ba**nee. Due to high inflation, bani have been withdrawn from circulation.

Coins: 1, 3, 5, 10, 20, 50, 100 lei
Notes: 200, 500, 1000, 5000 lei

Banks are open from Monday until Friday between 8.30am and 11.30am. Foreign currency can be changed at airports, banks and in most hotels, but exchange bureaus will generally offer the best rate. Avoid exchanging a large amount of money at the beginning of your visit as you may have difficulty changing it back into your own currency and it is illegal to import or export lei.

There are still two rates of exchange in operation: the official rate and the black market rate. High inflation has rendered the latter less advantageous; in addition such dealing is illegal and you are most likely to be cheated.

Personal cheques are not yet accepted in Romania but some big hotels accept payment by credit card, though you will not obtain the best exchange rate. Traveller's cheques are easy to cash at the National Tourist Office (ONT) or in most hotels.

| | | |
|---|---|---|
| Where's the nearest bank? | **Unde se află o bancă în apropiere?** | oondeh seh afler o bancer in apropyereh |
| Where's the nearest currency exchange office? | **Unde se află un birou de schimb prin apropiere?** | oondeh seh afler oon beero°° deh skeemb preen apropyereh |

### At the bank  La bancă

| | | |
|---|---|---|
| I want to change some dollars/pounds. | **Vreau să schimb nişte dolari/lire sterline.** | vra°° ser skeemb neeshteh dolar'/leereh sterleeneh |

| I want to cash a traveller's cheque. | Vreau să încasez niște cecuri de călătorie. | vra°° ser încasez neeshteh chehcoor<sup>y</sup> deh cerlertoree-eh |
| What's the exchange rate? | Care este cursul? | careh yesteh coorsool |
| How much commission do you charge? | Ce comision reţineţi? | cheh comeesyon retseenets<sup>y</sup> |
| Can you cash a personal cheque? | Puteţi încasa un cec personal? | pootets<sup>y</sup> încasa oon chec personal |
| Can you telex my bank in London? | Puteţi trimite un telex la banca mea din Londra? | pootets<sup>y</sup> treemeeteh oon telex la banca meh-a deen londra |
| I have a/an/some... | Am... | am |
| credit card | o carte de credit | o carteh deh credeet |
| Eurocheques | niște Eurocecuri | neeshteh e°°rochecoor<sup>y</sup> |
| letter of credit | o scrisoare acreditivă | o screeswareh acredeeteever |
| I'm expecting some money from New York. Has it arrived? | Aştept niște bani din New York. Au sosit cumva? | ashtept neeshteh ban<sup>y</sup> deen new york. a°° soseet coomva |
| Please give me... notes (bills) and some small change. | Vă rog să-mi daţi... bancnote și ceva bani mărunți. | ver rog serm<sup>y</sup> dats<sup>y</sup>... bancnoteh shee cheva ban<sup>y</sup> merroonts<sup>y</sup> |
| Give me... large notes and the rest in small notes. | Vă rog să-mi daţi... bancnote mari şi restul în bani mărunți. | ver rog serm<sup>y</sup> dats<sup>y</sup>... bancnoteh mar<sup>y</sup> shee restool în ban<sup>y</sup> merroonts<sup>y</sup> |

## Deposits—Withdrawals *Depuneri—Restituiri*

| I want to... | Vreau să... | vra°° ser |
| open an account | deschid un cont bancar | deskeed oon cont bancar |
| withdraw... lei | scot... lei | scot... lay |
| Where should I sign? | Unde trebuie să semnez? | oondeh trebooyeh ser semnez |
| I'd like to pay this into my account. | Aş vrea să depun aceşti bani în contul meu. | ash vreh-a ser depoon achesht<sup>y</sup> ban<sup>y</sup> în contool me°° |

NUMBERS, see page 147

## Business terms *Termeni de afaceri*

| English | Romanian | Pronunciation |
|---|---|---|
| My name is... | **Mă numesc...** | mer noo**mesc** |
| Here's my card. | **Poftim cartea mea de vizită.** | pof**teem** carteh-a meh-a deh **vee**zeeter |
| I have an appointment with... | **Am o întîlnire cu...** | am o întîl**nee**reh coo |
| Can you give me an estimate of the cost? | **Puteţi să-mi daţi un preţ estimativ?** | poo**tets**$^y$ serm$^y$ dats$^y$ oon prets esteema**teev** |
| What's the rate of inflation? | **Care este rata inflaţiei?** | careh **yes**teh rata deh een**flat**syey |
| Can you provide me with an interpreter/ a personal computer/ a secretary? | **Puteţi să-mi puneţi la dispoziţie un translator/un computer/o secretară?** | poo**tets**$^y$ serm$^y$ **poo**nets$^y$ la deespo**zeets**yeh oon trans**lator**/oon comp$^y$**oo**ter/o secre**tarer** |
| Where can I make photocopies? | **Unde pot face nişte fotocopii?** | **oon**deh pot **fa**cheh **neesh**teh foto**co**pee |

| amount | **cantitatea** | canteetateh-a |
|---|---|---|
| balance | **balanţa** | balantsa |
| capital | **capitalul** | capeetalool |
| cheque | **cec** | chec |
| contract | **contract** | contract |
| discount | **reduceri** | redoocher$^y$ |
| expenses | **cheltuieli** | keltooyel$^y$ |
| interest | **dobîndă** | dobînder |
| investment | **investiţie** | eenvesteetsyeh |
| invoice | **factură** | factoorer |
| loss | **pierderi** | pyerder$^y$ |
| mortgage | **ipotecă** | eepotecer |
| payment | **plată** | plater |
| percentage | **procentaj** | prochentazh |
| profit | **profit** | profeet |
| purchase | **achiziţii** | akeezeetsee |
| sale | **vînzare** | vînzareh |
| share | **acţiuni** | actsyoon$^y$ |
| transfer | **transfer** | transfer |
| value | **valoare** | valwareh |

Bancă

NUMBERS, see page 147

# At the post office

The sign PTTR indicates a post office in Romania. Post offices provide telegram and telephone facilities as well as postal services. They do not, however, have fax facilities, for which you will have to locate a private shop offering this service.

Post offices are open between 8am and 6pm. If you want to send a parcel overseas you should go to a special post office where you will be required to complete a customs declaration form. Take your passport with you when you go to collect a parcel or registered letter as you will need to show identification. To avoid the inevitable long queues in post offices, buy your stamps from tobacconists or at the hotel reception desk.

Post boxes are yellow and some have a separate box for local mail only (marked *loco*).

| | | |
|---|---|---|
| Where's the nearest post office? | **Unde se află o poştă prin apropiere?** | oondeh seh afler o poshter preen apropyereh |
| What time does the post office open/ close? | **La ce oră deschide/ închide la poştă?** | la cheh orer deskeedeh / înkeedeh la poshter |
| A stamp for this letter/postcard, please. | **Un timbru pentru această scrisoare/ vedere, vă rog.** | oon teembroo pentroo achaster screeswareh/ vedereh ver rog |
| A... -lei stamp, please. | **Un timbru de ... lei, vă rog.** | oon teembroo deh ... lay ver rog |
| What's the postage for a letter to London? | **Cît costă timbrul pentru o scrisoare la Londra?** | cit coster teembrool pentroo o screeswareh la londra |
| What's the postage for a postcard to Los Angeles? | **Cît costă un timbru pentru o vedere la Los Angeles?** | cit coster oon teembroo pentroo o vedereh la los angeles |

| Where's the letter box (mailbox)? | **Unde este cutia poştală?** | oondeh yesteh cooteea poshtaler |
| I want to send this parcel. | **Vreau să expediez coletul acesta.** | vra°° ser expedyez coletool achesta |
| I'd like to send this (by)... | **Aş vrea să expediez acesta (prin)...** | ash vreh-a ser expedyez achesta (preen) |
| airmail | **avion** | aveeon |
| express (special delivery) | **expres (de urgenţă)** | expres (deh oorjentser) |
| registered mail | **recomandată** | recomandater |
| At which counter can I cash an international money order? | **De la ce ghişeu pot încasa un mandat internaţional?** | deh la cheh geeshe°° pot incasa oon mandat eenternatsyonal |
| Where's the poste restante (general delivery)? | **Unde este ghişeul pentru post restant?** | oondeh yesteh geesheool pentroo post restant |
| Is there any post (mail) for me? My name is... | **Am vreo scrisoare? Numele meu este...** | am vro screeswareh. noomeleh me°° yesteh |

| **TIMBRE** | STAMPS |
| **COLETE** | PARCELS |
| **MANDAT POSTAL** | MONEY ORDER |

## Telegrams—Telex—Fax  *Telegrame—Telex—Fax*

| I'd like to send a telegram/telex. | **Aş dori să trimit o telegramă/un telex.** | ash doree ser treemeet o telegramer/oon telex |
| May I have a form, please? | **Puteţi să-mi daţi un formular, vă rog?** | pootetsʸ sermʸ datsʸ oon formoolar ver rog |
| How much is it per word? | **Cît costă un cuvînt?** | cit coster oon coovint |
| How long will a cable to Boston take? | **Cît durează pentru o legătură cu Boston?** | cit doorazer pentroo o legertoorer coo boston |
| How much will this fax cost? | **Cît o să coste fax-ul acesta?** | cit o ser costeh faxool achesta |

## Telephoning *La telefon*

Telephoning abroad is now much easier in Romania than previously but you should not expect Western standards of service; as yet, international direct dialling is not available to the general public and there are no card-operated public phones. You can make international calls from large post offices or from your hotel through an operator.

For local calls use a 10- or 20-lei coin.

| | | |
|---|---|---|
| Where's the telephone? | **Unde este un telefon?** | oondeh **yes**teh oon tele**fon** |
| I'd like a telephone token. | **Aş vrea o fişă (pentru telefon).** | ash vreh-**a** o **fee**ser (**pen**troo tele**fon**) |
| Where's the nearest telephone booth? | **Unde este un telefon prin apropiere?** | oondeh **yes**teh oon tele**fon** preen apro**pye**reh |
| May I use your phone? | **Îmi permiteţi să folosesc telefonul dumneavoastra?** | im<sup>y</sup> permee**tets**<sup>y</sup> ser folo**sesc** tele**fo**nool doomna**vwas**trer |
| Do you have a telephone directory for Bucharest? | **Aveţi un anuar telefonic pentru Bucureşti?** | a**vets**<sup>y</sup> oon an**war** tele**fo**neec **pen**troo boocoo**resht**<sup>y</sup> |
| I'd like to call... in England. | **Aş vrea să telefonez la numărul... în Anglia.** | ash vreh-**a** ser tele**fo**nez la **noo**merrool... în **an**glya |
| What's the dialling (area) code for...? | **Care este prefixul pentru...?** | **ca**reh **yes**teh pre**feex**ool **pen**troo |
| How do I get the international operator? | **Ce număr are centrala pentru convorbiri internaţionale?** | cheh **noo**merr areh **chen**trala **pen**troo convor**beer**<sup>y</sup> eenternatsyo**na**leh |

## Operator *Centrala*

| | | |
|---|---|---|
| I'd like Bucharest 23 45 67. | **Aş vrea o linie cu Bucureşti, numărul 23 45 67.** | ash vreh-**a** o **lee**nyeh coo boocoo**resht**<sup>y</sup> **noo**merrool 23 45 67 |
| Can you help me get this number? | **Mă puteţi ajuta să obţin acest număr?** | mer poo**tets**<sup>y</sup> azhoota ser ob**tseen** a**chest** **noo**merr |

NUMBERS, see page 147

| I'd like to place a personal (person-to-person) call. | Aş vrea să dau un telefon. | ash vreh-**a** ser da°° oon telefon |
| I'd like to reverse the charges (call collect). | Aş vrea să telefonez cu taxă inversă. | ash vreh-**a** ser telefo**nez** coo **tax**er **een**verser |

## Speaking *Convorbirea*

| Hello. This is... | Alo,... la telefon. | alo... la telefon |
| I'd like to speak to... | Aş vrea să vorbesc cu... | ash vreh-**a** ser vor**besc** coo |
| Extension... | Interior... | **een**ter**yor** |
| Speak louder/more slowly, please. | Vorbiţi mai tare/ mai rar, vă rog. | vor**beets**ᵛ migh tareh/migh rar ver rog |

## Bad luck *Ghinion*

| Would you try again later, please? | Puteţi încerca din nou, mai tîrziu, vă rog? | poo**tets**ᵛ incher**ca** deen no°° migh tîr**zee**°° ver rog |
| Operator, you gave me the wrong number. | Centrala, mi-aţi dat un număr greşit. | chen**tra**la myats°° dat oon **noo**merr gre**sheet** |
| Operator, we were cut off. | Alo, centrala, s-a întrerupt convorbirea. | alo chen**tra**la sa între**roopt** convor**beer**eh-a |

---

### Telephone alphabet *Codul telefonic de enunţare*

| A | **Ana** | ana | | O | **Olga** | olga |
| B | **Barbu** | barboo | | P | **Petre** | petreh |
| C | **Constantin** | constanteen | | Q | **qu** | kyoo |
| D | **Dumitru** | doomeetroo | | R | **Radu** | radoo |
| E | **Elena** | elena | | S | **Sandoo** | sandoo |
| F | **Florea** | floreh-a | | T | **Tudor** | toodor |
| G | **Gheorghe** | georgeh | | Ţ | **Ţară** | tsarer |
| H | **Haralambie** | haralambyeh | | U | **Udrea** | oodreh-a |
| I | **Ion** | eeon | | V | **Vasile** | vaseeleh |
| J | **Jiu** | zhee°° | | W | **dublu V** | doobloo veh |
| K | **kilogram** | keelogram | | X | **Xenia** | xenya |
| L | **Lazăr** | lazer | | Y | **I grec** | ee grec |
| M | **Maria** | mareea | | Z | **zahăr** | zaherr |
| N | **Nicolae** | neecolayeh | | | | |

### Not there *Nu-i aici, lipseşte*

| | | |
|---|---|---|
| When will he/she be back? | **Cînd se va întoarce?** | cînd seh va întwarcheh |
| Will you tell him/her I called? My name is... | **Vreţi să-i spuneţi că am sunat? Numele meu este...** | vrets<sup>y</sup> ser-y spoonets<sup>y</sup> cer am soonat. noomeleh me<sup>oo</sup> yesteh |
| Would you ask him/her to call me? My number is... | **Vreţi să-i spooneţi să mă sune? Numărul meu de telefon este...** | vrets<sup>y</sup> ser-y spoonets<sup>y</sup> ser mer sooneh. noomerrool me<sup>oo</sup> deh telefon yesteh |
| Would you take a message, please? | **Pot să las un mesaj, vă rog?** | pot ser las oon mesazh ver rog |

### Charges *Taxe*

| | | |
|---|---|---|
| What was the cost of that call? | **Cît a costat convorbirea aceasta?** | cît a costat convorbeereh-a achasta |
| I want to pay for the call. | **Vreau să plătesc convorbirea telefonică.** | vra<sup>oo</sup> ser plertesc convorbeereh-a telefoneecer |

---

| | |
|---|---|
| **Vă caută cineva la telefon.** | There's a telephone call for you. |
| **Ce număr aţi format?** | What number are you calling? |
| **Linia este ocupată.** | The line's engaged. |
| **Nu răspunde.** | There's no answer. |
| **Aţi greşit numărul.** | You've got the wrong number. |
| **Telefonul este deranjat.** | The phone is out of order. |
| **Un moment.** | Just a moment. |
| **Aşteptaţi, vă rog.** | Hold on, please. |
| **Nu este aici.** | He's/She's out at the moment. |

# Doctor

If you fall ill during your stay in Romania, ask for a *policlinică cu plată* (paying clinic); these are relatively inexpensive and can give you immediate attention by very good doctors. For minor complaints you can get advice from any pharmacy, in return for which it is polite to offer a gift, preferably foreign currency.

## General *Expresii de uz general*

| | | |
|---|---|---|
| Can you get me a doctor? | **Puteţi să chemaţi un doctor, vă rog?** | pootets<sup>y</sup> ser kemats<sup>y</sup> oon doctor ver rog |
| Is there a doctor here? | **Este un doctor aici?** | yesteh oon doctor aeech<sup>y</sup> |
| I need a doctor, quickly. | **E nevoie de un doctor, repede.** | yeh nevoyeh deh oon doctor repedeh |
| Where can I find a doctor who speaks English? | **Unde pot găsi un doctor care vorbeşte englezeşte?** | oondeh pot gersee oon doctor careh vorbeshteh englezeshteh |
| Where's the surgery (doctor's office)? | **Unde este cabinetul medical?** | oondeh yesteh cabeenetool medeecal |
| What are the surgery (office) hours? | **Care sînt orele de program?** | careh sint oreleh deh program |
| Could the doctor come to see me here? | **Poate doctorul să vină să mă vadă aici?** | pwateh doctorool ser veener ser mer vader aeech<sup>y</sup> |
| What time can the doctor come? | **La ce oră poate să vină doctorul?** | la cheh orer pwateh ser veener doctorool |
| Can you recommend a/an...? | **Puteţi să-mi recomandaţi...?** | pootets<sup>y</sup> serm<sup>y</sup> recomandats<sup>y</sup> |
| general practitioner | **un doctor de medicină generală** | oon doctor deh medeecheener generaler |
| children's doctor | **un medic pediatru** | oon medeec pedyatroo |
| eye specialist | **un doctor oculist** | oon doctor ocooleest |
| gynaecologist | **un ginecolog** | oon jeenecolog |
| Can I have an appointment...? | **Puteţi să-mi daţi un bon pentru o vizită la doctor...?** | pootets<sup>y</sup> serm<sup>y</sup> dats<sup>y</sup> oon bon pentroo o veezeeter la doctor |
| tomorrow | **mîine** | miyneh |
| as soon as possible | **cît de curînd posibil** | cit deh coorind poseebeel |

CHEMIST'S, see page 107

## Parts of the body *Corpul uman*

| appendix | apendice | apendeecheh |
|----------|----------|-------------|
| arm | braţ | brats |
| back | spate | spateh |
| bladder | vezica urinară | vezeeca ooreenarer |
| bone | os | os |
| bowel | intestin | eentesteen |
| breast | sîn | sîn |
| chest | piept | pyept |
| ear | ureche | oorekeh |
| eye(s) | ochi | ok$^y$ |
| face | faţă | fatser |
| finger | deget | dejet |
| foot | picior | peechyor |
| genitals | organe genitale | organeh jeneetaleh |
| gland | glandă | glander |
| hand | mînă | miner |
| head | cap | cap |
| heart | inimă | eeneemer |
| jaw | maxilar | maxeelar |
| joint | încheietură | inke-yetoorer |
| kidney | rinichi | reeneek$^y$ |
| knee | genunchi | jenoonk$^y$ |
| leg | picior | peechyor |
| ligament | ligament | leegament |
| lip | buză | boozer |
| liver | ficat | feecat |
| lung | plămîn | plermîn |
| mouth | gură | goorer |
| muscle | muschi | mooshk$^y$ |
| neck | gît | gît |
| nerve | nerv | nerv |
| nose | nas | nas |
| rib | coastă | cwaster |
| shoulder | umăr | oomer |
| skin | piele | pyeleh |
| spine | coloana vertebrală | colwana vertebraler |
| stomach | stomac | stomac |
| tendon | tendon | tendon |
| thigh | coapsă | cwapser |
| throat | gîtlej | gîtlezh |
| thumb | degetul mare | dejetool mareh |
| toe | deget de la picior | dejet deh la peechyor |
| tongue | limbă | leember |
| tonsils | amigdale | ameegdaleh |
| vein | venă | vener |

## Accident—Injury *Accident—Rănire*

| | | |
|---|---|---|
| There's been an accident. | **A fost un accident.** | a fost oon ac-cheedent |
| My child has had a fall. | **Copilul meu a căzut.** | copeelool me°° a cerzoot |
| He/She has hurt his/her head. | **El/ea s-a lovit la cap.** | yel/ya sa loveet la cap |
| He's/She's unconscious. | **El/ea şi-a pierdut cunoştinţa.** | yel/ya shya pyerdoot coonoshteentsa |
| He's/She's bleeding (heavily). | **El/ea sîngerează (puternic).** | yel/ya sinjerazer (pooterneec) |
| He's/She's seriously injured. | **El/ea e grav rănit(ă).** | yel/ya yeh grav rerneet(er) |
| His/Her arm is broken. | **Si-a rupt braţul.** | shya roopt bratsool |
| His/Her ankle is swollen. | **Are genunchiul umflat.** | areh jenoonkyool oomflat |
| I've been stung. | **M-a înţepat.** | ma intsepat |
| I've got something in my eye. | **Am ceva în ochi.** | am cheva in oky |
| I've got a/an... | **Am...** | am |
| blister | **o băşică** | o bersheecer |
| boil | **un furuncul** | oon foorooncool |
| bruise | **o vînătaie** | o vinertayeh |
| burn | **o arsură** | o arsoorer |
| cut | **o tăietură** | o ter-yetoorer |
| graze | **o julitură** | o jooleetoorer |
| insect bite | **o înţepătură de insectă** | o intsepertoorer deh eensecter |
| lump | **o umflatură** | o oomflertoorer |
| rash | **o egzemă** | o egzemer |
| sting | **o înţepătură** | o intsepertoorer |
| swelling | **o umflătură** | o oomflertoorer |
| wound | **o rană** | o raner |
| Could you have a look at it? | **Vreţi să va uitaţi la ea?** | vretsy ser ver ooytatsy la ya |
| I can't move my... | **Nu pot să-mi mişc...** | noo pot sermy meeshc |
| It hurts. | **Mă doare.** | mer dwareh |

| | |
|---|---|
| **Unde vă doare?** | Where does it hurt? |
| **Ce fel de durere este?** | What kind of pain is it? |
| **slabă/acută/cu zvîcnituri** | dull/sharp/throbbing |
| **continuă/întreruptă** | constant/on and off |
| **Este...** | It's... |
| **rupt/luxat** | broken/sprained |
| **dislocat/rupt** | dislocated/torn |
| **Trebuie să faceţi o radiografie.** | I'd like you to have an X-ray. |
| **Trebuie pus în gips.** | We'll have to put it in plaster. |
| **Este infectat.** | It's infected. |
| **Aţi făcut vaccin antitetanos?** | Have you been vaccinated against tetanus? |
| **O să vă dau un calmant.** | I'll give you a painkiller. |

## Illness *Boală*

| | | |
|---|---|---|
| I'm not feeling well. | **Nu mă simt bine.** | noo mer seemt **bee**neh |
| I'm ill. | **Sînt bolnav(a).** | sînt bol**nav**(a) |
| I feel... | **Mă simt...** | mer seemt |
| dizzy | **ameţit** | amet**seet** |
| nauseous | **mi-e greaţă** | myeh greh-**ats**er |
| shivery | **am frisoane** | am free**swan**eh |
| I have a temperature/fever. | **Am temperatură/febră.** | am tempera**too**rer/**febr**er |
| My temperature is 38 degrees. | **Am 38 de grade.** | am 38 deh **grad**eh |
| I've been vomiting. | **Am vomat.** | am vo**mat** |
| I'm constipated/I've got diarrhoea. | **Sînt constipat/Am diaree.** | sînt constee**pat**/am deeare-eh |
| My... hurt(s). | **Mă doare...** | mer **dwar**eh |
| I've got (a/an)... | **Am...** | |
| asthma | **astmă** | **ast**mer |
| backache | **o durere de spate** | o **door**ereh deh **spat**eh |
| cold | **o gripă** | o **gree**per |

| cough | o tuse | o **tooseh** |
|---|---|---|
| cramps | un cîrcel | oon **cîrchel** |
|   stomach cramps |   crampe |   **crampeh** |
| earache | o durere de ureche | o doorereh deh oorekeh |
| hay fever | alergie la polen | alerjee-eh la polen |
| indigestion | indigestie | eendeejestyeh |
| palpitations | palpitaţii | palpeetatsee |
| rheumatism | reumatism | re°°mateesm |
| sore throat | o durere în gît | o doorereh in git |
| stiff neck | o durere de ceafă | o doorereh deh **chafer** |
| stomach ache | o durere de burtă | o doorereh deh **boorter** |
| sunstroke | insolaţie | eensolatsyeh |

| I have a headache. | Am o durere de cap/Mă doare capul. | am o doorereh deh cap/mer **dwareh capool** |
|---|---|---|
| I have a nosebleed. | Îmi curge sînge din nas. | im**y coorjeh sinjeh** deen nas |
| I have difficulties breathing. | Respir greu. | respeer gre°° |
| I have chest pains. | Mă doare pieptul. | mer **dwareh pyep**tool |
| I had a heart attack... years ago. | Am avut un atac de cord... cu ani în urmă. | am a**voot** oon atac deh cord... coo an**y** in **oormer** |
| My blood pressure is too high/too low. | Am tensiunea prea mare/prea mică. | am ten**syoo**neh-a preh-**a** mareh/preh-**a mee**cer |
| I'm allergic to... | Sînt alergic la... | sint aler**jeec** la |
| I'm diabetic. | Sînt diabetic. | sint dya**be**teec |

## Women's section *Pentru femei*

| I have period pains. | Am dureri la ciclu. | am doorer**y** la **chee**cloo |
|---|---|---|
| I have a vaginal infection. | Am o infecţie vaginală. | am o een**fec**tsyeh vajeenaler |
| I'm on the pill. | Iau anticoncepţionale. | ya°° anteeconcheptsyonaleh |
| I haven't had a period for 2 months. | Nu mi-a venit ciclul de două luni. | noo mya ve**neet chee**clool deh **do**-wer loon**y** |
| I'm (3 months') pregnant. | Sînt gravidă (în trei luni). | sint gra**vee**der (in tray loon**y**) |

| De cînd vă simţiţi aşa? | How long have you been feeling like this? |
| E prima dată cînd aveţi aceasta? | Is this the first time you've had this? |
| Vă iau temperatura/pulsul. | I'll take your temperature/blood pressure. |
| Suflecaţi mîneca, vă rog. | Roll up your sleeve, please. |
| Vă rog dezbracaţi-vă (pînă la brîu). | Please undress (down to the waist). |
| Vă rog să vă întindeţi aici. | Please lie down over here. |
| Deschideţi gura. | Open your mouth. |
| Respiraţi adînc. | Breathe deeply. |
| Tuşiţi, vă rog. | Cough, please. |
| Unde vă doare? | Where does it hurt? |
| Aveţi... | You've got (a/an)... |
| apendicită | appendicitis |
| cistită | cystitis |
| gastrită | gastritis |
| gripă | flu |
| o imflamaţie a... | inflammation of... |
| o intoxicaţie alimentară | food poisoning |
| hepatită | hepatitis |
| icter | jaundice |
| o boală venerică | venereal disease |
| pneumonie | pneumonia |
| pojar | measles |
| Nu este contagioasă. | It's (not) contagious. |
| Este o alergie. | It's an allergy. |
| O să vă fac o injecţie. | I'll give you an injection. |
| Vreau un specimen de sînge/scaun/urină. | I want a specimen of your blood/stools/urine. |
| Trebuie să staţi în pat... zile. | You must stay in bed for... days. |
| Vreau să vă vadă un specialist. | I want you to see a specialist. |
| Trebuie să mergeţi la spital pentru un examen general. | I want you to go to the hospital for a general check-up. |

## Prescription—Treatment *Reţete—Tratament*

| This is my usual medicine. | **Acesta este medicamentul meu obişnuit.** | achesta yesteh medeecamentool me°° obeeshnooeet |
| Can you give me a prescription for this? | **Puteţi să-mi daţi o reţetă pentru aceasta.** | pootets<sup>y</sup> serm<sup>y</sup> dats<sup>y</sup> o retseter pentroo achasta |
| Can you prescribe a/an/some...? | **Puteţi să-mi prescrieţi...** | pootets<sup>y</sup> serm<sup>y</sup> prescree-ets<sup>y</sup> |
| antidepressant | **nişte antidepresante** | neeshteh anteedepresanteh |
| sleeping pills | **nişte somnifere** | neeshteh somneefereh |
| tranquillizer | **nişte tranchilizante** | neeshteh trankeleezanteh |
| I'm allergic to certain antibiotics/penicillin. | **Sînt alergic la anumite antibiotice/penicilină.** | sint alerjeec la anoomeeteh anteebyoteecheh/ peneecheeleener |
| I don't want anything too strong. | **Nu vreau ceva prea puternic.** | noo vra°° cheva preh-a pooterneec |
| How many times a day should I take it? | **De cîte ori pe zi trebuie să iau acest medicament?** | deh citeh or<sup>y</sup> peh zee trebooyeh ser ya°o achest medeecament |
| Must I swallow them whole? | **Trebuie să le inghit intregi?** | trebooyeh ser leh ingeet intrej<sup>y</sup> |

---

| | |
|---|---|
| **Ce tratament urmaţi?** | What treatment are you having? |
| **Pe cale injectabilă sau orală?** | By injection or orally? |
| **Luaţi... linguriţe din acest medicament...** | Take... teaspoons of this medicine... |
| **Luaţi o pastilă cu un pahar de apă...** | Take one pill with a glass of water... |
| **la... ore** | every... hours |
| **de... ori pe zi** | ... times a day |
| **înainte/după fiecare masă** | before/after each meal |
| **dimineaţa/seara** | in the morning/at night |
| **dacă aveţi dureri** | if there is any pain |
| **timp de... zile** | for... days |

CHEMIST'S, see page 107

### Fee *Plata*

| How much do I owe you? | **Cît vă datorez?** | cit ver dato**rez** |
| May I have a receipt for my health insurance? | **Pot să am o chitanţă pentru asigurări?** | pot ser am o kee**tant**ser **pen**troo aseegoo**rerr**ⁱ |
| Can I have a medical certificate? | **Pot să am un certificat medical?** | pot ser am oon cherteefee**cat** medee**cal** |
| Would you fill in this health insurance form, please? | **Vreţi să completaţi formularul de asigurări, vă rog.** | vretsⁱ ser comple**tats**ⁱ formoola**rool** deh aseegoo**rerr**ⁱ ver rog |

### Hospital *Spital*

| Please notify my family. | **Vă rog anunţaţi familia.** | ver rog anoon**tsats**ⁱ fa**mee**lya |
| What are the visiting hours? | **Care sînt orele de vizită?** | **care**h sint **o**releh deh **vee**zeeter |
| When can I get up? | **Cînd mă pot da jos din pat?** | cind mer pot da zhos deen pat |
| When will the doctor come? | **Cînd vine doctorul?** | cind **vee**neh **doc**torool |
| I'm in pain. | **Am dureri.** | am doo**rer**ⁱ |
| I can't eat/sleep. | **Nu pot mînca/dormi.** | noo pot **min**ca/dor**mee** |
| Where is the bell? | **Unde este soneria?** | **oon**deh **yes**teh sone**ree**-a |

| nurse | **soră (medicală)** | **so**rer (medee**ca**ler) |
| patient | **pacient** | pa**chy**ent |
| anaesthetic | **anestetic** | anes**te**teec |
| blood transfusion | **transfuzie de sînge** | trans**foo**zyeh deh **sin**jeh |
| injection | **injecţie** | een**zhec**tyeh |
| operation | **operaţie** | ope**ra**tsyeh |
| bed | **pat** | pat |
| bedpan | **oală de noapte/ploscă** | **wa**ler deh **nwap**teh/**plos**cer |
| thermometer | **termometru** | termo**me**troo |

## Dentist  *Dentist*

If you need to see the dentist while in Romania ask for a *cabinet dentar* at the *policlinică cu plată*. You will normally be able to get a quick appointment.

| | | |
|---|---|---|
| Can you recommend a good dentist? | **Puteţi să recomandaţi un dentist bun?** | pootets<sup>y</sup> ser recomandats<sup>y</sup> oon denteest boon |
| Can I make an (urgent) appointment to see Dr...? | **Puteţi să-mi faceţi o programare de urgenţă pentru doctorul...** | pootets<sup>y</sup> serm<sup>y</sup> fachets<sup>y</sup> o programareh deh oorjentser pentroo doctorool |
| Couldn't you make it earlier? | **Nu puteţi să o faceţi mai devreme?** | noo pootets<sup>y</sup> ser o fachets<sup>y</sup> migh devremeh |
| I have a broken tooth. | **Am un dinte spart.** | am oon deenteh spart |
| I have toothache. | **Mă doare dintele/ măseaua.** | mer dwareh deenteleh/ mersehawa |
| I have an abscess. | **Am un abces.** | am oon abches |
| This tooth hurts. | **Mă doare dintele acesta.** | mer dwareh deenteleh achesta |
| at the top | **sus** | soos |
| at the bottom | **jos** | zhos |
| at the front | **în faţă** | in fatser |
| at the back | **în spate** | in spateh |
| Can you fix it temporarily? | **Puteţi să-l trataţi provizoriu?** | pootets<sup>y</sup> serl tratats<sup>y</sup> proveezoryoo |
| I don't want it pulled out. | **Nu vreau să-l extrageţi.** | noo vra<sup>oo</sup> serl extrajets<sup>y</sup> |
| Could you give me an anaesthetic? | **Să-mi faceţi anestezie?** | serm<sup>y</sup> fachets<sup>y</sup> anestezee-eh |
| I've lost a filling. | **Mi-a căzut o plombă.** | my-a cerzoot o plomber |
| My gums... | **Gingia...** | jeenjea |
| are very sore | **mă doare** | mer dwareh |
| are bleeding | **sîngerează** | sinjerazer |
| I've broken my dentures. | **Mi s-a rupt proteza.** | mee sa roopt proteza |
| Can you repair my dentures? | **Puteţi să-mi reparaţi proteza?** | pootets<sup>y</sup> serm<sup>y</sup> reparats<sup>y</sup> proteza |
| When will they be ready? | **Cînd va fi gata?** | cind va fee gata |

# Reference section

## Where do you come from? *De unde veniți?*

| Africa | **Africa** | afreeca |
|--------|-----------|---------|
| Asia | **Asia** | asya |
| Australia | **Australia** | a°ostralya |
| Europe | **Europa** | e°oropa |
| North America | **America de Nord** | amereeca deh nord |
| South America | **America de Sud** | amereeca deh sood |
| Belgium | **Belgia** | beljya |
| Belorus | **Bielorusia** | byeloroosya |
| Bulgaria | **Bulgaria** | boolgarya |
| Canada | **Canada** | canada |
| China | **China** | keena |
| Czech Republic | **Republica Cehă** | repoobleeca cheher |
| Denmark | **Danemarca** | danemarca |
| England | **Anglia** | anglya |
| Finland | **Finlanda** | feenlanda |
| France | **Franța** | frantsa |
| Germany | **Germania** | jermanya |
| Great Britain | **Marea Britanie** | mareh-a breetanyeh |
| Greece | **Grecia** | grechya |
| India | **India** | eendya |
| Ireland | **Irlanda** | eerlanda |
| Italy | **Italia** | eetalya |
| Japan | **Japonia** | zhaponya |
| Luxembourg | **Luxemburg** | looxemboorg |
| Netherlands | **Olanda** | olanda |
| New Zealand | **Noua Zeelandă** | nowa zeh-ehlander |
| Norway | **Norvegia** | norvejya |
| Romania | **România** | romineea |
| Russia | **Rusia** | roosya |
| Scotland | **Scoția** | scotsya |
| Slovakia | **Slovakia** | slovakya |
| South Africa | **Africa de Sud** | afreeca deh sood |
| Spain | **Spania** | spanya |
| Sweden | **Suedia** | soo-edya |
| Switzerland | **Elveția** | elvetsya |
| Transylvania | **Transilvania** | transeelvanya |
| Tunisia | **Tunisia** | tooneesya |
| Turkey | **Turcia** | toorchya |
| Ukraine | **Ukraina** | oocrayna |
| United States | **Statele Unite** | stateleh ooneeteh |
| Wales | **Țara Galilor** | tsara galeelor |

**Numbers** *Numere*

| | | |
|---|---|---|
| 0 | **zero** | zero |
| 1 | **unu** | oonoo |
| 2 | **doi** | doy |
| 3 | **trei** | tray |
| 4 | **patru** | patroo |
| 5 | **cinci** | cheench<sup>y</sup> |
| 6 | **şase** | shaseh |
| 7 | **şapte** | shapteh |
| 8 | **opt** | opt |
| 9 | **nouă** | no-wer |
| 10 | **zece** | zecheh |
| 11 | **unsprezece** | oonsprezecheh |
| 12 | **doisprezece** | doysprezecheh |
| 13 | **treisprezece** | traysprezecheh |
| 14 | **paisprezece** | pighsprezecheh |
| 15 | **cincisprezece** | cheench<sup>y</sup>sprezecheh |
| 16 | **şaisprezece** | shighsprezecheh |
| 17 | **şaptesprezece** | shaptesprezeceh |
| 18 | **optsprezece** | optsprezecheh |
| 19 | **nouăsprezeche** | no-wersprezecheh |
| 20 | **douăzeci** | do-werzech<sup>y</sup> |
| 21 | **douăzeci şi unu** | do-werzech<sup>y</sup> shee oonoo |
| 22 | **douăzeci şi doi** | do-werzech<sup>y</sup> shee doy |
| 23 | **douăzeci şi trei** | do-werzech<sup>y</sup> shee tray |
| 24 | **douăzeci şi patru** | do-werzech<sup>y</sup> shee patroo |
| 25 | **douăzeci şi cinci** | do-werzech<sup>y</sup> shee cheench<sup>y</sup> |
| 26 | **douăzeci şi şase** | do-werzech<sup>y</sup> shee shaseh |
| 27 | **douăzeci şi şapte** | do-werzech<sup>y</sup> shee shapteh |
| 28 | **douăzeci şi opt** | do-werzech<sup>y</sup> shee opt |
| 29 | **douăzeci şi nouă** | do-werzech<sup>y</sup> shee no-wer |
| 30 | **treizeci** | trayzech<sup>y</sup> |
| 31 | **treizeci şi unu** | trayzech<sup>y</sup> shee oonoo |
| 32 | **treizeci şi doi** | trayzech<sup>y</sup> shee doy |
| 33 | **treizeci şi trei** | trayzech<sup>y</sup> shee tray |
| 40 | **patruzeci** | patroozech<sup>y</sup> |
| 41 | **patruzeci şi unu** | patroozech<sup>y</sup> shee oonoo |
| 42 | **patruzeci şi doi** | patroozech<sup>y</sup> shee doy |
| 43 | **patruzeci şi trei** | patroozech<sup>y</sup> shee tray |
| 50 | **cincizeci** | cheench<sup>y</sup>zech<sup>y</sup> |
| 51 | **cinzeci şi unu** | cheench<sup>y</sup>zech<sup>y</sup> shee oonoo |
| 52 | **cinzeci şi doi** | cheench<sup>y</sup>zech<sup>y</sup> shee doy |
| 53 | **cinzeci şi trei** | cheench<sup>y</sup>zech<sup>y</sup> shee tray |
| 60 | **şaizeci** | shighzech<sup>y</sup> |
| 61 | **şaizeci şi unu** | shighzech<sup>y</sup> shee oonoo |
| 62 | **şaizeci şi doi** | shighzech<sup>y</sup> shee doy |

| 63 | şaizeci şi trei | shighzech$^y$ shee tray |
| 70 | şaptezeci | shaptehzech$^y$ |
| 71 | şaptezeci şi unu | shaptehzech$^y$ shee oonoo |
| 72 | şaptezeci şi doi | shaptehzech$^y$ shee doy |
| 73 | şaptezeci şi trei | shaptehzech$^y$ shee tray |
| 80 | optzeci | optzech$^y$ |
| 81 | optzeci şi unu | optzech$^y$ shee oonoo |
| 82 | optzeci şi doi | optzech$^y$ shee doy |
| 83 | optzeci şi trei | optzech$^y$ shee tray |
| 90 | nouăzeci | no-werzech$^y$ |
| 91 | nouăzeci şi unu | no-werzech$^y$ shee oonoo |
| 92 | nouăzeci şi doi | no-werzech$^y$ shee doy |
| 93 | nouăzeci şi trei | no-werzech$^y$ shee tray |
| | | |
| 100 | o sută | o sooter |
| 101 | o sută unu | o sooter oonoo |
| 102 | o sută doi | o sooter doy |
| 110 | o sută zece | o sooter zecheh |
| 120 | o sută douăzeci | o sooter do-werzech$^y$ |
| 130 | o sută treizeci | o sooter trayzech$^y$ |
| 140 | o sută patruzeci | o sooter patroozech$^y$ |
| 150 | o sută cincizeci | o sooter cheench$^y$zech$^y$ |
| 160 | o sută şaizeci | o sooter shighzech$^y$ |
| 170 | o sută şaptezeci | o sooter shaptehzech$^y$ |
| 180 | o sută optzeci | o sooter optzech$^y$ |
| 190 | o sută nouazeci | o sooter no-werzech$^y$ |
| 200 | două sute | do-wer sooteh |
| 300 | trei sute | tray sooteh |
| 400 | patru sute | patroo sooteh |
| 500 | cinci sute | cheench$^y$ sooteh |
| 600 | şase sute | shaseh sooteh |
| 700 | şapte sute | shapteh sooteh |
| 800 | opt sute | opt sooteh |
| 900 | nouă sute | no-wer sooteh |
| | | |
| 1000 | o mie | o mee-eh |
| 1100 | o mie o sută | o mee-eh o sooter |
| 1200 | o mie două sute | o mee-eh do-wer sooteh |
| 2000 | două mii | do-wer mee |
| 5000 | cinci mii | cheench$^y$ mee |
| | | |
| 10,000 | zece mii | zecheh mee |
| 50,000 | cincizeci de mii | cheench$^y$zech$^y$ deh mee |
| 100,000 | o sută de mii | o sooter deh mee |
| 1,000,000 | un milion | oon meeleeon |
| 1,000,000,000 | un miliard | oon meeleeard |

| | | |
|---|---|---|
| first | **primul (prima)** | **pree**mool (**pree**ma) |
| second | **al doilea (a doua)** | al **doy**leh-a (a **do**-wer) |
| third | **al treilea (a treia)** | al **tray**leh-a (a **tre**-ya) |
| fourth | **al patrulea (a patra)** | al **pat**rooleh-a (a **pat**ra) |
| fifth | **al cincilea (a cincea)** | al **cheen**cheeleh-a (a **cheen**cheh-a) |
| sixth | **al saselea (a şasea)** | al **sha**seleh-a (a **sha**seh-a) |
| seventh | **al şapteleaa (a şapta)** | al **shap**tehleh-a (a **shap**ta) |
| eighth | **al optulea (a opta)** | al **op**tooleh-a (a **op**ta) |
| ninth | **al nouălea (a noua)** | al **no**-werleh-a (a **no**-wa) |
| tenth | **al zecelea (a zecea)** | al **ze**cheleh-a (a **ze**cheh-a) |
| once/twice | **o dată/de două ori** | o **da**ter/deh **do**-wer or$^y$ |
| three times | **de trei ori** | deh tray or$^y$ |
| a half | **o jumătate** | o **zhoo**mertateh |
| half a... | **jumătate...** | **zhoo**mertateh |
| half of... | **jumătate de ...** | **zhoo**mertateh deh |
| half (adj.) | **jumătate** | **zhoo**mertateh |
| a quarter/one third | **un sfert/o treime** | oon sfert/o treh-**ee**meh |
| a pair of | **o pereche de** | o **pe**rekeh deh |
| a dozen | **o duzină** | o doo**zee**ner |
| one per cent | **unu la sută** | **oo**noo la **soo**ter |
| 3.4% | **trei virgulă patru la sută** | tray **veer**gooler **pat**roo la **soo**ter |

## Date and time *Data şi anul*

| | | |
|---|---|---|
| 1981 | **o mie nouă sute optzeci şi unu** | o **mee**-eh **no**-wer **soo**teh opt**zech**$^y$ shee **oo**noo |
| 1993 | **o mie nouă sute nouă zeci şi trei** | o **mee**-eh **no**-wer **soo**teh **no**-wer zech$^y$ she tray |
| 2005 | **două mii cinci** | **do**-wer mee cheench$^y$ |

## Year and age *Anul şi vîrsta*

| | | |
|---|---|---|
| year | **an** | an |
| leap year | **an bisect** | an bee**sect** |
| decade | **deceniu** | de**cheh**-nyoo |
| century | **secol** | **se**col |
| this year | **anul acesta** | **a**nool a**ches**ta |
| last year | **anul trecut** | **a**nool tre**coot** |
| next year | **anul viitor** | **a**nool vee-ee**tor** |
| each year | **în fiecare an** | in **fee**-ecareh an |
| two years ago | **acum doi ani** | a**coom** doy an$^y$ |
| years ago | **cu ani în urm** | coo an$^y$ in **oor**mer |
| in one year | **într-un an** | intr-oon an |
| in the eighties | **în anii optzeci** | in **a**nee opt**zech**$^y$ |
| in the nineties | **în anii nouăzeci** | in **a**nee **no**-wer**zech**$^y$ |

| | | |
|---|---|---|
| the 16th century | **în secolul al şaisprezecelea** | in secolool al shighsprezecheleh-a |
| in the 20th century | **în secolul douăzeci** | in secolool do-werzech<sup>y</sup> |
| How old are you? | **Ce vîrstă aveţi?/ Cîţi ani ai?** | cheh virster avets<sup>y</sup>/cîts<sup>y</sup> an<sup>y</sup> igh |
| I'm 30 years old. | **Am treizeci de ani.** | am trayzech<sup>y</sup> deh an<sup>y</sup> |
| He/She was born in 1960. | **El/Ea s-a născut în o mie nouă sute şaizeci.** | yel/ya s-a nerscoot in o mee-eh no-wersooteh shighzech<sup>y</sup> |
| What is his/her age? | **Ce vîrsta are el/ea?** | cheh virster areh yel/ya |
| Children under 16 are not admitted. | **Copiii sub şaispre-zece ani nu sînt admişi.** | copee-ee soob shighsprezecheh an<sup>y</sup> noo sînt admeesh<sup>y</sup> |

## Seasons *Anotimpuri*

| | | |
|---|---|---|
| spring/summer | **primăvară/vară** | preemervarer/varer |
| autumn/winter | **toamnă/iarnă** | twamner/yarner |
| in spring | **primăvară** | preemervarer |
| during the summer | **în timpul verii** | in teempool veree |
| in autumn | **toamnă** | twamner |
| during the winter | **iarnă** | yarner |
| high season | **în sezon** | in sezon |
| low season | **în afara sezonului** | in afara sezonoolooy |

## Months *Lunile anului*

| | | |
|---|---|---|
| January | **ianuarie** | yanwaryeh |
| February | **februarie** | febrwaryeh |
| March | **martie** | martyeh |
| April | **aprilie** | apreelyeh |
| May | **mai** | migh |
| June | **iunie** | yoonyeh |
| July | **iulie** | yoolyeh |
| August | **august** | a°°goost |
| September | **septembrie** | septembryeh |
| October | **octombrie** | octombryeh |
| November | **noiembrie** | noyembryeh |
| December | **decembrie** | dechembryeh |
| in September | **în septembrie** | in septembryeh |
| since October | **din octombrie** | deen octombryeh |
| the beginning of January | **la începutul lunii ianuarie** | la inchepootool loonee yanwaryeh |
| the middle of February | **la mijlocul lunii februarie** | la meezhlocool loonee febrwaryeh |
| the end of March | **la sfîrşitul lui martie** | la sfîrsheetool looy martyeh |

### Days and date  *Zilele şi data*

| What day is it today? | Ce zi este azi? | cheh zee yesteh az<sup>y</sup> |
|---|---|---|

| | | |
|---|---|---|
| Sunday | duminică | doomeeneecer |
| Monday | luni | loon<sup>y</sup> |
| Tuesday | marţi | marts<sup>y</sup> |
| Wednesday | miercuri | myercoor<sup>y</sup> |
| Thursday | joi | zhoy |
| Friday | vineri | veener<sup>y</sup> |
| Saturday | sîmbătă | sîmberter |

| It's... | Este... | yesteh |
|---|---|---|
| July 1 | întîi iulie | intiy yoolyeh |
| March 10 | zece martie | zecheh martyeh |

| in the morning | dimineaţa | deemeenatsa |
|---|---|---|
| during the day | în timpul zilei | in teempool zeelay |
| in the afternoon | după amiază | dooper amyazer |
| in the evening | seara | sara |
| at night | noaptea | nwapteh-a |

| the day before yesterday | alaltăieri | alalter-yer<sup>y</sup> |
|---|---|---|
| yesterday | ieri | yer<sup>y</sup> |
| today | azi | az<sup>y</sup> |
| tomorrow | mîine | miyneh |
| the day after tomorrow | poimîine | poymiyneh |
| the day before | cu o zi înainte | coo o zee inaeenteh |
| the next day | ziua următoare | zeewa oormertwareh |
| two days ago | acum două zile | acoom do-wer zeeleh |
| in three days' time | peste trei zile | pesteh tray zeeleh |

| last week | săptămînă trecută | serperminer trecooter |
|---|---|---|
| next week | săptămîna viitoare | serperminer vee-eetwareh |
| for a fortnight (two weeks) | pentru două săptămîni | pentroo do-wer serpermin<sup>y</sup> |

| birthday | zi de naştere | zee deh nashtereh |
|---|---|---|
| day off | zi liberă | ze leeberer |
| holiday | sărbătoare legală | serbertwareh legaler |
| holidays/vacation | concediu/vacanţă | conchedyoo/vacantser |
| week | saptamînă | serperminer |
| weekend | sfîrşit de săptămînă | sfirsheet deh serperminer |
| working day | zi lucrătoare | zee loocrertwareh |

## Public holidays *Sărbători legale*

| | | |
|---|---|---|
| 1 January, New Year's Day | Întîi Ianuarie | intiy yanwaryeh |
| 1 May | Întîi Mai | intiy migh |
| Christmas Eve | Ajun | azhoon |
| Christmas Day | Crăciun | crerchyoon |
| **MOVEABLE DAYS** | | |
| Easter | Paşte | pashteh |

## Greetings and wishes *Salutări şi urări*

| | | |
|---|---|---|
| Merry Christmas! | **Sărbători fericite!** | serber**tor**y feree**chee**teh |
| Happy New Year! | **An Nou Fericit!** | an noh feree**cheet** |
| Happy Easter! | **Cristos a Inviat!** | crees**tos** a invee-**at** |
| Happy birthday! | **La mulţi ani!** | la **moolts**y an y |
| Best wishes! | **Noroc, şi numai bine!** | noroc shee **noo**migh **been**eh |
| Congratulations! | **Felicitări!** | feleechee**terr**y |
| Good luck/ All the best! | **Noroc/Toate cele bune!** | noroc/twa**teh cheleh boon**eh |
| Have a good trip! | **Călătorie plăcută!** | cerlerto**ree**-eh pler**coo**ter |
| Have a good holiday! | **Vacanţă plăcută!** | va**cantser** pler**coo**ter |
| Best regards from... | **Sincere salutări de la...** | **seen**chereh saloo**terr**y deh la |
| My regards to... | **Toate cele bune lui... /Complimente lui...** | twa**teh cheleh boon**eh looy/comple**emen**teh looy |

## What time is it? *Cît e ora?*

The 24-hour clock is generally used in timetables and often in everyday conversation too, for example when fixing appointments.

| | | |
|---|---|---|
| Excuse me. Can you tell me the time? | **Fiţi amabil, puteţi să-mi spuneţi cît este ceasul?** | **feets**y a**ma**beel poo**tets**y serm y **spoonets**y cît **yes**teh **cha**sool |

| It's... | Este... | yesteh |
|---|---|---|
| five past one | ora unu şi cinci minute | ora oonoo shee cheench<sup>y</sup> meenooteh |
| ten past two | ora două şi zece minute | ora do-wer shee zecheh meenooteh |
| a quarter past three | trei şi un sfert | tray shee oon sfert |
| twenty past four | patru şi douăzeci | patroo shee do-werzech<sup>y</sup> |
| twenty-five past five | cinci şi douăzeci şi cinci | cheench<sup>y</sup> shee do-werzech<sup>y</sup> shee cheench<sup>y</sup> |
| half past six | şase şi jumătate | shaseh shee zhoomertateh |
| twenty-five to seven | şapte fără douăzeci şi cinci | shapteh ferrer do-werzech<sup>y</sup> shee cheench<sup>y</sup> |
| twenty to eight | opt fară douăzeci | opt ferrer do-werzech<sup>y</sup> |
| a quarter to nine | nouă fară un sfert | no-wer ferrer oon sfert |
| ten to ten | zece fară zece | zecheh ferrer zecheh |
| five to eleven | unsprezece fară cinci | oonsprezecheh ferrer cheench<sup>y</sup> |
| twelve o'clock (noon/ midnight) | ora douăsprezece/ zero | ora do-wersprezecheh/zero |
| at noon | la amiază | la amyazer |
| at midnight | la miezul nopţii | la myezool noptsee |
| in the morning | dimineaţa | deemeenatsa |
| in the afternoon | după-amiază | dooper-amyazer |
| in the evening | seara | sara |
| The train leaves at... | Trenul pleacă la ora... | trenool pleh-acer la ora |
| 13.04 (1.04pm) | treisprezece zero patru/unu şi patru minute | traysprezecheh zero patroo/oonoo shee patroo meenooteh |
| 0.40 (0.40am) | ora zero şi patruzeci de minute | ora zero shee patroozech<sup>y</sup> deh meenooteh |
| in five minutes | în cinci minute | in cheench<sup>y</sup> meenooteh |
| in a quarter of an hour | într-un sfert de oră | intr-oon sfert deh orer |
| half an hour ago | acum jumătate de oră | acoom zhoomertateh deh orer |
| about two hours | vreo două ore | vro do-wer oreh |
| more than 10 minutes | mai mult de zece minute | migh moolt deh zecheh meenooteh |
| less than 30 seconds | mai puţin de treizeci de secunde | migh pootseen deh trayzech<sup>y</sup> deh secoondeh |
| The clock is fast/ slow. | Ceasul o ia înainte/ rămîne în urmă. | chasool o ya inaeenteh/ rermineh in oormer |

## Common abbreviations *Abreviere*

| | | |
|---|---|---|
| a.c. | anul curent | the current year |
| ACR | Automobil Clubul Român | Romanian Automobile Club |
| ap. | apartament | apartment |
| bd. | bulevardul | avenue/boulevard |
| BRCE | Banca Româna de Comerţ Exterior | Romanian Bank for Foreign Trade |
| BRD | Banca Româna pentru Dez-voltare | Romanian Bank for Development |
| BTT | Biroul de Turism pentru Tine-ret | Youth Travel Agency |
| CATT | Compania Autonomă de Turism pentru Tineret | Company for Youth Travel |
| CP | cai putere | horsepower |
| de ex. | de exemplu | for example |
| dl. | domnul | Mr |
| dlui. | dumnealui | he (formal) |
| dna. | doamna | Mrs |
| dşoara | domnişoara | Miss |
| dvs. | dumneavoastră | you (formal) |
| ONT | Oficiul Naţional de Turism | National Tourist Office |
| PTTR | Poşta, Telegraf, Telefon, Radio | Post Office |
| Pţa | piaţa | square |
| RATB | Regia Autonomă de Trans-porturi Bucureşti | Bucharest Public Transport Company |
| SA | Societate Anonimă | Incorporated (Inc.) |
| Sf. | sfîntul | Saint |
| SNCFR | Societatea Naţională a Căile Ferate Române | Romanian National Railways |
| SRL | Societate cu Răspundere Lim-itată | Public Limited Company (plc) |
| str. | strada | street |
| ş. a. m. d. | şi aşa mai departe | and so on |
| TAROM | Transporturile Aeriene Române | Romanian Airlines |
| TVR | Televizunea Română | Romanian Television |

**Signs and notices** *Semne și anunțuri*

| | |
|---|---|
| **Așteptați vă rog** | Please wait |
| **Atenție** | Caution |
| **Barbați** | Gentlemen |
| **Casa** | Cash desk |
| **Cîine rău** | Beware of the dog |
| **De închiriat** | For hire/To let |
| **Deschis** | Open |
| **De vînzare** | For sale |
| **Femei** | Ladies |
| **Fierbinte** | Hot |
| **Frig** | Cold |
| **Fumatul interzis** | No smoking |
| **Ieșire de incendiu** | Emergency exit |
| **Ieșire** | Exit |
| **Împingeți** | Push |
| **Informații** | Information |
| **...interzis** | ...forbidden |
| **Intrați fără să ciocăniți** | Enter without knocking |
| **Intrare** | Entrance |
| **Intrare interzisă** | No admittance |
| **Intrare gratuită** | Free admittance |
| **Jos** | Down |
| **Liber** | Vacant |
| **Lift** | Lift |
| **Nu atingeți** | Do not touch |
| **Nu avem locuri** | No vacancies |
| **Nu blocați intrarea** | Do not block entrance |
| **Nu deranjați** | Do not disturb |
| **Nu funcționează** | Out of order |
| **Ocupat** | Occupied |
| **Păstrați curățenia** | No littering |
| **Pericol de moarte** | Danger (of death) |
| **Proaspăt vopsit** | Wet paint |
| **Rezervat** | Reserved |
| **Solduri** | Sale |
| **Sunați vă rog** | Please ring |
| **Sus** | Up |
| **Trageți** | Pull |
| **Vîndut** | Sold out |

## Emergency *Urgenţă*

| Call the police | Chemaţi poliţia | kemats<sup>y</sup> poleetsya |
|---|---|---|
| Consulate | Consulat | consoolat |
| DANGER | PERICOL | pereecol |
| Embassy | Ambasadă | ambasader |
| FIRE | FOC | foc |
| Gas | gaz | gaz |
| Get a doctor | Chemaţi un doctor | kemats<sup>y</sup> oon doctor |
| Go away | Pleacă de aici | pleh-acer deh aeech<sup>y</sup> |
| HELP | AJUTOR | azhootor |
| Get help quickly | Chemaţi pe cineva repede | kemats<sup>y</sup> peh cheeneva repedeh |
| I'm ill | Sînt bolnav(a) | sînt bolnav(a) |
| I'm lost | M-am rătăcit | mam rertercheet |
| Leave me alone | Lasă-mă în pace | lasermer în pacheh |
| LOOK OUT | ATENŢIE | atentsyeh |
| Poison | Otravă | otraver |
| POLICE | POLIŢIA | poleetsya |
| Stop that man/ woman | Opriţi omul acela/ femeia aceea | opreets<sup>y</sup> omool achela/ femaya acheya |
| STOP THIEF | HOŢUL | hotsool |

## Emergency telephone numbers *Telefoane de urgenţă*

Here are some important emergency telephone numbers:

| | | | |
|---|---|---|---|
| 961 | Ambulance | 952 | Railway information |
| 955 | Police | 953 | Taxi |
| 981 | Fire brigade | 971 | International exchange |
| 927 | ACR (Romanian Automobile Club) | | |

## Lost property—Theft *Obiecte pierdute—Furt*

| Where's the ...? | Unde este ...? | oondeh yesteh |
|---|---|---|
| lost property (lost and found) office | biroul de obiecte pierdute | beero-ool deh obyecteh pyerdooteh |
| police station | centrul de poliţie | chentrool de poleetsyeh |
| I want to report a theft. | Vreau să raportez un furt. | vra<sup>oo</sup> ser raportez oon foort |
| My ... has been stolen. | Mi s-a furat ... | mee sa foorat |
| I've lost my ... | Am pierdut ... | am pyerdoot |
| handbag | poşeta/geanta | posheta/janta |
| passport | paşaportul | pashaportool |
| wallet | portmoneul | portmoneool |

CAR ACCIDENTS, see page 78

Informaţie

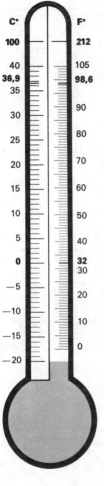

## Conversion tables

### Centimetres and inches

To change centimetres into inches, multiply by .39.

To change inches into centimetres, multiply by 2.54.

|        | in.   | feet  | yards |
|--------|-------|-------|-------|
| 1 mm   | 0.039 | 0.003 | 0.001 |
| 1 cm   | 0.39  | 0.03  | 0.01  |
| 1 dm   | 3.94  | 0.32  | 0.10  |
| 1 m    | 39.40 | 3.28  | 1.09  |

|        | mm    | cm    | m     |
|--------|-------|-------|-------|
| 1 in.  | 25.4  | 2.54  | 0.025 |
| 1 ft.  | 304.8 | 30.48 | 0.304 |
| 1 yd.  | 914.4 | 91.44 | 0.914 |

(32 metres = 35 yards)

### Temperature

To convert Centigrade into degrees Fahrenheit, multiply Centigrade by 1.8 and add 32.

To convert degrees Fahrenheit into Centigrade, subtract 32 from Fahrenheit and divide by 1.8.

REFERENCE SECTION

## Kilometres into miles

1 kilometre (km.) = 0.62 miles

| km. | 10 | 20 | 30 | 40 | 50 | 60 | 70 | 80 | 90 | 100 | 110 | 120 | 130 |
|------|----|----|----|----|----|----|----|----|----|-----|-----|-----|-----|
| miles | 6 | 12 | 19 | 25 | 31 | 37 | 44 | 50 | 56 | 62 | 68 | 75 | 81 |

## Miles into kilometres

1 mile = 1.609 kilometres (km.)

| miles | 10 | 20 | 30 | 40 | 50 | 60 | 70 | 80 | 90 | 100 |
|-------|----|----|----|----|----|----|-----|-----|-----|-----|
| km. | 16 | 32 | 48 | 64 | 80 | 97 | 113 | 129 | 145 | 161 |

## Fluid measures

1 litre (l.) = 0.88 imp. quart or 1.06 U.S. quart
1 imp. quart = 1.14 l.     1 U.S. quart = 0.95 l.
1 imp. gallon = 4.55 l.     1 U.S. gallon = 3.8 l.

| litres | 5 | 10 | 15 | 20 | 25 | 30 | 35 | 40 | 45 | 50 |
|--------|-----|-----|-----|-----|-----|-----|-----|------|------|------|
| imp. gal. | 1.1 | 2.2 | 3.3 | 4.4 | 5.5 | 6.6 | 7.7 | 8.8 | 9.9 | 11.0 |
| U.S. gal. | 1.3 | 2.6 | 3.9 | 5.2 | 6.5 | 7.8 | 9.1 | 10.4 | 11.7 | 13.0 |

## Weights and measures

1 kilogram or kilo (kg.) = 1000 grams (g.)

| 100 g. = 3.5 oz. | ½ kg. = 1.1 lb. |
|------------------|-----------------|
| 200 g. = 7.0 oz. | 1 kg. = 2.2 lb. |

1 oz. = 28.35 g.
1 lb. = 453.60 g.

Informaţie

# Basic Grammar

**Nouns and articles**

In Romanian, nouns belong to three genders: masculine, feminine and neuter. Nouns ending in a consonant are usually masculine or neuter, and nouns that end in a vowel are generally feminine. Although there are many exceptions in the plural form, masculine nouns usually end in **-i**; feminine nouns end in **-i**, and neuter nouns end in **-e** or **-uri**.

| | | |
|---|---|---|
| **pom – pomi** | tree – trees | (masc.) |
| **excursie – excursii** | trip – trips | (fem.) |
| **scaun – scaune** | chair – chairs | (neut.) |

## 1. Indefinite article (a)

The indefinite article is **un** for masculine nouns, **o** for feminine nouns and **un** for neuter nouns. With plural forms, the invariable article **nişte** "some" is used.

| | | | | |
|---|---|---|---|---|
| (masc.) | **un călător** | a traveller | **nişte călători** | some travellers |
| (fem.) | **o piesă** | a play | **nişte piese** | some plays |
| | **o librărie** | a bookshop | **nişte librării** | some bookshops |
| | **o carte** | a book | **nişte cărţi** | some books |
| (neut.) | **un spectacol** | a show | **nişte spectacole** | some shows |
| | **un taxi** | a taxi | **nişte taxiuri** | some taxis |

## 2. Definite article (the)

In Romanian, there is no separate word for the definite article; instead a particle is placed at the end of the noun, depending on its gender and number; the definite articles for singular nouns are **-l**, **-a**, **-le**, and for plural are **-i** and **-le**.

| | | | | | | |
|---|---|---|---|---|---|---|
| (masc.) | **copacu** | tree | **copacul** | the tree | **copacii** | the trees |
| (fem.) | **casă** | house | **casa** | the house | **casele** | the houses |
| (neut.) | **hotel** | hotel | **hotelul** | the hotel | **hotelurile** | the hotels |
| | **birou** | office | **biroul** | the office | **birourile** | the offices |

## Adjectives

The adjective agrees in number, case and gender with the noun it describes. It usually follows the noun but certain common adjectives precede the noun. The table below shows the declension of nouns, adjectives and indefinite articles.

|  | masc.<br>a good doctor | fem.<br>a good map | neut.<br>a good hotel |
|---|---|---|---|
| SINGULAR<br>subject<br>direct object | un doctor bun | o hartă bună | un hotel bun |
| possessive object<br>indirect object | unui doctor bun | unei hărți bune | unui hotel bun |
| PLURAL<br>subject<br>direct object | niște doctori buni | niște hărți bune | niște hoteluri bune |
| possessive object<br>indirect object | unor doctori buni | unor hărți bune | unor hoteluri bune |

Each case is illustrated in the examples below. Note the different forms of the possessive object (of ... or ...'s) and the indirect object (to ...).

| | |
|---|---|
| *Un doctor bun* este foarte ocupat. | *A good doctor* is very busy. |
| Puteți să chemați *un doctor bun?* | Can you get me *a good doctor?* |
| Biroul *unui doctor bun* est curat. | *A good doctor's* office is clean. |
| El a împrumutat cartea lui *unui doctor bun.* | He lent his book *to a good doctor.* |

### Demonstrative adjectives

|  | masc. | fem. | neut. |
|---|---|---|---|
| this<br>these | acest(a)<br>acești(a) | această (aceasta)<br>aceste(a) | acest(a)<br>aceste(a) |
| that<br>those | acel(a)<br>acei(a) | acea (aceea)<br>acele(a) | acel(a)<br>acele(a) |

These adjectives can be placed either before or, for particular emphasis, after the noun. When placed after the noun, they take the endings of the definte article form (shown in brackets).

## Possessive adjectives and pronouns

|  | | singular | | | plural | |
| --- | --- | --- | --- | --- | --- | --- |
|  | masc. | fem. | neut. | masc. | fem. | neut. |
| pronoun particle | al | a | al | ai | ale | ale |
| my | meu | mea | meu | mei | mele | mele |
| your | tău | ta | tău | tăi | tale | tale |
| his/her/its | său | sa | său | săi | sale | sale |
| our | nostru | noastră | nostru | noștri | noastre | noastre |
| your | vostru | voastră | vostru | voștri | voastre | voastre |

Invariable adjectives are used for "their" – **lor**, and the formal form of "you" – **dumneavoastră**. When they are not the subject of the sentence, **ei** "her" and **lui** "his" replace the forms of **său**.

The possessive pronoun is formed by preceding the possessive adjective with the pronoun particle.

**noastă pîine**   our bread      **cărţi sînt ale mele**   the books are mine

## Personal pronouns

|  | Subject | Direct Object | Indirect Object | Reflexive |
| --- | --- | --- | --- | --- |
| I | eu | mă | îmi | mă |
| you (sing.) | tu | te | îți | te |
| he, it | el | îl | îi | se |
| she | ea | o | îi | se |
| we | noi | ne | ne | ne |
| you (plur.) | voi/ dumneavoastră | vă | vă | vă |
| they (masc.) | el | îl | le | se |
| they (fem.) | ele | le | le | se |

Romanian has four forms for the word "you".

| | |
| --- | --- |
| **tu** | for adressing a close friend or child (singular) |
| **dumneata (d-ta)** | for addressing a colleague (singular) |
| **voi** | for addressing close friends (plural) |
| **dumneavoastră (dvs.)** | for addressing one or more strangers or people older than yourself; this is the most respectful term and should be used when in doubt |

### Verbs

There are four main conjugations of verbs in Romanian language. They are distinguished by the ending of the infinitive: **-a**, **-ea**, **-e** and **-i**.

The **present tense**:

|        | a învăţa<br>(to learn) | a vedea<br>(to see) | a face<br>(to make, do) | a vorbi<br>(to speak) |
|--------|------------------------|---------------------|-------------------------|-----------------------|
| eu     | învăţ                  | văd                 | fac                     | vorbesc               |
| tu     | înveţi                 | vezi                | faci                    | vorbeşti              |
| el/ea  | învaţă                 | vede                | face                    | vorbeşte              |
| noi    | învăţăm                | vedem               | facem                   | vorbim                |
| voi    | învăţaţi               | vedeţi              | faceţi                  | vorbiţi               |
| ei/ele | învaţă                 | văd                 | fac                     | vorbesc               |

Here are three common irregular verbs:

|        | a fi<br>(to be) | a avea<br>(to have) | a lau<br>(to take) |
|--------|-----------------|---------------------|--------------------|
| eu     | sînt            | am                  | iau                |
| tu     | eşti            | ai                  | iei                |
| el/ea  | este            | are                 | ia                 |
| noi    | sîntem          | avem                | luăm               |
| voi    | sînteţi         | aveţi               | luaţi              |
| ei/ele | sînt            | au                  | iau                |

Note: Verbs often appear in Romanian without a personal pronoun because the ending of the verb is sufficient to indicate the subject. Personal pronouns precede the verb only for emphasis.

The **perfect tense** is formed with the help of the auxilliary verb **a avea** "to have" followed by the past participle of the verb used.

Verbs with infinitives ending in **-a** and **-i** form the past participle by adding **-t**; those with an **-ea** ending replace it with **-ut**; others ending in **-e** replace it with either **-ut** or **-s**:

| infinitive | past participle | | |
|---|---|---|---|
| **a invita** | **invitat** | **am invitat** | I (have) invited |
| **a vedea** | **vazut** | **a vazut** | he/she/it saw (has seen) |
| **a face** | **făcut** | **aţi făcut** | you did (have done) |
| **a se duce** | **dus** | **s-au dus** | they went (have gone) |

The **future tense** is formed in two main ways:

1. by using the colloquial **o să** plus the subjunctive (similar to the present tense in all forms except the third person).

> **O să stau o lună.** I'll be staying a month.
> **O să venim la ora opt.** We'll come at eight.

2. by using the auxiliary forms **voi**, **vei**, **va**, **vom**, **veţi** and **vor** placed in front of the infinitive form of the verb without **a**.

| | | | |
|---|---|---|---|
| **eu voi pleca** | I shall leave | **noi vom pleca** | we shall leave |
| **tu vei pleca** | you shall leave | **voi veti pleca** | you shall leave |
| **el/ea va pleca** | he/she shall leave | **ei vor pleca** | they shall leave |

### The negative

The negative is formed by putting the negation **nu** in front of the verb; eg:

> **eu nu locuiesc aici** I do not live here
> **eu nu am locuit aici** I did not live here
> **eu nu voi locui aici** I will not live here

With the verb **a avea** "to have", the negative is often reduced to **n-**:

> **n-am** I don't have   **n-aveţi** you don't have

# Dictionary
and alphabetical index

## English—Romanian

| f feminine | m masculine | nt neuter | pl plural |

**A**

**abbey** mînăstire f 81
**abbreviation** abreviere nt 154
**about** *(approximately)* vreo 153
**above** deasupra 15, 63
**abscess** abces nt 145
**absent** nu-i aici 136
**absorbent cotton** vată f 108
**accept, to** a accepta 102
**accessories** accesorii nt 115, 125
**accident** accident nt 139
**account** cont bancar 130
**ache** durere f 141
**adaptor** adaptor nt 118
**address** adresă f 21, 31, 76, 102; locuiţ 79
**address book** agendă de adrese f 104
**adhesive** colant 105
**adhesive tape** scoci nt 104
**admission** intrare f 82, 155
**admitted** admis 150
**Africa** Africa f 146
**after** după 15, 77
**after-shave lotion** loţiune după ras nt 109
**afternoon, in the** după-amiaza nt 151, 153
**again** din nou 96
**age** vîrstă f 149, 150
**ago** în urmă 149
**air bed** saltea pneumatică f 106
**air conditioning** aer condiţionat 23, 28
**air mattress** saltea pneumatică f 106
**airmail** par avion 133
**airplane** avion nt 65
**airport** aeroport nt 16, 21, 65
**aisle seat** loc la culoar nt 65
**alarm clock** radio-ceas nt 118
**alcohol** alcool nt 37, 59
**alcoholic** alcoolic 59

**all** tot 103
**allergic** alergic 141, 143
**almond** migdală f 55
**alphabet** alfabet nt 9
**also** de asemenea 15
**alter, to** *(garment)* a modifica 114
**altitude sickness** rău de altitudine 107
**amazing** uluitor 84
**amber** chihlimbar nt 122
**ambulance** salvare f 79
**American** american 93, 105, 126
**American plan** pensiune completă nt 24
**amethyst** ametist nt 122
**amount** suma f 62
**amplifier** amplificator nt 118
**anaesthetic** anestetic nt 144
**analgesic** calmant nt 107
**and** şi 15
**animal** animal nt 85
**aniseed** anason nt 54
**ankle** genunchi m 139
**anorak** hanorac nt 115
**another** altul 123
**answer** răspuns 136
**antibiotic** antibiotic nt 143
**antidepressant** antidepresant 143
**antique shop** magazin de antichităţi nt 98
**antiques** antichităţi fpl 83
**antiseptic cream** cremă antiseptică f 107
**any** nici un 13
**anyone** cineva 16
**anything** ceva 17, 24, 112; nimic 101
**anywhere** pe undera 89
**apartment** apartament nt 21
**aperitif** aperitiv nt 60
**appendicitis** apendicită 142
**appendix** apendice nt 138

DICTIONARY

Dicţionar

**appetizer** antreu *f* 41
**apple** măr *nt* 63, 119
**appliance** aparatură *nt* 118
**appointment** programare *f* 145;
întâlnire *f* 131
**apricot** caisă *f* 55
**April** aprilie 150
**archaeology** arheologie *f* 83
**architect** arhitect *m* 83
**area code** prefix *nt* 134
**arm** braţ *nt* 138, 139
**around** *(approximately)* în jur de 31
**arrangement** *(set price)* tarif *ntpl* 20
**arrival** sosiri *f* 16
**arrive, to** a ajunge 68, 70; a veni 68; a
sosi 130
**art** artă *f* 83
**art gallery** galerie de artă *f* 81, 98
**artichoke** anghinare *f* 51
**article** obiect *nt* 101
**artificial** artificial 124
**artificial light** lumină artificială *f* 124
**artist** artist *m* 83
**ashtray** scrumieră *f* 36
**Asia** Asia 146
**ask for, to** a spune 136; a comanda
61
**asparagus** sparanghel *m* 51
**aspirin** aspirină *f* 107
**asthma** astmă *f* 140
**astringent** loţiune astringentă *f* 109
**at** la 15
**at least** cel puţin 24
**at once** imediat 31
**aubergine** vînătă *f* 51
**August** august 150
**aunt** mătuşă *f* 93
**Australia** Australia 146
**Austria** Austria 146
**automatic** automat 20, 122, 124
**average** în medie 91
**awful** groaznic 84; urît 94

**B**

**baby** copil *m* 24, 110
**babysitter** îngrijitoare de copii *f* 27
**back** spate *nt* 138
**back, to be/to get** a se întoarce 21,
80, 136
**backache** durere de spate *f* 140
**backpack** rucsac *nt* 106
**bacon** şuncă *f* 40
**bacon and eggs** şuncă şi ouă 40

**bad** rău 14, 95
**bag** sac *m* 18; pungă *f* 103
**baggage** bagaj *nt* 18, 26, 31, 71
**baggage cart** cărucior de bagaje *nt*
18, 71
**baggage check** birou de bagaje *nt*
67; înregistrarea bagajelor *f* 71
**baggage locker** cabină de bagaje *f*
18; birou de bagaje *nt* 67, 71
**baked** copt 44, 47
**baker's** brutărie *f* 98
**balance** *(finance)* balanţă *f* 131
**balcony** balcon *nt* 23
**ball-point pen** pix cu pastă *nt* 104
**ball** *(inflated)* minge *nt* 128
**ballet** balet *nt* 87
**banana** banană *f* 55, 63
**Band-Aid**® pansamente *nt* 108
**bandage** bandaj *nt* 108
**bangle** brăţară *f* 121
**bangs** breton *nt* 30
**bank** *(finance)* bancă *f* 98, 129
**banknote** bancnote *f* 130
**bar** *(room)* bar *nt* 33
**barber's** frizer *m* 30, 98
**basil** busuioc *nt* 54
**basketball** baschet *nt* 89
**bath** baie *f* 23, 25, 27
**bath salts** săruri de baie *fpl* 109
**bath towel** prosop de baie *nt* 27
**bathing cap** cască de înot *f* 115
**bathing hut** cabină de schimb *f* 90
**bathing suit** costum de baie *nt* 115
**bathrobe** halat de baie *nt* 115
**bathroom** baie *f* 27
**battery** baterie *f* 75, 78, 121, 125
**be, to** a fi 162
**beach** plajă *f* 90
**beach ball** minge de plajă *f* 128
**bean** fasole *f* 51
**beard** barbă *f* 31
**beautiful** frumos 14, 84
**beauty salon** salon de cosmetică *nt*
30, 98
**bed** pat *nt* 24, 28, 142, 144
**bed and breakfast** cazare şi micul
dejun 24
**bedpan** oală de noapte *f* 144
**beef** vacă *f* 45
**beer** bere *f* 63
**beet(root)** sfeclă roşie *f* 51
**before** *(time)* înainte 15
**beginner** începător *m* 91
**beginning** început *nt* 150
**behind** înapoi 15; in spate 77

**beige** bej 112
**Belgium** Belgia 146
**bell** *(electric)* sonerie *f* 144
**Belorus** Bielorusia 146
**below** dedesubt 15
**belt** curea *f* 116
**bend** *(road)* curbă *f* 79
**berth** cuşetă de dormit *f* 69, 70
**better** mai bine 14, 25, 101
**between** între 15
**bicycle** bicicletă *f* 74
**big** mare 14, 101
**bilberry** afină *f* 55
**bill** notă de plată *f* 28, 31, 62, 102; *(banknote)* bancnotă *f* 130
**billion** *(Am.)* bilion 148
**binoculars** binoclu *nt* 123
**bird** pasăre *f* 85
**birth** naştere 25
**birthday** zi de naştere 151
**biscuit** *(Br.)* biscuit *nt* 63
**bitter** amar 62
**black** negru 112
**black and white** *(film)* alb-negru 124, 125
**black coffee** cafea neagră *(turcească)* *f* 40
**blackberry** mură *f* 55
**blackcurrant** coacăz negru *nt* 55
**bladder** vezică urinară *f* 138
**blade** lamă *f* 110
**blanket** pătură *f* 27
**bleach** decolorant *nt* 30
**bleed, to** a sîngera 139, 145
**blind** *(window shade)* jaluzea *f* 29
**blister** băşică *f* 139
**blocked** înfundat 28
**blood** singe *nt* 142
**blood pressure** tensiune arterială *f* 141; puls *nt* 142
**blood transfusion** transfuzie de sînge *f* 144
**blouse** bluză *f* 115
**blow-dry** un pieptănat *nt* 30
**blue** albastru 112
**blueberry** afină *f* 55
**blusher** ruj de obraz *nt* 109
**boat** barcă *f* 73, 74
**bobby pin** agrafă *f* 110
**body** corp *nt* 138
**boil** furuncul *m* 139
**boiled** fiert 40
**boiled egg** ou fiert *nt* 40
**bone** os *nt* 138
**book** carte *f* 12, 104

**booking office** agenţie de voiaj *f* 19, 67
**booklet** *(of tickets)* carnet de bilete *nt* 72
**bookshop** librărie *f* 98, 104
**boot** cizmă *f* 117
**born** născut 150
**botanical gardens** grădină botanică *f* 81
**botany** botanică 83
**bottle** sticlă *f* 17, 59
**bottle-opener** deschizător de sticle *nt* 120
**bottom** jos *nt* 145
**bow tie** papion *nt* 115
**bowel** intestin *nt* 138
**box** cutie *f* 120
**boxing** box *nt* 89
**boy** băiat *m* 111, 128
**boyfriend** prieten *m* 93
**bra** sutien *nt* 115
**bracelet** brăţară *f* 121
**braces** *(suspenders)* bretele *f* 115
**braised** fiert înăbuşit 46
**brake** frînă *f* 78
**brake fluid** lichid de frînă *nt* 75
**brandy** ţuică *f* 60
**bread** pîine *f* 36, 40, 64
**break, to** a sparge 123; a rupe 145
**break down, to** a avea de pană de motor 78
**breakdown** pană *f* 78
**breakdown van** maşină de depanare *f* 78
**breakfast** micul dejun *nt* 24, 27, 34, 38
**breast** sîn *m* 138
**breathe, to** a respira 141, 142
**bridge** pod *nt* 85
**bring down, to** a aduce 31
**bring, to** a aduce 13, 59
**British** britanic 93
**broken** defect 118; spart, rupt 123
**brooch** broşă *f* 121
**brother** frate *m* 93
**brown** maro 112
**bruise** vînătaie *f* 139
**Brussels sprouts** varză de Bruxelles *f* 52
**bubble bath** spumă de baie *f* 109
**bucket** găleată *f* 128
**buckle** cataramă *f* 116
**build, to** a construi 83
**building** clădire *f* 81, 83
**building blocks/bricks** cuburi *ntpl*

128
**bulb** *(light)* bec *nt* 28
**Bulgaria** Bulgaria 146
**bump** *(lump)* umflătură *f* 139
**burn** arsură *f* 139
**burn out, to** *(bulb)* a se arde 28
**bus** autobuz *nt* 18, 19, 65, 72, 80
**bus stop** stație de autobuz *f* 73
**business** afaceri *fpl* 131
**business class** clasa business 65
**business district** zona băncilor *f* 81
**business trip** scop de serviciu *nt* 94
**busy** ocupat 96
**but** dar 15
**butane gas** butan 32, 106
**butcher's** măcelărie *f* 98
**butter** unt *nt* 36, 40, 64
**button** nasture *m* 29, 117
**buy, to** a cumpăra 82, 100, 104, 123

**C**
**cabana** cabană *f* 90
**cabbage** varză *f* 49
**cabin** *(ship)* cabină *f* 74
**cable** legătură *f* 133
**cable car** teleferic *nt* 74
**cable release** declanșator *nt* 125
**café** cafe *f* 33
**cake** prăjitură *f* 37
**calculator** calculator *nt* 105
**calendar** calendar *nt* 104
**call** *(phone)* apel telefonic *nt* 135, 136
**call, to** *(give name)* a se zice 11;
  *(phone)* a telefona 134, 136
**call, to** *(summon)* a da 78; a chema
  156
**call back, to** a suna înapoi 136
**calm** liniștit 90
**cambric** batist 113
**camel-hair** păr de cămilă *nt* 113
**camera** aparat de filmat *nt* 124;
  aparat de fotografiat 125
**camera case** port-aparat *nt* 125
**camera shop** magazin de aparate
  foto *nt* 98
**camp site** teren de camping *nt* 32
**camp, to** a merge la camping 32
**campbed** pat de camping *nt* 106
**camping** camping *nt* 32
**camping equipment** echipament de
  camping *nt* 106
**can opener** deschizător de conserve
  *nt* 120
**can** *(be able to)* pot să 12

**can** *(container)* cutie de conservă *f*
  120
**Canada** Canada 146
**Canadian** canadian *m* 93
**cancel, to** a anula 65
**candle** lumânare *f* 120
**candy** dropsuri *ntpl* 126
**cap** șapcă *f* 116
**capers** capere *fpl* 54
**capital** *(finance)* capital *nt* 131
**car** mașină *f* 19, 20, 32, 78
**car hire** auto închiriere 20
**car mechanic** mecanic auto *m* 78
**car park** parcare *f* 77
**car racing** raliu *nt* 89
**car radio** radio de mașină *nt* 118
**car rental** agenție de închiriat mașini
  *f* 20
**carafe** carafă *f* 59
**carat** carat *nt* 121
**caraway** chimen *m* 54
**carbon paper** hîrtie indigou *nt* 104
**carbonated** *(fizzy)* gazos 60
**carburettor** carburator *nt* 78
**card** carte de joc *f* 93; carte de visita *f*
  131
**card game** joc de cărti *nt* 128
**cardigan** jachetă *f* 116
**carp** crap *m* 44
**carpet** carpetă *f* 127
**carrot** morcov *m* 52
**cart** cărucior *nt* 18
**carton** *(of cigarettes)* cartuș *nt* 17;
  pachet *nt* 126
**cartridge** *(camera)* încărcător de film
  *nt* 124
**case** port(-aparat) 123, 125
**cash desk** casa *f* 103, 155
**cash, to** a încasa 130, 133
**cassette** casetă *f* 118, 127
**cassette recorder** casetofon *nt* 118
**castle** castel *nt* 81
**catalogue** catalog *nt* 82
**cathedral** catedrală *f* 81
**Catholic** catolic 84
**cauliflower** conopidă *f* 52
**caution** atenție 155
**cave** peșteră *f* 81
**celery** țelină *f* 52
**cemetery** cimitir *nt* 81
**centimetre** centimetru *m* 111
**centre** centru *nt* 19, 21, 81
**century** secol *nt* 149
**ceramics** ceramică *f* 83

**cereal** cereală *f* 40
**certain** sigur 144
**certificate** certificat *nt* 144
**chain** *(jewellery)* lănţişor *nt* 121
**chain bracelet** brăţară de lănţişor *f* 121
**chair** scaun *nt* 106
**chamber music** muzică de cameră *f* 128
**change, to** a schimba 18, 61, 68, 73, 123, 129; banî mărunţi 130
**chapel** capelă *f* 81
**charcoal** cărbune pentru grătar *m* 106
**charge** cost 20, 32, 77, 89; tarif 24; tax *f* 136
**charge, to** a plăti 24; reţineţi 130
**charm bracelet** brăţară cu talismanuri *f* 121
**charm** *(trinket)* talisman *nt* 121
**cheap** ieftin 14, 24, 25, 101
**check** *(Am.)* cec *nt* 130, 131
**check** *(restaurant)* nota de plată *f* 62
**check, to** a verifica 75; a controla 123; *(luggage)* a înregistra 71
**check-up** *(medical)* examen medical *nt* 142
**check in, to** *(airport)* a înregistra 65
**check out, to** a pleca, a părăsi 31
**cheers!** noroc *nt* 56
**cheese** brînză 55, 64
**chemist's** farmacie *f* 98, 107
**cheque** cec *nt* 130, 131
**cherry** cireşe *f* 55
**chess** şah *nt* 94
**chess set** joc de şah *nt* 128
**chest** piept *nt* 138, 141
**chestnut** castană *f* 54
**chewing gum** gumă de mestecat *f* 126
**chewing tobacco** tutun de mestecat *nt* 126
**chicken** pui *m* 48
**chicken breast** piept de găină *m* 48
**chicory** andive *f* 52
**chiffon** şifon *nt* 113
**child** copil *m* 24, 61, 82, 93, 139, 150
**children's doctor** doctor pediatru *m* 137
**China** China 146
**chips** cartofi prăjiţi *mpl* 50, 64
**chives** arpagic *nt* 54
**chocolate** ciocolată *f* 40, 64, 126
**chocolate bar** baton de ciocolată *nt* 64

**chop** *(meat)* cotlet *nt* 46
**Christmas** Crăciun 152
**chromium** crom *nt* 122
**church** biserică *f* 81, 84
**cigar** trabuc *nt* 126
**cigarette** ţigară *f* 17, 95, 126
**cigarette case** tabacheră *f* 121, 126
**cigarette holder** port-ţigaret *nt* 126
**cigarette lighter** brichetă *f* 121, 126
**cine camera** cameră de filmat *f* 124
**cinema** cinema *nt* 86, 96
**cinnamon** scorţişoară *f* 54
**circle** *(theatre)* balcon *nt* 87
**city** oraş *nt* 81
**city centre** centrul oraşului *nt* 81
**classical** clasic 128
**clean** curat 62
**clean, to** a spăla 76
**cleansing cream** lapte demachiat *nt* 110
**cliff** stîncă *f* 85
**clip** clamă *f* 121
**cloakroom** garderoba *f* 87
**clock** ceas *nt* 121, 153
**clock-radio** radio cu ceas *nt* 118
**close, to** a închide 11, 82, 107, 132
**clothes** haine *fpl* 115
**clothes peg/pin** cîrlig de rufe *nt* 120
**clothing** îmbrăcăminte *f* 111
**cloud** nor *m* 94
**clove** cuişoare *f* 54
**coach** *(bus)* autocar *nt* 72
**coat** haină *f* 116
**coconut** nucă de cocos *f* 55
**coffee** cafea *f* 40, 64
**coins** numismatica *f* 83
**cold** rece 14, 25; frig 94, 155
**cold** *(illness)* răceală *f* 107; gripă 140
**cold cuts** salamuri *npl* 64
**collar** guler *nt* 116
**collect call** cu taxă inversă 135
**colour** culoare *f* 103, 111; color 124, 125
**colour chart** paletă de culori *nt* 30
**colour rinse** şampon colorant *nt* 30
**colour shampoo** şampon colorant *nt* 110
**colour slide** diapozitiv color *nt* 124
**colourfast** nu iese la spălat 113
**comb** pieptene *m* 110
**comedy** comedie *f* 86
**commission** *(fee)* comision *nt* 130
**common** *(frequent)* curent 154
**compact disc** compact disc *nt* 127
**compartment** *(train)* loc *nt* 70

**compass** busolă f 106
**complaint** reclamaţie f 61
**concert** concert nt 87
**concert hall** sală de concerte f 81, 88
**condom** preservativ nt 108
**conductor** (orchestra) dirijor m 88
**conference room** sală de conferinţă f 23
**confirm, to** a confirma 65
**confirmation** confirmare f 23
**congratulation** felicitări fpl 152
**connection** (transport) legătura de tren f 65, 68
**constipation** constipaţie f 140
**consulate** consulat nt 156
**contact lens** lentile de contact f 123
**contagious** contagios 142
**contain, to** a conţine 37
**contraceptives** anticoncepţionale ntpl 108
**contract** contract nt 131
**control** control nt 16
**convent** mînăstire f 81
**cookie** fursec n 64
**cool box** geantă frigorifică f 106
**copper** cupru nt 122
**coral** coral m 122
**corduroy** velur nt 113
**corkscrew** tirbuşon nt 120
**corn plaster** leucoplast de bătătură f 108
**corn** (sweet) porumb nt 52
**corn** (foot) bătătură f 108
**corner** colţ nt 21, 36, 77
**cost** preţ nt 131; cost nt 136
**cost, to** a costa 11, 80, 133
**cot** patuţ nt 24
**cotton** bumbac nt 113
**cotton wool** vată f 108
**cough** tuse f 108, 141
**cough drops** picături de tuse fpl 108
**cough, to** a tuşi 142
**counter** ghişeu nt 133
**country** ţară f 93
**countryside** la ţară 85
**courgette** dovlecel m 52
**court house** tribunal nt 81
**cousin** văr m 93
**crab** crab m 44
**cramp** cîrcel m 141
**crayfish** (river) rac m 44
**crayon** creion nt 104
**cream** frişcă f 61
**cream** (toiletry) cremă f 109
**crease resistant** nu se şifonează 113

**credit** credit nt 130
**credit card** carte de credit f 20, 31, 63, 102, 130
**crepe** crep 113
**crisps** cartofi cipşi mpl 64
**crockery** veselă f 120
**cross** cruce f 121
**crossing** (maritime) traversare f 74
**crossroads** intersecţie f 77
**cruise** croazieră f 74
**crystal** cristal nt 122
**cucumber** castravete m 51
**cuff link** buton de manşetă nt 121
**cuisine** mîncăruri f 34
**cup** ceaşcă f 36
**curler** bigudiu nt 110
**currants** stafide f 55
**currency** schimb nt 129
**currency exchange office** birou de schimb valutar 18, 67; birou de schimb prin apropriere 129
**current** curent de apă nt 90
**curtain** perdea f 28
**curve** (road) curbă f 79
**customs** vamă f 17, 102
**cut** (wound) tăietură f 139
**cut, to** (with scissors) a tunde 30
**cut off, to** (interrupt) a întrerupe 135
**cut glass** sticlă şlefuită 122
**cuticle remover** substanţă de înlăturat cuticula f 109
**cutlery** tacîmuri ntpl 120
**cutlet** cotlet nt 46
**cycling** ciclism nt 89
**cystitis** cistită f 142
**Czech Republic** Republica Cehă 146

**D**
**dairy** magazin de brînzeturi şi lapte nt 98
**dance** dans nt 88, 96
**dance, to** a dansa 88, 96
**danger** pericol nt 155, 156
**dangerous** periculos 90
**dark** întuneric 25; închis 101, 111, 112
**date** (appointment) întîlnire f 95
**date** (day) dată f 25
**date** (fruit) curmale f 55
**daughter** fată f 93
**day** zi f 20, 24, 32, 80, 94, 150, 151
**day off** zi liberă f 151
**daylight** lumină de zi f 124
**decade** deceniu nt 149

**DICTIONARY**

**decaffeinated** decafeinat 40
**December** decembrie 150
**decision** decizie f 25, 102
**deck chair** şezlong nt 90, 106
**deck** (ship) punte f 74
**declare, to** (customs) a declara 17
**deep** adînc 142
**degree** (temperature) grad nt 140
**delay** întîrziere f 69
**delicatessen** magazin de delicatese nt 98
**deliver, to** a livra 102
**delivery** livrare f 102
**denim** doc nt 113
**Denmark** Danemarca 146
**dentist** dentist m 145
**denture** proteză f 145
**deodorant** deodorant nt 109
**department store** magazin universal nt 98
**department** (museum) departament nt 83; (shop) raion nt 100
**departure** plecări f 65
**deposit** (down payment) depunere f 130; avans nt 20
**dessert** desert nt 56
**detour** (traffic) diverune f 79
**develop, to** a developa 125
**diabetic** diabetic 37, 141
**dialling code** prefix telefonic nt 134
**diamond** diamant nt 122
**diaper** scutec de unică folosinţă nt 110
**diarrhoea** diaree f 140
**dictionary** dicţionar nt 104
**diesel** motorină f 75
**diet** regim alimentar n 37
**difficult** greu 14
**difficulty** dificultate 28, 102
**digital** ceas digital nt 122
**dill** mărar nt 54
**dine, to** a lua masa 95
**dining car** vagon restaurant nt 68, 71
**dining room** sufragerie f 27; sala de mese f 27
**dinner** cina f 34; masa de seară f 95
**direct** direct 65
**direct, to** a îndruma 12
**direction** directie 76
**director** (theatre) regizor m 86
**directory** (phone) anuar nt 134
**disabled** persoane invalide m 82
**disc** disc nt 127
**discotheque** discotecă 88, 96
**discount** reducere 131

**disease** boală f 142
**dish** mîncare f 36
**dishwashing detergent** detergent de vase nt 120
**disinfectant** desinfectant nt 108
**dislocated** dislocat 140
**dissatisfied** nemulţumit 103
**disturb, to** a deranja 155
**diversion** (traffic) diversiune f 79
**dizzy** ameţit 140
**do, to** a face 161
**doctor** doctor m 79, 137, 144, 145
**doctor's office** cabinet medical nt 137
**dog** cîine m 155
**doll** păpuşă f 128
**dollar** dolar m 19, 102, 129
**double bed** pat dublu nt 23
**double room** cameră de două persoane f 19, 23
**down** jos 15
**downtown** centru nt 81
**dozen** duzină f 149
**drawing paper** hîrtie de desenat f 104
**drawing pins** pioneze f 104
**dress** rochie f 115
**dressing gown** capot nt 115
**drink** băutură f 59, 60, 95
**drink, to** a bea 35, 36, 37
**drinking water** apă potabilă f 32
**drip, to** a curge 28
**drive, to** a conduce 21, 76
**driving licence** carnet de conducere nt 20, 79
**drop** (liquid) picătură f 108
**drugstore** farmacie f 98, 107
**dry** uscat 30, 110; sec 59
**dry cleaner's** curăţătorie f 29, 98
**dry shampoo** şampon nt 110
**duck** raţă f 48
**dummy** (baby's) suzetă f 110
**during** în timp ce 15, 150, 151
**duty** (customs) vamă f 17
**duty-free shop** magazin pentru duty-free nt 19
**dye** vopsea f 30, 110

**E**
**each** fiecare 149
**ear** ureche f 138
**earache** durere de urechi f 141
**early** devreme 14
**earring** cercel m 121

**Dicţionar**

east Est 77
Easter Paște 152
easy ușor 14
eat, to a mînca 36, 37, 144
eel țipar m 44
egg ou nt 40, 64
eggplant vînătă f 51
eight opt 147
eighteen optsprezece 147
eighth al optulea 149
eighty optzeci 148
elastic bandage bandaj elasticat nt 108
electrical appliance aparatură electrică f 118
electrical goods shop magazin de aparate electrice 98
electricity electricitate f 32
electric(al) electric(e) 118
electronic electronic 128
elevator lift nt 27, 100
eleven unsprezece 147
embarkation point punct de îmbarcare 74
embassy ambasadă f 156
embroidered brodat 127
embroidery broderie f 127
emerald smarald nt 122
emergency urgență 156
emergency exit ieșire de incendiu f 27, 100
emery board pilă f 109
empty gol 14
enamel email nt 122
end sfîrșit 150
engaged (phone) ocupat 136
engagement ring inel de logodnă nt 122
engine (car) motor nt 78
England Anglia 134, 146
English englez 16, 93; englezesc 80, 82, 84, 104
enjoy oneself, to a se distra 96
enjoyable minunat 31
enlarge, to a mări 125
enough destul 14, 68
entrance intrare f 67, 100, 155
entrance fee intrare f 82
envelope plic nt 104
equipment echipament nt 91, 106
eraser gumă f 104
escalator escalatorul nt 100
estimate (cost) estimativ nt 78, 131
Eurocheque Eurocec 130
Europe Europa 146

evening seară f 95, 96
evening dress toaletă de seară f 88; (woman's) rochie de seară f 115
evening, in the seara 151, 153
everything tot, toate 31, 63
exchange, to a schimba 103
exchange rate cursul 130
excursion excursie f 80
excuse me pardon 11
exercise book caiet nt 104
exhaust pipe țeavă de eșapament f 78
exhibition expoziție f 81
exit ieșire f 67, 100, 155
expect, to a aștepta 130
expenses cheltuieli 131
expensive scump 14, 19, 24, 101
exposure (photography) expunere 124
exposure counter dispozitiv de numărătoare nt 125
express expres 133
expression expresie f 10, 100
expressway autostradă f 76
extension (phone) interior nt 135
extension cord/lead prelungitor nt 118
extra în plus 27
eye ochi m 138, 139
eye drops picături de ochi f 108
eye shadow fard de pleope nt 109
eye specialist doctor oculist m 137
eyebrow pencil creion de sprîncene nt 109
eyesight vedere f 123

F
fabric (cloth) pînzeturi f 112
face față f 138
face pack mască f 30
face powder pudră de obraz f 109
factory uzina f 81
fair tîrg nt 81
fall (autumn) toamnă f 149
fall, to a cădea 139
family familie f 93, 144
fan belt curea de ventilator f 76
far departe 14, 100
fare (ticket) costul (biletului) 68, 73
farm fermă f 85
fast rapid 124
fat (meat) gras 37
father tată m 93
faucet robinet nt 28

**fax** fax *nt* 133
**February** februarie 150
**fee** *(doctor's)* plată *f* 144
**feeding bottle** biberon *nt* 110
**feel, to** *(physical state)* a simți 140, 142
**felt** fetru *nt* 113
**felt-tip pen** carioca *nt* 104
**ferry** bac *nt* 74
**fever** febră *f* 140
**few** puțini 14; *(a few)* cîțiva 14
**field** cîmp *nt* 85
**fifteen** cinisprezece 147
**fifth** al cincilea 149
**fifty** cincizeci 147
**fig** smochină *f* 55
**file** *(tool)* pilă *f* 109
**fill in, to** a completa 26, 144
**filling** *(tooth)* plombă *f* 145
**filling station** PECO *f* 75
**film** film *nt* 86, 124, 125
**film winder** maneta de rulat a filmului *nt* 125
**filter** filtru *nt* 125
**filter-tipped** cu filtru 126
**find, to** a găsi 11, 12, 84, 100
**fine** *(OK)* bine 25, 92
**fine arts** artele frumoase 83
**finger** deget *nt* 138
**Finland** Finlanda 146
**fire** foc *nt* 156
**first** primul 68, 73, 77, 149
**first-aid kit** trusă de prim ajutor *f* 108
**first class** clasa întîia 69
**first name** prenumele *nt* 25
**fish** pește *m* 44
**fishing** a pescui 90
**fishing tackle** unelte de pescuit *ntpl* 106
**fishmonger's** pescărie *f* 98
**fit, to** a proba 114
**fitting room** cabin de probă *f* 114
**five** cinci 147
**fix, to** a trata 145
**fizzy (mineral water)** (apă minerală) gazoasă *f* 60
**flannel** flanelă *f* 113
**flash** *(photography)* blitz *nt* 125
**flash attachment** legătur de blitz *ntpl* 125
**flashlight** lanterna *f* 106
**flat** *(apartment)* apartament *nt* 23
**flat** *(shoe)* plați 117
**flat tyre** roată dezumflată 78
**flea market** talcioc *nt* 81

**flight** zbor *nt* 65
**floor** palier *nt* 27
**floor show** spectacol în mijlocul publicului *nt* 88
**florist's** florărie *f* 98
**flour** făină *f* 37
**flower** floare *f* 85
**flu** gripă *f* 142
**fluid** lichid *nt* 75, 123
**foam rubber mattress** saltea de burete de cauciuc *f* 106
**fog** ceață *f* 94
**folding chair** scaun pliant *nt* 106
**folding table** masă pliantă *f* 106
**folk music** muzică populară *f* 128
**follow, to** a urma 77
**food** mîncare *f* 37
**food poisoning** intoxicație alimentară *f* 142
**foot** picior *nt* 138
**foot cream** cremă de picioare *f* 109
**football** fotbal 89
**footpath** potecă *f* 85
**for** pentru 15
**forbidden** interzis 155
**forecast** prevedere 94
**forest** pădure *f* 85
**forget, to** a uita 62
**fork** furculiță *f* 36, 61, 120
**form** *(document)* formular *nt* 25, 26, 133, 144
**fortnight** două săptămîni 151
**fortress** cetate *f* 81
**forty** patruzeci 147
**foundation** *cosmetic* fond de ten *nt* 109
**fountain** fîntînă *f* 81
**fountain pen** stilou cu cerneală *nt* 105
**four** patru 147
**fourteen** paisprezece 147
**fourth** al patrulea 149
**fowl** pasăre *f* 48
**frame** *(glasses)* ramă *f* 123
**France** Franța 146
**free** liber 14, 70, 80, 96; gratuit 82, 155
**French bean** fasole fidreluța *f* 52
**Friday** vineri 151
**fried** prăjit 46
**fried egg** ou prăjit 40
**friend** prieten *m* 93, 95
**fringe** breton *nt* 30
**from** de la 15
**frost** ger *nt* 94

**fruit** fruct *nt* 55
**fruit cocktail** cocteil de fructe *n* 55
**fruit juice** suc de fructe *nt* 60
**fruit salad** salată de fructe *f* 56
**frying pan** tigaie *f* 120
**full** plin 14
**full board** pensiune completă 24
**full insurance** asigurare totală *f* 20
**furniture** mobilă stil *f* 83
**furrier's** blănărie *f* 98

## G

**gabardine** gabardină *f* 113
**gallery** galerie de artă *f* 81, 98
**game** joc *nt* 128
**game** *(food)* vânat 48
**garage** garaj *nt* 26; servis *nt* 78
**garden** grădină *f* 85
**gardens** grădin *nt* 81
**garlic** usturoi *m* 54
**gas** gaz *nt* 156
**gasoline** benzină *f* 75, 78
**gastritis** gastrită *f* 142
**gauze** tifon *nt* 108
**gem** piatră prețioasă *f* 121
**general** uzuale 100; general 137
**general delivery** post restant 133
**general practitioner** doctor de medicină generală *m* 137
**genitals** organe genitale *ntpl* 138
**gentlemen** bărbați *mpl* 155
**geology** geologie *f* 83
**Germany** Germania 146
**get, to** *(find)* alua 19, 21
**get off, to** a coborî 73
**get past, to** a face loc 70
**get to, to** a ajunge 19; a lua 19
**get up, to** a se da jos din pat 144
**gherkin** castravete murat *m* 54, 64
**gift** cadou *nt* 17
**gin** gin *nt* 60
**gin and tonic** gin cu apă tonică 60
**ginger** ghimber *m* 54
**girdle** centură *f* 115
**girl** fată *f* 111, 128
**girlfriend** prietenă *f* 93
**give, to** a da 13, 63, 123, 126, 130, 135; a pune 75
**give way, to** *(traffic)* a ceda (trecerea) 79
**gland** glandă *f* 138
**glass** pahar *nt* 36, 59, 61, 143
**glasses** ochelari *fpl* 123
**gloomy** sumbru 84

**glove** mănuşă *f* 115
**glue** lipici *nt* 105
**go, to** a merge 21, 72, 77
**go away!** pleacă de aici 156
**go back, to** a se întoarce 77
**go out, to** a ieşi 96
**gold** aur *nt* 121, 122
**gold plated** aurit 122
**golden** auriu 112
**golf** golf *nt* 89
**golf course** teren de golf *nt* 89
**good** bun 14, 86, 101
**good afternoon** bună ziua 10
**good-bye** la revedere 10
**good evening** bună seara 10
**good morning** bună dimineaţa 10
**good night** noapte bună 10
**goose** gâscă *f* 48
**gooseberry** agrişă *f* 55
**gram(me)** gram *nt* 119
**grammar** gramatică *f* 159
**grammar book** carte de gramatică *f* 105
**grape** struguri *mpl* 55, 64
**grapefruit** grepfrut *nt* 55
**grapefruit juice** suc de grepfrut *nt* 40, 60
**gray** gri 112
**graze** julitură *f* 139
**greasy** *(păr)* gras 30, 110
**Great Britain** Marea Britanie 146
**Greece** Grecia 146
**green** verde 112
**green bean** fasole verde *f* 51
**greengrocer's** aprozar *nt* 98
**greeting** salut *f* 10, 152
**grey** gri 112
**grilled** grătar *nt* 44, 47
**grocery (grocer's)** băcănie *nt* 99, 119
**groundsheet** folie de muşama *f* 106
**group** grup *nt* 82
**guesthouse** hotel pensiune *f* 19
**guide** ghid *nt* 80
**guidebook** ghid *nt* 82, 104, 105
**guinea fowl** bibilică *f* 48
**gum** *(teeth)* gingie *f* 145
**gynaecologist** ginecolog *m* 137

## H

**hair** păr *nt* 30, 110
**hair dryer** uscător de păr *nt* 118
**hair gel** gel de păr *nt* 30, 110
**hair lotion** loţiune de păr *f* 110
**hair spray** fixativ de păr *nt* 31, 110

**hairbrush** perie de păr f 110
**haircut** o tunsoare f 30
**hairdresser** coafor nt 30, 99
**hairgrip** clam f 110
**hairpin** ac de păr nt 110
**half** jumătate 149
**half an hour** jumătate de oră f 153
**half board** demipensiune 24
**half price** jumătate de preț f 69
**hall porter** valet m 26
**ham** șuncă f 40, 63
**ham and eggs** șuncă și ouă 40
**hammer** ciocan nt 120
**hammock** hamac nt 106
**hand** mînă f 138
**hand cream** cremă de mîini f 109
**hand washable** de spălat de mînă 112
**handbag** geantă f 115, 156; poșeta f 156
**handicrafts** artizanat nt 127
**handkerchief** batistă f 115
**handmade** făcut de mînă 112
**hanger** umeraș nt 27
**happy** fericit 152
**harbour** port nt 74, 81
**hard** dur 123
**hard-boiled (egg)** (ou) tare 40
**hardware store** magazin de obiecte fieroase nt 99
**hare** iepure m 48
**hat** pălărie f 115
**have, to** a avea 162
**have to, to** (must) a trebui, a fi necesar 17, 68, 69, 77, 140
**hay fever** alergie la polen f 107, 141
**hazelnut** alune de pădure f 55
**he** el 160
**head** cap nt 138, 139
**head waiter** ospătar șef m 62
**headache** durere de cap f 141
**headphones** căști fpl 118
**health food shop** magazin dietetic nt 99
**health insurance form** formular de asigurare 144
**heart** inimă f 138
**heart attack** atac de cord nt 141
**heat, to** a încălzi 90
**heavy** greu 14, 101; puternic 139
**heel** toc nt 117
**height** înălțime f 85
**helicopter** helicopter nt 74
**hello** bună 10; (telephone) alo 135
**help!** ajutor 156

**help, to** a ajuta 12, 21, 71, 100, 134
**her** a ei 161
**herb tea** ceai de plante medicinale nt 60
**herbs** mirodenii fpl 54
**here** aici 14
**hi** bună 10
**high** înălțime 85; mare 141
**high season** în sezon 150
**hill** deal nt 85
**hire** închiriere 20, 74
**hire, to** a închiria 19, 20, 74, 90, 91, 155
**his** a lui 161
**history** istorie f 83
**hitchhike, to** a face autostop 74
**hold on!** (phone) așteptați 136
**hole** gaură f 30
**holiday** vacanță f 151, 152
**holidays** vacanță 16, 151; concediu nt 151
**home** casă nt 96
**home address** adresa de acasă f 31
**home town** orașul nt 25
**honey** miere f 41
**hope, to** a spera 96
**horse racing** curse de cai f 89
**horseback riding** călărie 89
**hospital** spital nt 99, 142, 144
**hot water** apă caldă f 28
**hot-water bottle** buiotă cu apă fierbinte f 27
**hot** cald 25, 94; (boiling) fierbinte 14
**hotel** hotel nt 19, 21, 22, 26, 80, 96, 102
**hotel directory/guide** ghid nt 19
**hotel reservation** rezervare la hotel f 19
**hour** oră f 80, 143, 153
**house** casă f 83, 85
**household article** articol de uz nt 120
**how far** cît de departe 11, 76, 85
**how long** cît timp 11, 24
**how many** cîți 11
**how much** cît 11, 24
**hundred** o sută 148
**hungry** foame f 13, 35
**hunting** vînătoare f 90
**hurry, to be in a** a se grăbi 21
**hurt** (to be) a durea 139
**hurt, to** a durea 140, 142, 145
**husband** soț m 93
**hydrofoil** nava cu aripi portante f 74

**I**

**I** eu 160
**ice** gheață f 94
**ice cream** înghețată 56
**ice cube** cuburi de gheață ntpl 27
**ice pack** pungă cu cuburi de gheață f 106
**iced tea** ceai rece nt 61
**icon** icoană 127
**if** dacă 143
**ill** bolnav 140
**illness** boală f 140
**important** important 13
**imported** importat 112
**impressive** impresionant 84
**in** în 15
**include, to** a include 24, 31, 32, 80
**included** inclus 20, 31, 32, 61, 80
**India** India 146
**indigestion** indigestie f 141
**inexpensive** nu prea scump 35, 124
**infected** infectat 140
**infection** infecție 141
**inflammation** inflamație 142
**inflation** inflație f 131
**inflation rate** rată inflației f 131
**influenza** gripă f 142
**information** informație f 67, 155
**injection** injecție f 142,143, 144
**injure, to** a (se) răni 139
**injured** rănit 79, 139
**injury** rană f 139
**ink** cerneală f 105
**inquiry** informație f 68
**insect bite** înțepătură de insectă f 107, 139
**insect repellent** spray contra insectelor nt 108
**insect spray** insecticid nt 106
**inside** înăuntru 15
**instrument (musical)** instrument muzical nt 127
**insurance** asigurare f 20, 144
**insurance company** companie de asigurări f 79
**interest (finance)** dobîndă f 131
**interested, to be** a fi interesat 83, 96
**interesting** interesant 84
**international** internațional 133, 134
**interpreter** translator m 131
**intersection** intersecție f 77
**introduce, to** a prezenta 92
**introduction (social)** prezentare f 92
**investment** investiție f 131
**invitation** invitație f 95

**invite, to** a invita 95
**invoice** factură f 131
**iodine** iod nt 108
**Ireland** Irlanda 146
**Irish** irlandez 93
**iron (for laundry)** fier de călcat nt 118
**iron, to** a călca 29
**ironmonger's** fierărie f 99
**it** acest 160
**Italy** Italia 146
**its** al său, a sa, ai săi, ale sale 161
**ivory** fildeș nt 122

**J**

**jacket** jachetă f 115
**jade** jad nt 122
**jam (preserves)** gem nt 40
**jam, to** a se bloca 28, 125
**January** ianuarie 150
**Japan** Japonia 146
**jar (container)** borcan nt 119
**jaundice** icter nt 142
**jaw** maxilar nt 138
**jazz** jazz nt 128
**jeans** blugi mpl 115
**jersey** jerseu nt 115
**jewel box** cutie de bijuterii f 121
**jeweller's** magazin de bijuterii nt 99; bijuterie f 121
**joint** încheietură f 138
**journey** călătorie f 72
**juice** suc nt 37, 60
**July** iulie 150
**jumper** pulover nt 115
**June** iunie 150
**just (only)** doar 16, 100

**K**

**keep, to** a ține 63
**kerosene** gaz nt 106
**key** cheie f 26
**kidney** rinichi m 138
**kilo(gram)** kilogram nt 119
**kilometre** kilometru m 20
**kind** amabil 95
**kind (type)** fel nt 85
**knee** genunchi m 138
**kneesocks** șosete lungi fpl 116
**knife** cuțit nt 36, 61, 120
**knock, to** a ciocăni 155
**know, to** a ști 16, 96

**L**

**label** etichetă f 105
**lace** dantelă f 113
**ladies** femei fpl 155
**lake** lac nt 81, 85, 90
**lamb** *(meat)* miel m 45
**lamp** lampă f 29, 106
**landscape** peisaj nt 93
**language** limbă f 104
**lantern** felinar nt 106
**large** mare 20, 101, 130
**last** ultimul 14, 68, 73; trecut 149
**last name** numele de familie nt 25
**late** tîrziu 14, 69
**late, to be** a rămîne în urmă 153
**laugh, to** a rîde 95
**launderette** spălătorie Nufărul f 99
**laundry service** servicii de spălătorie
  ntpl 24
**laundry** *(clothes)* rufe de spălat fpl 29
**laundry** *(place)* spălătorie f 29, 99
**laxative** laxativ nt 108
**lead** *(metal)* plumb nt 75
**lead** *(theatre)* rol principal nt 86
**leap year** an bisect m 149
**leather** piele f 113, 117
**leave, to** a pleca 31, 68, 95; *(deposit)*
  a lăsa 26, 71
**leeks** praz nt 52
**left** stînga 21, 69, 77
**left-luggage office** birou de bagaje nt
  67, 71
**leg** picior nt 138
**lemon** lămîie f 37, 41, 60
**lemonade** limonadă f 60
**lens** *(camera)* obiectiv nt 125
**lens** *(glasses)* lentilă f 123
**lentils** linte f 52
**less** mai puțin 14
**lesson** lecție f 91
**let, to** *(hire out)* a închiria 155
**letter** scrisoare f 132
**letter box** cutie poștală f 133
**letter of credit** scrisoare acreditivă f
  130
**lettuce** salată verde f 52
**library** bibliotecă f 81, 99
**licence** *(driving)* carnet de conducere
  nt 20, 79
**lie down, to** a se întinde 142
**life belt** colac de salvare nt 74
**life boat** barcă de salvare f 74
**life guard** *(beach)* salvamar nt 90
**lift** *(elevator)* lift nt 27, 100
**light** ușor 14; *(colour)* deschis 101

**light** *(lamp)* lumina f 28, 124
**light** *(for cigarette)* foc 95
**light meter** celulă fotoelectrică f 125
**lighter** brichetă f 126
**lighter fluid/gas** gaz de brichetă nt
  126
**lightning** fulger nt 94
**like** ca 111
**like, to** a vrea 20, 23, 61, 96, 112;
  *(please)* a place 92, 102
**linen** *(cloth)* in nt 113
**lip** buză nt 138
**lipsalve** strugurel de buze nt 109
**lipstick** ruj de buze nt 109
**liqueur** lichior nt 60
**listen, to** a asculta 128
**litre** litru nt 75
**little** *(a little)* puțin 14
**live, to** a locui 83
**liver** ficat nt 138
**lobster** homar m 44
**local** local 69
**long** lung 114, 115, 116
**long-sighted** prezbit 123
**look, to** a se uita 100, 123, 139
**look for, to** a căuta 13
**look out!** atenție 156
**loose** *(clothes)* largi 114
**lose, to** a pierde 123, 156
**loss** pierdere f 131
**lost** rătăcit 13
**lost and found office/lost property
  office** birou de obiecte pierdute nt
  67, 156
**lot** *(a lot)* mult 14
**lotion** loțiune f 109
**loud** *(voice)* *(cu voce)* tare 135
**lovely** frumos 94
**low** mic 141
**low season** în afara sezonului 150
**lower** de jos 69
**luck** noroc nt 152
**luggage** bagaj nt 17, 18, 21, 26, 31, 71
**luggage locker** cabină de bagaje f 18;
  birou de bagaje 67, 71
**luggage trolley** cărucior de bagaje nt
  18, 71
**lump** *(bump)* umflătură f 139
**lunch** dejun nt 34; masa f 80, 95
**lung** plămîn nt 138

**M**

**machine (washable)** (care se spală
  la) mașină 113

**mackerel** macrou *n* 44
**magazine** revistă *f* 105
**magnificent** magnific 84
**maid** cameristă *f* 26
**mail** poşta *f* 28, 133
**mail, to** a pune la poştă 28
**mailbox** cutia de scrisori *f* 133
**main** important 80; principal 100
**make, to** a face 131, 161
**make up, to** *(prepare)* a face 28, 71
**make-up** machiaj *nt* 109
**make-up remover pad** tampon pentru demachiant *f* 109
**mallet** ciocan *nt* 106
**man** bărbat *m* 114, 155; om *m* 156
**manager** director *m* 26
**manicure** manichiură *f* 30
**many** mulţi 14
**map** hartă *f* 76, 105
**March** martie 150
**marinated** marinată 44
**marjoram** măghiran *nt* 54
**market** piaţă *f* 81, 99
**marmalade** marmeladă *f* 40
**married** căsătorit 93
**mass** *(church)* slujbă *f* 84
**matt** *(finish)* mat 125
**match** *(matchstick)* chibrit *nt* 106, 126
**match** *(sport)* meci *m* 89
**match, to** *(colour)* a potrivi 111
**material** *(cloth)* material *nt* 113
**matinée** matineu *nt* 87
**mattress** saltea *f* 106
**May** mai 150
**may** *(can)* a permite 12
**meadow** pajişte *f* 85
**meal** masă *f* 24, 34, 143
**mean, to** a însemna 11, 25
**means** mijloace 74
**measles** pojar *nt* 142
**measure, to** a măsura 112
**meat** carne *f* 37, 45, 47, 62
**meatball** chiftele *f* 46
**mechanic** mecanic *m* 78
**mechanical pencil** creon mecanic *nt* 105, 121
**medical certificate** certificat medical *nt* 144
**medicine** medicină *f* 83; *(drug)* medicament *nt* 143
**medium-sized** de capacitate medie 20
**medium** *(meat)* bine făcut potrivit 46
**meet, to** a întîlni 96

**melon** pepene gelben *m* 56
**memorial** monument comemorativ *nt* 81
**mend, to** a repara 29, 75
**menthol** *(cigarettes)* ţigări mentolate *fpl* 126
**menu** meniu *nt* 37, 39
**merry** fericit 152
**message** masaj *nt* 28, 136
**metre** metru *m* 111
**mezzanine** *(theatre)* balcon *nt* 87
**middle** mijloc 69, 150
**midnight** miezul nopţii 153
**mild** *(light)* slab 126
**mileage** kilometraj *f* 20
**milk** lapte *f* 41, 60, 64
**milliard** miliard *nt* 148
**million** milion *nt* 148
**mineral water** apă minerală *f* 60
**minister** *(religion)* pastor *m* 84
**mint** mentă *f* 54
**minute** minut *f* 21, 69, 153
**mirror** oglindă *f* 114, 123
**miscellaneous** diverse 127
**Miss** domnişoară *f* 10
**miss, to** a lipsi 18, 61
**mistake** greşală *f* 31, 61, 62, 102
**moccasin** mocasini *mpl* 117
**modified American plan** demipensiune 24
**moisturizing cream** cremă hidratantă *f* 109
**moment** moment *nt* 12, 136
**monastery** mînăstire *f* 81
**Monday** luni 151
**money** bani *mpl* 18, 129, 130, 156
**money order** mandat *nt* 133
**month** lună *f* 16, 150
**monument** monument *nt* 81
**moon** lună *f* 94
**moped** motoretă *nt* 74
**more** mai mult 14
**morning, in the** dimineaţa 143, 151, 153
**mortgage** ipotecă *f* 131
**mosque** moschee 84
**mosquito net** plasă de ţînţari *f* 106
**motel** motel *nt* 22
**mother** mamă *f* 93
**motorbike** motocicletă *f* 74
**motorboat** barcă cu motor *f* 90
**motorway** autostradă *f* 76
**mountain** munte *m* 85
**mountaineering** alpinism *nt* 89
**moustache** mustaţă *f* 31

DICTIONARY

**mouth** gură f 138, 142
**mouthwash** apă de gură f 108
**move, to** a mișca 139
**movie** film m 86
**movie camera** cameră de filmat f 124
**movies** films ntpl 86, 96
**Mr.** domnul m 10
**Mrs.** doamna f 10
**much** mult 14
**mug** cană f 120
**muscle** mușchi m 138
**museum** muzeu nt 81
**mushroom** ciupercă f 52
**music** muzică f 83, 128
**musical** comedie muzicală f 86
**must** (have to) a trebui 31, 142; avea nevoie 37; a crede 61
**mustard** muștar nt 64
**my** al meu 161

**N**

**nail** (human) unghie f 109
**nail brush** periuță de unghii f 109
**nail clippers** foarfece de unghii cu arc nt 109
**nail file** pilă de unghii f 109
**nail polish** ojă de unghii f 109
**nail polish remover** acetonă f 109
**nail scissors** foarfece de unghii nt 109
**name** nume nt 23, 25, 79, 92, 131, 136
**napkin** șervețel m 36, 105
**nappy** scutec nt 110
**narrow** strîmt 117
**nationality** naționalitate f 25
**natural** natural 83
**natural history** științele naturale f 83
**nausea** greață f 140
**near** aproape 14; lîngă 15
**nearby** în apropiere 32, 77
**nearest** cel mai aproape 75, 78, 98, 104, 132
**neat** (drink) (băutură) simplă 60
**neck** gît nt 30, 138
**necklace** colier nt 121
**need, to** a avea nevoie 29, 90, 137
**needle** ac nt 27
**negative** negativ 124, 125
**nephew** nepot m 93
**nerve** nerv m 138
**Netherlands** Olanda 146
**never** niciodată 15
**new** nou 14
**New Year** Anul Nou 152

**New Zealand** Noua Zeelandă 146
**newsagent's** chioșc de ziare m 99
**newspaper** ziar nt 104, 105
**newsstand** chioșc de ziare nt 19, 67, 99, 104
**next** următorul 14, 68, 73, 76, 151; viitor 149, 151
**next to** lîngă 15, 77
**nice** (beautiful) frumos 94
**niece** nepoată f 93
**night** noapte f 10, 24, 151
**night, at** la noapte 151
**night cream** cremă de noapte f 109
**nightclub** club de noapte nt 88
**nightdress/-gown** pijama f 115
**nine** nouă 147
**nineteen** nouăsprezece 147
**ninety** nouăzeci 148
**ninth** al nouălea 149
**no** nu 10
**noisy** zgomotos 25
**nonalcoholic** nealcoolic 60
**none** niciuna 15
**nonsmoker** nefumător 36, 70
**noodle** tăiței m 50
**noon** la amiază f 31, 153
**normal** normal 30
**north** nord 77
**North America** America de Nord 146
**Norway** Norvegia 146
**nose** nas nt 138
**nose drops** picături de nas f 108
**nosebleed** a curge sînge din nas 141
**not** nu 15, 163
**note paper** hîrtie de scris f 105
**note** (banknote) bancnotă f 130
**notebook** carnet nt 105
**nothing** nimic 15, 17
**notice** (sign) anunț nt 155
**notify, to** a înștiința 144
**November** noiembrie 150
**now** acum 15
**number** număr 25, 65, 135, 136, 147
**nurse** soră (medicală) f 144
**nutmeg** nucșoară f 54

**O**

**o'clock** ora f 153
**occupation** (profession) ocupație f 25
**occupied** ocupat 14, 155
**October** octombrie 150
**office** birou nt 19, 99
**oil** ulei nt 37, 75

Dicționar

**DICTIONARY**

oily *(greasy)* gras 30, 110
old vechi, bătrîn 14
old town oraş vechi 81
olive măslin *m* 41
on pe 15
on foot pe jos 76
on request facultativă 73
on time la timp 68
once o dată 149
one unu 147
one-way *(traffic)* sens unic *nt* 79
one-way ticket un (bilet) dus 65, 69
onion ceapă *f* 52
only numai 15, 24, 108; doar 80, 87
onyx onix *nt* 122
open deschis 14, 82, 155
open, to a deschide 11, 17,
open-air în are liber 90
opera operă *f*
opera house opera *f* 81, 88
operation operaţie *f* 144
operator centrala *f* 134
opposite vis-a-vis 77
optician optician *m* 99, 123
or sau 15
orange *(fruit)* portocaliu 113
orange *(colour)* portocală *f* 64
orange juice suc de portocale *nt* 40,
60
orchestra orchestră *f* 88
orchestra *(seats)* stal *nt* 87
order *(goods, meal)* comandă *f* 102
order, to *(goods, meal)* a comanda
61, 102, 103
oregano sovîrv *m* 54
ornithology ornitologie *f* 83
other alt 101
our al nostru 161
out of order deranjat 136; nu
funcţionează 155
out of stock stoc terminat 103
outlet *(electric)* priză *f* 27
outside afară 15, 36
oval oval 101
overalls salopete *f* 115
overdone *(meat)* prea prăjită 62
overheat, to *(engine)* a încălzi peste
măsură 78
overtake, to a depăşi 79
owe, to a datora 144

**P**

pacifier *(baby's)* suzetă *f* 110
packet pachet *nt* 126

pail găletică *f* 120, 128
pain durere *f* 140, 141, 144
painkiller calmant *nt* 140
paint vopsea *f* 155
paint, to a picta 83
paintbox cutie de culori *f* 105
painter pictor *m* 83
painting pictură *f* 83, 127; tablou *f*
127
pair pereche *f* 149
pajamas pijama *f* 116
palace palat *nt* 81
palpitations palpitaţii *f* 141
panties chiloţi *mpl* 115
pants *(trousers)* pantaloni *m* 115
panty girdle burtieră *f* 115
panty hose ciorapi cu chilot *m* 115
paper hîrtie *f* 105
paper napkin şerveţel de hîrtie *nt* 105
paperback carte *f* 105
paperclip agrafă pentru hîrtie *f* 105
paraffin *(fuel)* parafină *f* 106
parcel colet *nt* 133
pardon, I beg your poftiţi 10
parents părinţi *mpl* 93
park parc *nt* 81
park, to a parca 26, 77
parking parcaj *nt* 77, 79
parking lot parcare *f* 79
parliament building clădirea
parlamentului *f* 81
parsley pătrunjel *m* 54
partridge potîrniche *f* 48
party *(social gathering)* petrecere *f*
95
pass *(mountain)* trecătoare *f* 85
pass, to *(driving)* a trece 79
pass through, to a trece 16
passport paşaport *nt* 16, 25, 26, 156
passport photo fotografie de
paşaport *f* 124
pasta tăiţei 50
paste *(glue)* clei *nt* 105
pastry shop peăcintărie *f* 99
patch, to *(clothes)* a pune un petec
29
path potecă *f* 85
patient pacient *m* 144
pattern model *nt* 112
pay, to a plăti 17, 31, 62, 102, 136
payment plată *f* 102, 131
pea mazăre *f* 52
peach piersică *f* 56
peak vîrf *nt* 85
peanut arahidă *f* 56

**Dictionar**

pear pară f 56
pearl perlă f 122
pedestrian pieton m 79
peg *(tent)* cîrlig de cort nt 106
pen stilou m 105
pencil creion m 105
pencil sharpener ascuțitoare f 105
pendant pandantiv m 121
penicillin penicilină f 143
penknife briceag m 120
pensioner pensionar m 82
people oameni 93
pepper piper 37, 41, 51, 64
per cent procent 149
per day pe zi 20, 32, 89
per hour pe oră 77, 89
per night pe noapte 24
per person de persoană 32
per week pe săptămînă 20, 24
percentage procentaj 131
perch biban 44
perform, to *(theater)* a juca 86
perfume parfum m 109
perhaps poate 15
period pains dureri la ciclu 141
period *(monthly)* ciclu 141
permanent wave permanent 30
permit permis m 90
person persoană f 32, 36
personal personal 130
personal call/person-to-person call a
   da un telefon 135
personal cheque cec personal nt 130
petrol benzină f 75, 78
pewter aliaj cu cositor 122
pharmacy farmacie f 107
pheasant fazan nt 48
photo poză f 82, 125; fotografie f 124
photocopy fotocopie f 131
photographer atelier de fotografiat
   m 99
photography fotografie f 124
phrase frază f 12
pick up, to *(person)* a lua 80, 96
picnic picnic nt 63
picnic basket coş de picnic nt 106
picture *(painting)* tablou nt 83
picture *(photo)* poză f 82
pig porc m 46
pigeon porumbel m 48
pike știucă f 44
pill somnifer 143
pillow pernă f 27
pin ac nt 110, 121; agrafă f 110
pineapple ananas m 56

pink roz 112
pipe pipă f 126
pipe cleaner instrument pentru pipă
   nt 126
pipe tobacco tutun de pipă nt 126
pipe tool dispozitiv de curăţat pipă nt
   126
place, to a da 135
place loc f 25, 76
place of birth locul de naştere 25
plain *(colour)* simplă 112
plane avion n 65
planetarium planetar m 81
plaster pansament gipsat nt 140
plastic plastic 120
plastic bag pungă de plastic f 120
plate farfurie f 36, 61, 120
platform *(station)* peron nt 67, 68, 69,
   70
platinum platină f 122
play *(theatre)* piesă f 86
play, to a cînta 88; a juca 89
playground teren de joc nt 32
playing card cărţi de joc f 105, 128
please vă rog 10
plimsolls tenişi mpl 117
plug *(electric)* ştecher nt 29, 118
plum prună f 56
pneumonia pneumonie f 142
poached fiert în apă 44
pocket buzunar nt 116
pocket calculator calculator de
   buzunar f 105
pocket watch ceas de buzunar nt 121
point of interest *(sight)* obiectiv
   turistic imporant m 80
point, to a arăta 12
poison otravă f 108, 156
poisoning intoxicaţie (alimentară)
   142
pole *(ski)* prăjină f 91
pole *(tent)* stîlp de cort m 106
police poliţie f 79, 156
police station post de poliţie nt 99;
   centru de poliţie nt 156
pond iaz nt 85
poplin poplin nt 113
pork porc m 45
port port nt 74
portable portabil 118
porter hamal m 18, 71; portar 26
portion porţie f 61
Portugal Portugalia 146
possible, (as soon as) *(cît de curînol)*
   posibil 137

**post office** poşta f 99, 132
**post** *(mail)* poşta f 28, 133
**post, to** a pune la poştă 28
**postage** costul (prin poştă) nt 132
**postage stamp** timbru nt 28, 126, 132, 133
**postcard** vedere 105, 126, 132
**poste restante** post restant nt 133
**potato** cartof m 52
**pottery** olărit nt 83, 127
**poultry** păsări fpl 48
**pound** liră sterlină f 19, 102, 129
**powder** pudră f 109
**powder compact** pudră compactă f 121
**powder puff** puf de pudră nt 110
**pregnant** gravidă f 141
**premium** *(gasoline)* benzină super f 75
**prescribe, to** a prescrie 143
**prescription** reţetă f 107, 143
**present** cadou nt 17
**press stud** capsă f 116
**press, to** *(iron)* a călca 29
**pressure** presiune f 75; tensiune f 141
**pretty** drăguţ 84
**price** preţ nt 69; cost nt 24; tarif nt 24
**priest** preot m 84
**print** *(photo)* poză f 125
**private** particular 23, 80, 91
**processing** *(photo)* developat 124
**profession** *(occupation)* ocupaţie f 25
**profit** profit nt 131
**programme** program nt 87
**pronounce, to** a pronunţa 12
**pronunciation** pronunţare f 6
**propelling pencil** creion mecanic nt 105, 121
**Protestant** protestant m 84
**provide, to** a puna la dispoziţie 131
**prune** prune uscate 56
**public holiday** sărbătoare legală f 152
**pull, to** a trage 155; *(tooth)* a extrage 145
**pullover** pulovăr nt 115
**pump** pompă f 106
**puncture** *(flat tyre)* pană de cauciuc f 78
**purchase** achiziţie f 131
**pure** pur 113
**purple** purpuriu 112
**push, to** a împinge 155

**put, to** a pune 24
**pyjamas** pijama f 116

**Q**
**quail** prepeliţă f 48
**quality** calitate f 103, 112
**quantity** cantitate f 14, 103
**quarter** sfert nt 149
**quarter of an hour** sfert de oră nt 153
**quartz** cuarţ nt 122
**question** întrebare f 11
**quick(ly)** repede 14, 137, 156
**quiet** linişte f 23, 25

**R**
**rabbi** rabin m 84
**rabbit** iepure m 49
**race course/track** hipodrom nt 89
**racket** *(sport)* rachetă f 90
**radiator** *(car)* radiator nt 78
**radio** radio nt 23, 28, 118
**radish** ridiche f 52
**railroad crossing** trecere peste cale ferată f 79
**railway** cale ferată f 154
**railway station** gară 19, 21, 67
**rain** ploaie f 94
**rain, to** a ploua 94
**raincoat** haină de ploaie f 116
**raisin** stafidă f 56
**rangefinder** telemetru nt 125
**rare** *(meat)* crudă 62; singe 46
**rash** egzemă f 139
**raspberry** smeură f 56
**rate** *(inflation)* rată f 131
**rate** *(price)* cost nt 20
**razor** aparat de ras nt 110
**razor blades** lamă de ras f 110
**reading lamp** lampă de cetit f 27
**ready** gata 29, 123, 125, 145
**real** *(genuine)* veritabil 117, 121
**rear** coada f 69
**receipt** chitanţă f 103, 144
**reception** recepţie f 23
**receptionist** recepţionist m 26
**recommend, to** a recomanda 35, 36, 80, 88, 137, 145
**record** *(disc)* disc nt 128
**record player** pick-up nt 118
**rectangular** rectangular 101
**red** roşu 105, 112; *wine* vin roşu 59
**reduction** reduce f 24, 82
**refill** *(pen)* rezervă de stilou f 105

**refund** *(to get a)* plata înapoi *f* 103
**regards** salutări *fpl* 152
**register, to** *(luggage)* a înregistra 71
**registered mail** recomandată *f* 133
**registration** înregistrare *f* 25
**registration form** formular de înregistrare *nt* 25, 26
**regular (petrol)** (benzină) normală *f* 75
**religion** religie *f* 83
**religious service** slujbă *f* 84
**rent, to** a închiria 19, 20, 90, 91, 155
**rental** închiriere *f* 20, 24, 74
**repair** a repara 125
**repair, to** a repara 29, 118, 121, 123, 125, 145
**repeat, to** a repeta 12
**report, to** *(a theft)* a raporta 156
**request** facultativă 73
**required** cerut 88
**reservation** rezervaţie *f* 19, 23, 69
**reservations office** birou de rezervări *nt* 19
**reserve, to** a rezerva 19, 23, 36, 69, 87
**reserved** rezervat 155
**rest** restul *nt* 130
**restaurant** restaurant *nt* 19, 32, 35, 67
**return, to** *(come back)* a se întoarce 21, 80; *(give back)* a înapoia 103
**return ticket** bilet dus întors *nt* 65, 69
**rheumatism** reumatism *nt* 141
**rib** coastă *nt* 138
**ribbon** panglică *nt* 105
**rice** orez *nt* 50
**right** *(correct)* bine 14
**right** *(direction)* dreapta 21, 69, 77
**ring** *(jewellery)* inel *nt* 122
**ring, to** *(doorbell)* a suna 155
**river** rîu *nt* 85, 90
**river trip** croazieră *f* 74
**road** drum *nt* 77, 85
**road assistance** asistenţă rutieră 78
**road map** harta drumurilor *f* 105
**road sign** semn de circulaţie *nt* 79
**roast beef** friptură de vacă *f* 47
**roasted** prăjit 46
**roll** chiflă *f* 41, 64
**roll-neck** pulover cu guler pe gît *nt* 116
**roll film** bobină de film *nt* 124
**roller skate** patine cu rotile *f* 128
**Romania** România *f* 146
**Romanian** *(language)* româneşte 11, 95

**room** cameră *f* 19, 23, 24, 25, 27
**room number** număr camerei 26
**room service** serviciu de cameră 23
**room** *(space)* spaţiu *nt* 32
**rope** frînghie *f* 106
**rosary** rozar *nt* 122
**rosemary** rozmarin *m* 54
**rouge** ruj *nt* 110
**round** rotund 101
**round-neck** pulover cu guler în jurul gîtului *nt* 116
**round-trip ticket** bilet dus-întors *nt* 65, 69
**round up, to** a rotunji 63
**route** traseu *nt* 85
**rowing boat** barcă cu rame *nt* 90
**rubber** *(eraser)* gumă *f* 105
**rubber** *(material)* cauciuc *nt* 117
**ruby** rubin *nt* 122
**rucksack** rucsac *nt* 106
**ruin** ruină *f* 82
**ruler** *(for measuring)* linie *f* 105
**rum** rom *nt* 60
**running water** apă curentă *f* 24
**Russia** Rusia 146

**S**
**safe** seif *n* 26
**safe** *(free from danger)* lipsit de pericol 90
**safety pin** ac de siguranţă *nt* 110
**saffron** şofran *m* 54
**sage** salvie *f* 54
**sailing** navigaţie *f* 91
**sailing boat** barcă cu pînze *nt* 91
**salad** salată *f* 42
**sale** *(bargains)* solduri *ntpl* 100; *(commerce)* vînzare *f* 131
**salt** sare *nt* 37, 41, 64
**salty** sărat 38
**same** acelaşi 117
**sand** nisip 90
**sandal** sandale *f* 117
**sandwich** sendvici *f* 63
**sanitary napkin/towel** tampon extern *nt* 108
**sapphire** safir *nt* 122
**sardine** sardele *f* 44
**satin** satin *nt* 113
**Saturday** sîmbătă *f* 151
**sauce** sos 51
**saucepan** cratiţă *f* 120
**saucer** farfurioară *f* 120
**sauerkraut** varză acră *f* 49

**sausage** cîrnaţi *mpl* 46, 64
**scarf** fular *nt* 116
**scarlet** stacojiu 112
**scenery** peisaj *nt* 93
**scenic route** traseu turistic spre *f* 85
**scissors** foarfece *f* 120
**scooter** scuter *m* 74
**Scotland** Scoţia 146
**scrambled eggs** scrob *nt* 40
**screwdriver** şurubelniţă *f* 106
**sculptor** sculptor *m* 83
**sculpture** sculptură *f* 83
**sea** mare *f* 85, 90
**seafood** fructe de mare *ntpl* 44
**season** anotimp *nt* 150
**seasoning** condimente *ntpl* 37
**seat** loc *nt* 65, 69, 70, 86, 87
**second** al doilea 149; secundă *f* 153
**second class** clasa a doua 69
**second-hand shop** consignaţie *f* 99
**second hand** *(watch)* secundar 122
**secretary** secretară *f* 27, 131
**section** raion *nt* 104
**see, to** a vedea 12, 25, 89, 121, 161; a întîlni 96
**self-service shop** magazin cu autoservire *nt* 33
**sell, to** a vinde 100
**send, to** a trimete 78; a livra 102; a expedia 103, 133
**sentence** propoziţie *f* 12
**separately** separat 62
**September** septembrie 150
**seriously** grav 139
**service** serviciu *nt* 24, 62, 98, 100
**service** *(church)* slujbă *f* 84
**serviette** şerveţel *nt* 36
**set menu** meniu fix *nt* 36, 39
**set** *(hair)* bigudiuri *nt* 30
**setting lotion** fixativ *nt* 30, 110
**seven** şapte 147
**seventeen** şaptesprezece 147
**seventh** al şaptelea 149
**seventy** şaptezeci 148
**sew, to** a coase 29
**shade** *(colour)* culoare *f* 111
**shampoo** şampon *nt* 30, 110
**shampoo and set** şampon şi bigudiuri 30
**shape** masură *f* 103
**share** *(finance)* acţiune *f* 131
**sharp** *(pain)* durere acută 140
**shave** ras 31
**shaver** aparat de ras *nt* 27, 118
**shaving brush** pămătuf de ras *nt* 110

**shaving cream** cremă de ras *f* 110
**she** ea 160
**shelf** raft *nt* 119
**ship** vapor *f* 74
**shirt** cămaşă *f* 116
**shivery** frisoane *n* 140
**shoe** pantof *nt* 116
**shoe polish** cremă de pantofi *f* 117
**shoe shop** magazin de încalţaminte *nt* 99
**shoelace** şiret de pantofi *nt* 117
**shoemaker's** cizmar *m* 99
**shop** magazin *nt* 98
**shop window** vitrină *f* 101, 111
**shopping area** centu comercial *nt* 82, 100
**shopping centre** centru comercial *nt* 99
**short** scurt 30, 115, 116
**short-sighted** miop 123
**shorts** şort *nt* 116
**shoulder** umăr *nt* 138
**shovel** lopăţică *f* 128
**show** spectacol *nt* 87, 88
**show, to** a arăta 12, 13, 100, 101, 103, 119, 124
**shower** duş *nt* 23, 32
**shrimp** crevete *m* 44
**shrink, to** a intra la apă 113
**shut** închis 14
**shutter**
**shutter** *(window)* oblon *nt* 29; *(camera)* obturator *nt* 125
**sick** *(ill)* bolnav 140
**sickness** *(illness)* boală *f* 140
**side** parte *f* 30
**sideboards/-burns** perciuni *m* 31
**sightseeing** excursie 80
**sightseeing tour** traseu *nt* 80
**sign** *(notice)* semna *f* 77, 79, 155
**sign, to** a semna 26, 130
**signet ring** inel cu sigiliu *nt* 122
**silk** mătase *f* 113
**silver** argint *nt* 121, 122; *(colour)* argintiu 112
**silver plated** argintat 122
**silverware** argintărie *f* 122
**simple** simplu 124
**since** de, din 15
**sing, to** a cînta 88
**single cabin** cabină pentru o persoană *f* 74
**single room** cameră cu un pat *f* 19, 23
**single** *(ticket)* un dus 65, 69

DICTIONARY

**single** *(unmarried)* necăsătorit 93
**sister** soră f 93
**sit down, to** a sta jos 95
**six** şase 147
**sixteen** şaisprezece 147
**sixth** al şaselea 149
**sixty** şaizeci 147
**size** mărime 124
**size** *(clothes, shoes)* măsură f 113, 117
**skate** patină f 91
**skating rink** patinuar nt 91
**ski** schi nt 91
**ski, to** a schia 91
**ski boot** ghete de schi f 91
**ski lift** teleski nt 91
**ski run** pistă f 91
**skiing** schiind 89, 91
**skiing equipment** echipament de schi nt 91, 106
**skiing lessons** lecţii de schi f 91
**skin** piele f 138
**skin-diving** a plonja 91
**skin-diving equipment** echipament de plonjat nt 91, 106
**skirt** fustă f 116
**sky** cer nt 94
**sleep, to** a dormi 144
**sleeping bag** sac de dormit nt 106
**sleeping car** vagon de dormit 66, 68, 69, 70
**sleeping pill** somnifer m 108, 143
**sleeve** mînecă f 115, 116, 142
**sleeveless** fără mînecă 116
**slice** felie f 119
**slide** *(photo)* diapozitiv nt 124
**slip** *(underwear)* jupon m 116
**slipper** papuc m 117
**Slovakia** Slovakia 146
**slow down, to** a reduce viteza 79
**slow(ly)** încet 14, 21; mai rar 135
**small** mic 14, 25, 101
**smoke, to** a fuma 95
**smoked** afumat 44
**smoker** fumător m 70
**snack** gustare f 63
**snack bar** chioşcul cu gustări nt 67
**snap fastener** capsă f 116
**sneaker** pantofi de tenis m 117
**snorkel** tub de scafandru nt 128
**snow** zăpadă f 94
**snuff** tutun de brizat nt 126
**soap** săpun nt 27, 110
**soccer** fotbal 89
**sock** şosetă f 116

**socket** *(electric)* priză f 27
**soft-boiled (egg)** (ou) moale 40
**soft drink** băutură răcoritoare f 64
**soft** *(lens)* flexibile 123
**sole** *(shoe)* talpă f 117
**soloist** solist m 88
**some** nişte 14
**someone** cineva 95
**something** ceva 30, 36, 112, 125, 139
**somewhere** undeva 87
**son** băiat m 93
**song** cîntec nt 128
**soon** curînd 15
**sore throat** durere în gît f 141
**sore** *(painful)* dureros 145
**sorry** scuzaţi 10; regret 16, 87, 103
**sort** *(kind)* fel 119
**soup** supă f 43
**south** sud 77
**South Africa** Africa de Sud 146
**South America** America de Sud 146
**souvenir** suvenir nt 127
**souvenir shop** magazin de suveniruri nt 99
**spade** lopăţică f 128
**Spain** Spania 146
**sparkling (wine)** (vin) spumos nt 59
**spark(ing) plug** bujie f 76
**speak, to** a vorbi 11, 16, 84, 135
**speaker** *(loudspeaker)* difuzor nt 118
**special** special 37
**special delivery** de urgenţă 133
**specialist** specialist m 142
**speciality** specialitate 47, 53
**specimen** *(medical)* specimen nt 142
**spectacle case** port ochelari ntpl 123
**speed** viteză f 79
**spell, to** a se scrire 12
**spend, to** a cheltui 101
**spice** condiment f 54
**spinach** spanac nt 52
**spine** coloană vertebrală f 138
**sponge** burete m 110
**spoon** lingură f 36, 61, 120
**sport** sport nt 88
**sporting goods shop** magazin cu articole de sport nt 99
**sprained** luxat 140
**spring** *(season)* primăvară f 150
**spring** *(water)* izvor nt 85
**square** pătrat 101; *(town)* piaţă f 82
**stadium** stadion nt 82
**staff** *(personnel)* personal 26
**stain** pată f 29

Dicţionar

**stalls** *(theatre)* stal *nt* 87
**stamp** *(postage)* timbru *nt* 28, 126, 132, 133
**staple** capsă *f* 105
**star** stea *f* 94
**start, to** a începe 80, 88
**starter** *(meal)* antreu *nt* 41
**station** *(railway)* gară *f* 19, 21, 67
**station** *(underground, subway)* metrou *nt* 72
**stationer's** papetărie *f* 99, 104
**statue** statuie *f* 82
**stay** sejur *nt* 31
**stay, to** a sta 16, 24, 26, 142; *(reside)* a locui 93
**steal, to** a fura 156
**steamed** în aburi 44
**stew** tocană *f* 48
**stewed** fiert 46
**stiff neck** durere de ceafă 141
**still (mineral water)** (apă) simplă *f* 60
**sting** înțepătură *f* 139
**sting, to** a înțepa 139
**stitch, to** a coase 29
**stock exchange** bursa *f* 82
**stocking** ciorap *m* 116
**stomach** stomac *nt* 138
**stomach ache** durere de burtă *f* 141
**stools** scaun *nt* 142
**stop** *(bus)* stație de autobuz *f* 73
**stop, to** a opri 21, 68, 72; a sta 70
**stop!** oprește! 156
**stop thief!** hoții! 156
**store** *(shop)* magazin *nt* 98
**straight ahead** drept înainte 21, 77
**straight (drink)** băutură simplă *f* 60
**strange** straniu 84
**strawberry** căpșună *f* 56
**street** stradă *f* 25, 77
**street map** hartă străzilor *f* 105; hartă orașului *f* 19
**streetcar** tramvai *nt* 72
**string** sfoară *f* 105
**strong** tare 126; puternic 143
**student** student *m* 82, 93
**study, to** a studia 94
**stuffed** umplut 41
**sturdy** durabilă 101
**sturgeon** sturion *m* 44
**subway** *(railway)* metrou *nt* 71
**suede** piele de căprioară *f* 113, 117
**sugar** zahăr *nt* 37, 64

**suitcase** valiză *f* 18
**summer** vară *f* 150
**sun** soare *m* 94
**sun-tan cream** cremă de bronzat *f* 110
**sun-tan oil** ulei de bronzat *nt* 110
**sunburn** arsură de soare *f* 107
**Sunday** duminică 151
**sunglasses** ochelari de soare *nt* 123
**sunstroke** insolație *f* 141
**super** *(petrol)* super 75
**superb** superb 84
**supermarket** magazin alimentar *nt* 99
**suppository** supozitoare *fpl* 108
**surgery** *(consulting room)* cabinet medical *nt* 137
**surname** numele de familie *nt* 25
**suspenders** *(Am.)* bretele *f* 116
**swallow, to** a înghiți 143
**sweater** pulover *nt* 116
**sweatshirt** bluză de trening din bumbac *nt* 116
**Sweden** Suedia 146
**sweet** dulce 59, 62
**sweet corn** porumb *nt* 52
**sweet shop** magazin de dulciuri *nt* 99
**sweet** *(confectionery)* dulciuri 126
**sweetener** zaharină *f* 37
**swell, to** a (se) umfla 139
**swelling** umflătură *f* 139
**swim, to** a înota 90
**swimming** înot 89, 91
**swimming pool** piscină *f* 32, 90
**swimming trunks** costum de baie *nt* 116
**swimsuit** costum de înot *nt* 116
**switch** *(electric)* buton *nt*, întrerupător *nt* 29
**switchboard operator** telefonist(ă) *m/f* 26
**Switzerland** Elveția 146
**swollen** umflat 139
**synagogue** sinagogă *f* 84
**synthetic** sintetic 113
**system** sistem *nt* 138

**T**
**T-shirt** cămașă *f* 116
**table** masă *f* 36
**tablet** *(medical)* tabletă *f* 108
**tailor's** croitor *m* 99
**take, to** a lua 18, 72, 143; a merge 73;

*(time)* a dura 102
**take away, to** a lua acasă 63
**taken** *(occupied)* liber 70
**talcum powder** pudră de talc f 110
**tampon** tampon intern nt 108
**tangerine** mandarină f 56
**tap (water)** (apă de la) robinet 28
**tape recorder** casetofon nt 118
**tapestry** tapiserie 127
**tarragon** tarhon m 54
**tart** tartă f 56
**tax** taxă f 32; TVA 102
**taxi** taxi nt 19, 21, 31, 67
**taxi rank/stand** staţie de taxi nt 21
**tea** ceai nt 41, 60, 64
**team** echipă f 89
**teaspoon** linguriţă nt 120, 143
**telegram** telegramă f 133
**telegraph office** birou PTT nt 99
**telephone** telefon nt 28, 78, 79, 134
**telephone, to** *(call)* a telefona 134
**telephone booth** telefon nt 134
**telephone call** apel telefonic m 135, 136
**telephone directory** anuar telefonic nt 134
**telephone number** număr de telefon nt 135, 136
**telephoto lens** teleobiectiv nt 125
**television** televizor nt 23, 28, 118
**telex** telex nt 133
**telex, to** a trimete un telex 130
**tell, to** a spune 12, 73, 76, 136, 152
**temperature** temperatură f 90, 140, 142
**temporary** provizoriu 145
**ten** zece 147
**tendon** tendon nt 138
**tennis** tenis nt 89
**tennis court** teren de tenis nt 90
**tennis racket** rachetă de tenis f 89
**tent** cort nt 32, 106
**tent peg** cîrlig de cort nt 106
**tent pole** stîlp de cort nt 106
**tenth** al zecelea 149
**term** *(word)* termen nt 131
**terrace** terasă f 36
**terrifying** îngrozitor 84
**tetanus** tetanus nt 140
**than** decît 14
**thank you** mulţumesc 10
**thank, to** a mulţumi 10, 96
**that** acela 101
**theatre** teatru nt 82, 86
**theft** furt nt 156

**their** al lor 161
**then** atunci 15
**there** acolo 14
**thermometer** termometru nt 108, 144
**these** acestea 160
**they** ei 160
**thief** hoţ m 156
**thigh** coapsă f 138
**thin** subţire 112
**think, to** *(believe)* a crede 31, 62, 94, 102
**third** al treilea 149
**thirsty, to be** a-i fi sete 13, 35
**thirteen** treisprezece 147
**thirty** treizeci 147
**this** acesta 11, 101
**those** acelea 160
**thousand** o mie 148
**thread** aţă f 27
**three** trei 147
**throat** gît nt 138, 141
**throat lozenge** pastile de gît f 108
**through** prin 15
**through train** tren direct nt 68
**thumb** degetul mare nt 138
**thumbtack** pioneză f 105
**thunder** tunet nt 94
**thunderstorm** furtună f 94
**Thursday** joi 151
**thyme** cimbru m 54
**ticket** bilet nt 65, 69, 72, 87, 89
**ticket office** casa de bilete f 67
**tie** cravată f 116
**tie clip** clamă de cravată f 122
**tie pin** ac de cravată nt 122
**tight** *(close-fitting)* strîmt 114
**tights** dresuri ntpl 116
**time** oră f 68, 80, 153
**time** *(occasion)* oră f 95; zi nt 143
**timetable** *(trains)* mers trenurilor nt 68
**tin** *(container)* cutie de conserve f 119
**tin opener** deschizător de conserve nt 120
**tint** vopsea f 110
**tinted** fumuriu 123
**tire** *(tyre)* roată f 75
**tired** obosit 13
**tissue** *(handkerchief)* batistă de hîrtie f 110
**to** pînă la 15
**to get** *(fetch)* a comanda 31
**to get** *(go)* a ajunge 100

DICTIONARY

**to get** *(obtain)* a obține 90, 134; a cumpăra 107
**toast** pîine prăjită *f* 40
**tobacco** tutun *nt* 126
**tobacconist's** tutungerie *f* 99, 126
**today** azi 29, 151
**toe** deget de la picior *nt* 138
**toilet paper** hîrtie igienică *f* 110
**toilet water** apă de toaletă *f* 110
**toiletry** parfumerie *f* 109
**toilets** toaleta *f* 23, 27, 32, 37, 67
**tomato** roșie *f* 52
**tomato juice** suc de roșii *nt* 60
**tomb** mormînt *nt* 82
**tomorrow** mîine 29, 96, 151
**tongue** limbă *f* 138
**tonic water** apă tonică *f* 60
**tonight** diseară 29, 86, 88, 96
**tonsils** amigdale *f* 138
**too** prea 14; *(also)* de asemenea 15
**too much** prea mult 14
**tools** scule *f* 120
**tooth** dinte *m* 145
**toothache** durere de dinți *f* 145
**toothbrush** perie de dinți *f* 110, 118
**toothpaste** pastă de dinți *f* 110
**top, at the** la vîrf 30; sus 145
**torch** *(flashlight)* lanternă *f* 106
**torn** rupt 140
**touch, to** a atinge 155
**tough** *(meat)* (carne) tare 62
**tour** croazieră *f* 74; traseu *nt* 80
**tourist office** agenția de voiaj *f* 19; oficiul de turism *nt* 80
**tourist tax** taxă turistică *f* 32
**tow truck** mașină de depanare *f* 78
**towards** spre 15
**towel** prosop *nt* 27, 110
**towelling** *(terrycloth)* material flașat *nt* 113
**tower** turn *nt* 82
**town** oraș *nt* 19, 88
**town center** centru *nt* 21, 76
**town hall** primăria *f* 82
**toy** jucărie *f* 128
**toy shop** magazin de jucării *nt* 99
**tracksuit** trening *nt* 116
**traffic** trafic *nt* 79
**traffic light** semafor *nt* 77
**trailer** rulotă *f* 32
**train** tren *nt* 66, 68, 69, 70
**tram** tramvai *nt* 72
**tranquillizer** tranchilizante *nt* 108, 143
**transfer** *(finance)* transfer *nt* 131

**transformer** transformator *nt* 118
**translate, to** a traduce 12
**transport, means of** mijloace de transport 74
**Transylvania** Transilvania 146
**travel agency** agenție de voiaj *f* 99
**travel guide** ghid *nt* 105
**travel sickness** rău de călătorie 107
**travel, to** a călători 94
**traveller's cheque** cec de voiaj *nt* 18, 63; cec de călătorie 102, 130
**travelling bag** sac de voiaj *m* 18
**treatment** tratament *nt* 143
**tree** copac *m* 85
**tremendous** nemaipomenit 84
**trim, to** *(a beard)* a aranja 31
**trip** călătorie *f* 72, 94, 152
**trolley** cărucior *nt* 18, 71
**trousers** pantaloni *m* 116
**trout** păstrăv *m* 45
**truck** camion *nt* 79
**try on, to** a proba 114
**tube** tub *nt* 119
**Tuesday** marți 151
**tumbler** pahar *nt* 120
**turkey** curcă *f* 48
**Turkey** Turcia 146
**turn, to** *(change direction)* a (se) întoarce 21
**turnip** nap *m* 52
**turquoise** turcuaz 122; *colour* turcoaz 112
**turtleneck** guler pe gît *nt* 116
**tweezers** pensetă *f* 110
**twelve** doisprezece 147
**twenty** douăzeci 147
**twice** de două ori 149
**twin beds** cu două paturi 23
**two** doi 147
**typewriter** mașină de scris *f* 27
**typing paper** hîrtie pentru mașină de scris *f* 105
**tyre** cauciuc *f* 75

## U

**ugly** urît 14, 84
**Ukraine** Ukraina 146
**umbrella** umbrelă *f* 116
**umbrella** *(beach)* umbrelă de soare *f* 91
**uncle** unchi *m* 93
**unconscious (to be)** a pierde conștiința 139
**under** sub 15

Dicționar

**underdone** *(meat)* cu puţin sînge 46
**underground** *(railway)* metrou *nt* 72
**underpants** chiloţi *m* 116
**undershirt** maiou *nt* 116
**understand, to** a înţelege 12, 16
**undress, to** a *(se)* dezbrăca 142
**United States** Statele Unite 146
**university** universitate *f* 82
**unleaded** fără plumb 75
**until** pînă 15
**up** sus 15
**upper** de sus 69
**upset stomach** stomacul deranjat *nt* 107
**upstairs** la etaj 15
**urgent** urgent 13, 145
**urine** urină *f* 142
**use, to** a folosi 134
**useful** util 14
**usually** de obicei *nt* 94; obişnuit 143

**V**
**V-neck** cu guler în formă de V 116
**vacancy** liber 23
**vacant** liber 14, 155
**vacation** vacanţă *f* 151
**vaccinate, to** a *(se)* vaccina 140
**vacuum flask** termos *f* 120
**vaginal infection** infecţie vaginală *f* 141
**valley** vale *f* 85
**value** valoare *f* 131
**value-added tax** taxă pe valoare adăugată *f* 102
**vanilla** vanilie *f* 56
**veal** viţel *m* 45
**vegetable** legume *f* 51
**vegetable store** aprozar *nt* 99
**vegetarian** vegetarian 37
**vein** venă *f* 138
**velvet** catifea *f* 113
**velveteen** bumbac pluşat *f* 113
**venereal disease** boală venerică *f* 142
**venison** căprioară *f* 48
**vermouth** vermut *nt* 60
**very** foarte 15
**vest** *(Am.)* vestă *f* 117
**vest** *(Br.)* maiou *nt* 116
**veterinarian** veterinar *m* 99
**video camera** cameră video *f* 124
**video cassette** casetă video 118, 124, 127
**video recorder** aparat video *nt* 118

**view** *(panorama)* vedere *f* 23
**village** sat *m* 85
**vinegar** oţet *nt* 37
**vineyard** vie *f* 85
**visit** vizită *f* 92
**visit, to** a vizita 95
**visiting hours** orele de vizită 144
**vitamin pill** vitamine tablete *fpl* 108
**vodka** vodcă *f* 60
**volleyball** voleibal 89
**voltage** voltaj *nt* 27, 118
**vomit, to** a voma 140

**W**
**waist** brîu *f* 142
**waistcoat** vestă *f* 116
**wait, to** a aştepta 21, 96
**waiter** chelner *m* 26, 36
**waiting room** sala de aşteptare *f* 67
**waitress** chelneriţă *f* 26
**wake, to** a se scula 26, 71
**Wales** Ţara Galilor 146
**walk, to** a merge 74
**wall** zid *m* 85
**wallet** portmoneu *nt* 156
**walnut** nuc *m* 56
**want, to** a dori 13; a vrea 101, 102
**warm** cald 94; fierbinte 155
**wash, to** a spăla 29
**washable** care se spală 113
**washbasin** chiuvetă *f* 28
**washing-up liquid** detergent de vase *nt* 120
**washing powder** detergent de rufe *nt* 120
**watch** ceas *nt* 121, 122
**watchmaker's** ceasornicar *m* 99, 121
**watchstrap** curea de ceas *f* 122
**water** apă *f* 28, 75, 90
**water flask** termos *nt* 107
**water melon** pepene roşu *m* 56
**watercress** măcriş *n* 54
**waterfall** cascadă *f* 85
**waterproof** antiacvatic 122
**water-skis** schi nautic 91
**wave** val *nt* 90
**way** drum *nt* 76
**we** noi 160
**weather** vreme *f* 94
**weather forecast** prevederi meteorologice 94
**wedding ring** verighetă *f* 122
**Wednesday** miercuri 151
**week** săptămînă *f* 16, 20, 24, 80, 92,

151

**weekday** zi lucrătoare *f* 151
**weekend** sfîrşit de săptămînă *nt* 20, 151
**well** bine 10, 140
**well-done** *(meat)* bine prăjit 46
**west** vest 77
**what** ce 11
**wheel** roată *f* 78
**when** cînd 11
**where** unde 11
**where from** de unde 93, 146
**which** care 11
**whipped cream** frişcă *f* 56
**whisky** whisky 17, 60
**white** alb 59
**who** cine 11
**whole** întreg 143
**why** de ce 11
**wick** meşă *nt* 126
**wide** larg 117
**wide-angle lens** obiectiv superangular *nt* 125
**wife** soţie *f* 93
**wig** perucă *f* 110
**wild boar** porc mistreţ *m* 48
**wind** vînt *nt* 94
**window** fereastră *f* 28, 36, 65, 69; *(shop)* vitrină *f* 101, 111
**windscreen/shield** parbriz *nt* 76
**windsurfer** windsurfer 91
**wine** vin *nt* 17, 59
**wine list** listă de vinuri *f* 59
**wine merchant's** magazin de vinuri *nt* 99
**winter** iarnă *f* 150
**winter sports** sporturi de iarnă ntpl 91
**wiper** *(car)* ştergătoare *nt* 76
**wish** urare *f* 152
**with** cu 15
**withdraw, to** *(from account)* a scoate 131
**withdrawal** restituire 130

**without** fără 15
**woman** femeie *f* 114
**wonderful** minunat 96
**wood** pădure *f* 85
**wool** lînă *f* 113
**word** cuvînt *nt* 12, 133
**work, to** a funcţiona 28
**working day** zi lucrătoare *f* 151
**worse** mai rău 14
**worsted** lînă toarsă 113
**wound** rană *f* 139
**wrap up, to** a împacheta 103
**wrinkle-free** neşifonat 113
**wristwatch** ceas de mînă 122
**write, to** a scrie 12, 101
**writing pad** bloc notes *nt* 105
**writing paper** hîrtie de scris *f* 27, 105
**wrong** greşit 77, 135; rău 14

## X
**X-ray** radiografie *f* 140

## Y
**year** an 149
**yellow** galben 112
**yes** da 10
**yesterday** ieri 151
**yet** încă 15, 16, 25
**yoghurt** iaurt *nt* 40, 64
**you** tu, Dumneavoastră 160
**young** tînăr *m* 14
**your** a ta, al tău, a Dumneavoastră 161
**youth hostel** cămin *nt* 22; cazare *f* 32

## Z
**zero** zero 147
**zip(per)** fermoar *nt* 116
**zoo** grădină zoologică *f* 82
**zoology** zoologie *f* 83
**zucchini** dovlecel *m* 52

# Indice Român

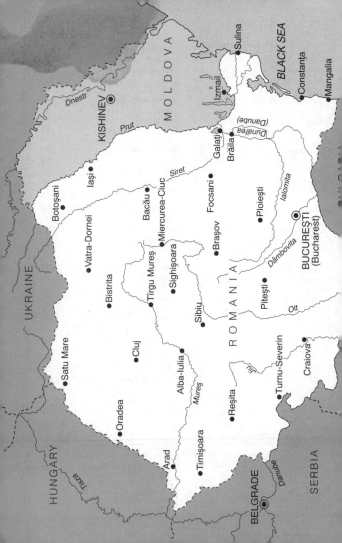